ONE FAMILY

A TALE OF DIVISION, DEVOTION AND RESTITUTION

IN ULSTER

BY HENRY MACRORY

CURLY BURN
BOOKS

Cover design: Curly Burn Books.

Printed and bound by:
Zing Design and Print, Loughanhill Industrial Estate, Coleraine, County Londonderry. www.zingdp.com

To Helen, Conolly and Eila

and the home where they grew up

The McCausland Tree

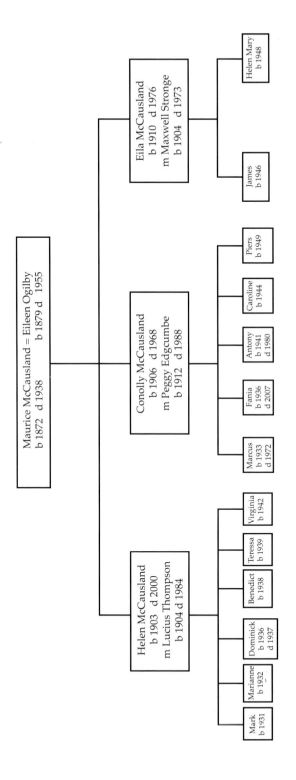

Maurice McCausland = Eileen Ogilby
b 1872   d 1938   b 1879 d 1955

Helen McCausland
b 1903 d 2000
m Lucius Thompson
b 1904 d 1984

Mark
b 1931

Marianne
b 1932

Dominick
b 1936
d 1937

Benedict
b 1938

Teressa
b 1939

Virginia
b 1942

Conolly McCausland
b 1906 d 1968
m Peggy Edgcumbe
b 1912 d 1988

Marcus
b 1933
d 1972

Fania
b 1936
d 2007

Antony
b 1941
d 1980

Caroline
b 1944

Piers
b 1949

Eila McCausland
b 1910 d 1976
m Maxwell Stronge
b 1904   d 1973

James
b 1946

Helen Mary
b 1948

Contents

Chapter   Page

Introduction

1.   A Gun Too Hot to Hold   1

2.   Princely Paradise   13

3.   The Young Master   29

4.   Home Fun   40

5.   Ninety Fateful Words   56

6.   A Fine Romance   66

7.   Jewel of a Bride   88

8.   The Approaching Storm   102

9.   The Die is Cast   116

10.   Change of Heart   133

11.   Preparing the Ground   145

12.   The Wheels Turn   156

13.   A Dagger Pointed at my Heart   164

14.   Strained Relations   179

15.   Endgame   189

16.   Peaceful Days   205

17.   Time moves on   215

        Appendix: The Battle of Be'long   235

        Bibliography   239

Introduction

The great estate of Drenagh, home to ten generations of the McCausland family, lies just to the north of the old market town of Limavady in County Londonderry. The Georgian house, set in a thousand acres of parkland, exudes a quiet elegance that belies its turbulent past. In 1940, Captain Conolly McCausland, who had succeeded to Drenagh on the death of his father shortly before the war, converted to Roman Catholicism. His action sparked widespread condemnation in Protestant-dominated Ulster. It also led to an extraordinary family conflict because his father – a staunch Protestant - had made legal provision years earlier to prevent the estate from falling into Catholic hands. By becoming a Catholic, Conolly automatically forfeited all his interest and his children's interest in Drenagh, and the property passed to his elder sister Helen.

To begin with, Conolly reluctantly acquiesced to his father's unusual – indeed possibly unique - stipulation, but he subsequently changed his mind and began a court action to win Drenagh back. The thirteen-year saga cost the family a vast sum in legal fees and threatened to tear it apart. At one point, no fewer than twelve barristers, including five KCs and the Attorney General of Northern Ireland, appeared at an eleven-day High Court hearing to argue the consequences of the conversion. Later, eight barristers, including four KCs, were present when the case went before the Court of Appeal. This book tells for the first time the full story of a remarkable legal drama that created interest throughout Northern Ireland and led to a bizarre and unworkable judgment that took everyone – lawyers and family alike - by surprise.

Although the four main characters in the tale - Conolly, his wife Peggy, his sister Helen, and Helen's husband Lucius – are long dead, many of their children are alive, and it was at their request that I began researching this unique story. The process was sparked by Helen and Lucius's eldest daughter, Marianne More-Gordon, who lived through the events as a child and who, after Helen's death, realised that boxes, drawers, shelves and bags around the house held a remarkable and unique source of information on a tumultuous period of family history.

In 2008 all five of Helen and Lucius's children spent several days collating papers from the case with a view to lodging copies with the Public Records Office of Northern Ireland. Virginia 'Squobe' Armstrong, the youngest, then set about the Herculean task of sorting through and putting in order a large cache of legal correspondence. Later she sifted through hundreds of personal letters and old photographs which gave colour and flavour to the dry facts. All these papers were passed to me. Relatives on both sides of the family – including Conolly and Peggy's surviving children - subsequently made further important contributions to the story, although Virginia remained my main point of contact throughout the enterprise.

It helped enormously that all the central characters in the story were inveterate letter writers, pouring out their thoughts and emotions to one another at great length, particularly during the war when they were often parted for long periods and when the Drenagh controversy was at its height. This, of course, was long before the days of electronic communications when even telephone calls were the exception rather than the rule. In the modern age, it is unlikely there would have been anything like as much contemporary documentation. Fortunately, many of the letters they wrote to one another have survived the passage of time, making it possible to create a comprehensive picture of what happened seven decades and more ago.

A by-product of relating the Drenagh story is that it creates an opportunity to provide a glimpse of the privileged and rarefied life led by one of Northern Ireland's foremost land-owning families during the early years of the twentieth century. An army of servants saw to their needs, a coach and horses took them on their travels, and shooting and fishing were the order of the day. Embossed invitations requested their attendance at coronations and investitures, and visitors to the house included the brilliant lawyer and revered Ulster Unionist leader Sir Edward Carson. It was a true Upstairs Downstairs existence that now belongs to a vanished age.

As for the telling of the tale, why me? Much of my living over four decades has been made out of writing, and my family's connection to the McCauslands dates back nearly two centuries. My great-great grandfather and great-grandfather were tenant farmers and millers on the Drenagh demesne. My grandparents were contemporaries of Conolly's parents, Maurice and Eileen (they once received an angry letter from Maurice informing them that one of their house guests had attended a shoot at Drenagh and walked off with a brace of pheasants without his permission), and my father was a close friend of Conolly in the 1930s. My own memories of Drenagh date back to family holidays in Northern Ireland in the 1950s and 1960s. As a small boy in 1954 I was roped into a boisterous flag game in the Glen at Drenagh organised by Conolly's son, Marcus, then aged twenty-one, and I vividly remember the dreadful thrill of being 'taken prisoner' by some of his friends, who were many years older than me. More than half a century later I was delighted to be asked to piece together the various strands of a family drama that had only just ended when I was 'captured' in the Glen.

By a strange coincidence, all five of Helen and Lucius's children met on September 28 2012 to celebrate Marianne's 80th birthday and to review the book's progress – exactly a hundred years to the day after nearly half a million people in Ireland, including their grandparents, Maurice and Eileen McCausland, signed the famous Ulster Covenant and Declaration in protest against the third Irish Home Rule Bill. Two months later, in another event that resonated powerfully with the family, the Coalition

Government published legislation to end the ban on anyone in the line of succession to the British throne from marrying a Roman Catholic.

In telling the story I have been at pains not to take sides. For the most part, the lengthy litigation was conducted in a remarkably friendly and civilised manner, but at times there were displays of petulance, irritation, and bloody-mindedness, as well as the occasional flash of anger. However, having read all the surviving correspondence and other documentation, I am convinced that - financially disastrous though the case was - none of the four main characters at its heart ever behaved maliciously, let alone dishonestly.

Writing the full story of the Drenagh controversy would not have been possible without the co-operation of both sides of the family. For their help and guidance I would like to express my great thanks to Helen and Lucius's five children, Mark, Marianne, Benedict, Tessa and Virginia, as well as to Conolly and Peggy's two surviving children, Caroline and Piers, who also gave me access to scores of personal letters and documents relevant to the story. I also owe a debt of gratitude to Conolly and Peggy's daughters-in-law June Welsh, and Elizabeth and Priscilla McCausland. I am especially grateful to Conolly's grandson, Conolly Patrick, for welcoming me to Drenagh, talking me through various aspects of McCausland family history and allowing me to rummage without restriction through many drawers of old documents and letters. Conolly's brother Shane kindly gave me access to documentation about their father, Marcus.

My thanks also to my brother Patrick, who at an early stage cast his lawyer's eye over the hundreds of pages of legal correspondence relating to the case and produced a lengthy 'opinion' (he was appalled by the behaviour of some of the lawyers involved) which I used as the starting point for this

book. I am also grateful to Gill Sargent for her stories of
Drenagh in the 1960s, to Harry Boyle for supplying me with his
father's reminiscences of Limavady in Edwardian times, and
to Barney Grimes for telling me about his grandfather, William
Grimes, the legendary Drenagh butler.

My thanks also to the staff of the Public Records Office of
Northern Ireland, the staff of Coleraine Public Library, and
to the Eton College archivist, Penny Hatfield, for supplying
me with details of Conolly's and Maurice's schooldays.
Acknowledgement also goes to BBC researchers for providing
documents they had found in preparing Alexander
Armstrong's "Who do you think you are" programme. A ten-
page memoir by Conolly's first cousin, Denis Gibbs, entitled
'Early Irish Recollections', provided an invaluable insight
into life at Drenagh in the first two decades of the twentieth
century. Finally my thanks to my wife Francie for taking some
of the photographs that appear in this book and for sharing my
enthusiasm for what has been an enthralling project. While I am
indebted to all of the above, the responsibility for any mistakes,
misunderstandings or omissions very much rests with me.

Henry Macrory

March 2014

Chapter One

A Gun Too Hot to Hold

Come all ye loyal Irishmen, the border is erased,
By North and South a fighting man will equally be praised,
Set light to your tobacco boys, while I give you a song
Of Captain C McCausland at the Battle of Be'long

From The Battle of Boulogne, by Capt J F Marnon

On May 10 1940, the German armoured crocodile invaded Belgium, Luxembourg and the Netherlands with quick and shocking success. Breaking through the French lines at Sedan, Hitler's troops began a rush for the English Channel, putting Britain at the greatest risk of invasion since Napoleon. Men from the British Expeditionary Force - sent to France eight months earlier to check any German advance – found themselves in full and ignominious retreat towards the coast with the Germans breathing down their necks. The aim of the German Blitzkrieg was their encirclement and annihilation.

The situation was so grave that King George VI called for an unprecedented week of national prayer. In the House of Commons Winston Churchill described the events in France as 'a colossal military disaster.' He warned that 'the whole root and core and brain of the British Army' had been stranded at the coastal town of Dunkirk and seemed about to perish or be captured. In churches throughout the country people prayed for a miraculous delivery.

The miracle happened. In the course of nine days during May and June nearly 230,000 British troops were evacuated from the alien hell of Dunkirk and brought back to England. Some came home on destroyers. Others were ferried across the Channel by a rag-tag rescue fleet of trawlers, fishing smacks, pleasure craft, barges and lifeboats. To this day the 'miracle of the little ships' remains a vivid folk memory in Britain. Churchill dubbed it Britain's Finest Hour.

Many brave men helped bring about the miracle, and one of these was Conolly McCausland, a 33-year-old Captain in the 2nd Battalion of the elite Irish Guards. As the human flotsam from one of the country's greatest defeats prepared to head back to Britain, Conolly and his men crossed the Channel the other way in a daring and dangerous bid to stall the enemy and so help the evacuation to take place. Their orders were to defend the port of Boulogne – some 45 miles from Dunkirk - against the overwhelming and inexorable advance of battle-hardened German veterans for as long as possible. Many never made it back to Britain, but all played their part with valour and distinction. Conolly especially.

It was not the first time he had faced danger that month. A week earlier he and 650 other members of the 2nd Battalion – using the codename 'Harpoon Force' - had dashed to the Hook of Holland to safeguard the return of British diplomats and citizens and, if necessary, cover the evacuation of Queen Wilhelmina and the Dutch Government. Arriving in the early dawn of May 13 they found enormous fires blazing near the quayside and almost immediately came under attack from German planes, which dropped salvos of bombs and raked their positions with machine-gun fire. Several of Conolly's fellow guardsmen - Patrick Carroll, James Burke, Thomas Power – were blown to pieces yards from where he was standing. They were among the first British infantry casualties of the war, and he was shocked by the loss of life among men he knew and liked. 'One thing I am convinced of is the hopelessness of being caught in the open air in an air raid such as this', he wrote to his mother from the Guards Club in London on his return from Holland. 'A cat could not have escaped   without a bullet or a bomb splinter.'

The next morning the Battalion's makeshift HQ in a local hotel was attacked repeatedly. 'Off went the sirens and with a roar like Niagara these blasted German bombers were at it again,' wrote Conolly. Amid the deafening noise, he spent what he described as 'the ten most terrifying minutes of my life' crouching in the ladies' lavatory with ten other men as the building collapsed around them. The house next door was flattened, killing several women and children. 'The noise was quite indescribable,' he wrote. 'You could hear the brutes diving to the attack and then Bang, Bang, Bang, BANG as they dropped their four bombs in a line, one after the other. The last bang seemed to be inside one's ear drum. In the intervals of the crashes of bombs, falling glass and masonry, you could hear the rat-tat-tat of their machine guns.'

In the midst of the mayhem Conolly strode nonchalantly into the town centre and wrote a postcard to his wife, Peggy, assuring her he was 'safe and well.' Later that day the Irish Guards retreated with a clutch of terrified evacuees to three waiting destroyers (Queen Wilhelmina had been spirited out of the port several hours earlier) and returned to England after what Conolly called a 'disastrous' expedition in which eleven of their number had been killed and twelve wounded. Ever practical, he 'liberated' three bottles of eau de cologne from the railway station on his way to the ship, one each for his mother and two sisters.

'I did not expect to come back alive,' he wrote to his mother. 'It is only by the grace of God that any of us did. The slaughter amongst the poor civilians was simply terrible. God only knows who is to blame for things such as that and I can't believe they will get away with it when the Day of Judgement comes. Whatever sights I may see or whatever fear I may feel will not be any more terrible because that would be quite impossible. Thank God that I had been able to get out of the ruins alive. I do not know when we will be sent off again, but it won't be long I feel.'

His instincts were right. After the briefest of respites, the order came to cross the Channel a second time, this time to France. The directive reached Battalion headquarters at Old Dean Common near Camberley at 11 a.m. on Tuesday May 21. The men had just completed a 24-hour field exercise in the Surrey countryside and had spent an uncomfortable night in makeshift trenches. Like everyone else Conolly had barely slept. The new instruction could not have arrived at a worse time, but if he had strong feelings about the matter he did not let them show. As the officer in charge of No 1 Company he had 100 'other ranks' under his command, and his priority was to have them ready for departure in four and a half hours flat.

Exhausted though they were, Conolly and his men were on the move at the appointed time of 3.30 p.m., setting off at the head of a column which also included the Welsh Guards. They reached Dover six hours later where they had a hurried meal of stew, bread and tea before loading their vehicles and equipment on to the cross-channel steamer *Queen of the Channel*. It soon became clear the ship was not big enough for the battalion's needs, and another vessel, Mona's Star, was provided as back-up. It was on this second ship that Conolly and his men eventually set sail several hours behind the rest of the battalion. As the white cliffs of Dover faded into the distance, he must have wondered if he would ever see them again.

Events moved with alarming speed the following day. It was the start of what Conolly described in an under-stated letter home as a 'memorable 36 hours.' With inadequate weaponry and very little transport, the Irish Guards were allotted a sector near the village of Outreau, a mile south of Boulogne, and 'dug in like beavers' as rapidly and as deeply as they could with picks and shovels to protect themselves against German tanks approaching from the south. Most of the battalion had several hours to prepare their defences, but Conolly's company was denied even that small advantage. Arriving much later on the second ship, they found themselves at the sharp end of the German advance almost at once. Barely had Conolly got his men into their positions on the battalion's left flank at three p.m. than parties of Germans appeared on the ridge overlooking the village behind a curtain of shells. They were accompanied by tanks from General Heinz Guderian's II Panzer Division, which had been given the job of capturing Boulogne.

The first German shells fell on Conolly's company almost before they had broken the ground with their shovels. After a brief lull the German tanks moved forward, and again Conolly and his men took the brunt of the incoming fire. Despite this they knocked out two enemy tanks with several direct hits from an anti-tank gun and kept up a fusillade of deadly fire. One of Conolly's men, Sgt Arthur Evans, recalled later: 'I could clearly see the tank commander's head above the open turret with his field glasses to his eyes. We opened fire and the tank rocked as we scored two direct hits. The crew baled out and abandoned it. Soon a second appeared and that too was effectively disposed of.'

Gradually the German advance towards Boulogne began to falter. A German motor-cycle platoon commander later published a graphic account in the Army magazine Die Militarwoche of what it was like to be under fire from Conolly's men during the advance towards Outreau: 'Hell is let loose. The houses ahead of us and the little wood are occupied by the enemy. Burst after burst of machine-gun fire come whipping into the long green grass. We crouch in the thorns and nettles while the bullets whistle over us. Where are the bastards? We can't find where the shots are coming from. It seems to be a field fortification, as if there wasn't enough to deal with already. Meanwhile we have found that a direct attack on the enemy anti-tank guns is impossible. Now it has grown dark. Every attempt to get within grenade-throwing distance of the enemy fails because of his defensive fire. The enemy is shooting too damned well.'

At this stage, Conolly's company was the only unit in the Battalion to have engaged the Germans and halt their advance. Still holding their position, they were at the receiving end of vicious German shellfire for much of that night and at one point came under attack from enemy aircraft. The following morning the Germans shelled them with guns and mortars, and inflicted heavy casualties as they finally started to drive them back towards the centre of Outreau. With each small advance, the Germans were met with withering fire from behind garden walls, the churchyard, the girls' school and the village square. A frustrated General Guderian wrote in his war diary at 2.45 pm: 'In and around Boulogne the enemy is fighting tenaciously for every inch of ground in order to prevent the harbour from falling into German hands.'

The Guards' Roman Catholic chaplain, Father Julian Stonor, who was helping to tend the wounded in a garage behind the railway line, observed later: 'The Bren-gunners were using up magazines as fast as their comrades could fill them. It needed a constant stream of fire to stop the Germans slipping across the railway and down between the houses into the town. Some of the barrels got so hot that they warped and jammed, leaving the section with only their rifles.'

Fierce skirmishes continued for the rest of the day, and at one stage the surviving Irish Guards hid in houses on either side of the road as enemy tanks passed within a few yards of them. The effect on the Germans of finding the streets deserted when they expected to find them filled with troops was disquieting.

They thought they were heading into a trap, and this slowed them down even further. Conolly found this particular episode exhilarating, describing it in a letter home as an 'exciting game of hide and seek between the enemy tanks and ourselves.'

Soon afterwards, as he arrived back in the centre of Boulogne, Conolly had a bizarre experience. During a lull in the fighting he took shelter outside a small shop and happened to glance at some picture postcards on a pavement rack. One of the postcards – which portrayed a small kilted boy with curly blonde hair - looked oddly familiar and he thrust it into his tunic pocket before moving on. Only when he looked properly at the postcard did he realise that the small boy was his own son, Marcus. Conolly himself had taken the picture in Ireland some three or four years previously with a Leica camera which he had subsequently lost during a holiday in Deauville in 1938. Extraordinarily - miraculously even - the picture had been made into a postcard which, two years later, happened to be on display when Conolly, in mortal danger, was passing by. Not surprisingly, he attributed the episode to the work of a particularly benign God, and would say afterwards that for a few moments he had felt himself in the very presence of The Almighty.

At 8 p.m. an air battle between the Luftwaffe and the R.A.F. raged over Boulogne. By now the remnants of the Irish Guards had retreated to the town and, when the air battle was over, they ran to the quayside with orders from Churchill himself to evacuate as quickly as possible on to waiting British destroyers. The Germans kept up a tornado of fire at very short range, but the troops remained completely disciplined and only boarded the ships when the order was given. By now three officers and 36 men were all that was left of Conolly's company. The entire battalion had suffered 200-plus casualties in one of the bloodiest British/German engagements yet of World War II.

A watching naval officer wrote later in Blackwood's Magazine: 'The fine discipline of the Guards earned the awed, open-mouthed respect of all. Watching them in perfect order, moving exactly together, engaging target after target as though on parade ground drill, it was difficult to realise that this was the grim reality of battle. They were truly magnificent and no sailor who saw them could ever forget the feeling of pride he experienced.'

Conolly was equally impressed by the actions of the Royal Navy. He wrote to his mother: 'The Germans thought they had got the whole lot of us into a trap, and so they had! But the Navy handled their guns so well and manoeuvered their ships so marvellously that we all got out of it. It was an example of efficiency and heroism such as I have never seen, or thought possible. Our own men were wonderful too – they did not turn a hair – but then they are very fine men. I'm beginning to feel quite an old soldier now after the bombs at the Hook and tanks, shells, shrapnel and machine guns at this place!!'

The 500 or so survivors – Conolly among them - arrived back on British soil at 6.30 on the morning of May 24, having won precious time for the quarter of a million men trapped at Dunkirk. After their departure, French troops managed to hold Boulogne's old citadel for another 24 hours before surrendering. So ended an episode which, the following day, the London *Daily Mirror* reported under the banner headline THE HELL THAT WAS BOULOGNE. Jon Cooksey, in his book *Boulogne*, described it as a 'story of remarkable discipline amid the utmost confusion of reckless courage and devotion to duty.'

While not as famous as the defence of Calais, which was being conducted at almost the same time, the three-day defence of Boulogne played a significant part in delaying the German advance towards Dunkirk, and gave the British and French time to consolidate their defensive positions as the evacuation of the

British Expeditionary Force got underway. Operation Dynamo –
the evacuation from Dunkirk – finally began on May 26.

Conolly's bravery undoubtedly contributed to the subsequent
'miracle of the little ships' and he exemplified Britain's 'Finest
Hour.' Military historians wrote later that the Guards held
out for longer than anyone had believed possible against the
advancing panzers. The commander of the 2nd battalion, Lt Col
Charles Haydon, described No 1 Company's role in resisting
the Germans as 'invaluable,' even though it had been reduced
to 'microscopic' numbers by the end of the fighting. He was
emphatic that Conolly's role as company commander had been
crucial.

He wrote in a despatch: 'They had been in close contact
with the enemy for nearly two hours at a range of not much
more than 30-50 yards. Throughout that time the posts had
exchanged bursts of fire one with the other and all attempts
to outflank No. 1 Company's position had each in turn been
defeated. In my opinion, the holding of this post by No. 1
Company, which might quite easily have been somewhat
demoralised by the very heavy losses which the Company
had suffered, reflects the very greatest credit on Capt. C.R.
McCausland and 2/Lt. G.G. Romer, and on the other ranks
who held the post. I was very apprehensive as to whether they
would be able to withdraw from such close contact without
further heavy losses. The fact that they were able to do so
shows that they must have made the fullest and most effective
use of the ground.'

A fellow Guards officer, Captain John Marnon, later wrote a
rip-roaring poem of twenty-six stanzas – reproduced in full at
the end of this book - about the Battle of Boulogne, in which
Conolly featured prominently:

So forward went the Germans and approached the village square,
When suddenly twenty muskets and a Bren gun rent the air,
Says Hans to Fritz 'It's still the Micks, who called this a
withdrawal?
There's Captain C McCausland up behind the garden wall.'

Says Captain C McCausland 'Boys, the range is thirty yards,
We'll teach them limbs of Satan to obstruct the Irish Guards,
For every shot they loose, me lads, we give them back the same,
And an extra one for Ireland's sake, or Conolly's not me name.'

The Germans concentrated every gun and every tank
From village square to garden wall the firing was point blank,
But every shot was answered by the rifles and the Bren
Of Captain C McCausland and his one and twenty men.

And every man that saw that sight pronounced the self same
thing,
The stand remains unrivalled since the Siege of Mafeking,
Like Hougemont and Rorkes' Drift the story will be told
Of Captain C McCausland with his gun too hot to hold.

As a result of his exploits at Boulogne, Conolly was awarded the Military Cross for gallantry in action against the enemy. His was one of only three MCs awarded to 2nd Battalion members in the wake of the Hook of Holland and Boulogne operations, and reflected the outstanding part he had played while ignoring all danger to himself. His citation read:

Captain McCAUSLAND commanded No. 1 Company during the BOULOGNE operations. His company was attacked twice during the afternoon and evening of Wednesday 22nd May, and continuously during the following day. Very heavy casualties were suffered, and only 3 Officers and 36 Other Ranks were present for re-embarkation on the evening of 23rd May. Throughout the final move, Captain

*McCAUSLAND set the finest example to his men and after the
initial withdrawal of what remained of his Company on the morning
of the 23rd May, he took personal command of a most important
post in the village of OUTREAU. This post was not more than 30-
50 yards distant from the enemy's advanced elements and despite
repeated attacks and efforts to out-flank them, they held their ground
for nearly two hours. The spirit and courage which animated those
in the post was due in a large measure to the example set by Captain*
McCAUSLAND, *who ignoring all danger himself, refused to allow
his men to become in any way depressed by the heavy casualties
they had suffered earlier in the day. Later, despite being in such close
contact with the enemy, Captain McCAUSLAND was able, by skilful
handling, to extricate his men without loss when the moment came to
make a further withdrawal. This officer showed courage and ability of
very high order throughout the operations.*

Conolly was profoundly affected by his battlefield experiences,
and they remained vivid memories until his dying day. A week
after the battle he wrote to his mother: 'Your good prayers
and those of many others were over me, my Darling, and so
I came out unscathed.' As if he had not already been through
enough, another trauma was awaiting him on his return to
Britain. Three days after the Battle of Boulogne his wife's
brother, Piers Edgcumbe, was killed forty miles away near the
village of Wormhoudt in France. His armoured car was at the
head of a column reconnoitering the area for enemy positions
when, rounding a bend in the road, it came face to face with a
stationary German tank. The first shot from the tank hit Piers'
car and exploded the ammunition magazine. The car and its
occupants literally vanished into thin air.

In a letter to his mother, Conolly described it as 'a terrible
tragedy,' adding: 'He was a dear, good-hearted creature and in
all the time I knew him I never heard him say an unkind word
about anyone…each day I see the names of people I knew and
loved - always the very best, kindest and wisest of men seem to

be killed. That foul brute Hitler, what crimes are not upon his evil soul?'

May 1940 had been the most dramatic month in Conolly's life, a rush of intense emotion and experience in which he saw action in two battles, won the M.C. and lost a brother-in-law. Topping these experiences during that extraordinary month was yet another event which was to affect his life more profoundly than all the others combined. On May 3 - ten days before his narrow escape from the Hook of Holland - Conolly went quietly to the chapel of St Mary's School, Ascot, close to his battalion headquarters at Old Dean Common, and was there received into the Roman Catholic church.

The news came as a shock - if not a surprise - to his friends and relations, for he came from a staunchly Protestant Ulster family. Indeed, so steeped were the McCauslands in Protestant history and values that his late father had made legal provision to prevent the family estate in County Londonderry from falling into Roman Catholic hands. Conolly's conversion on that Friday morning in May was a simple act of faith, but it would have consequences more far-reaching than he could have ever foreseen, and sparked a family dispute that lasted thirteen difficult and expensive years.

Chapter Two

Princely Paradise

> *Mountains stretch'd around, gloomy was their tinting,*
> *And the horse's hoofs made a dismal clinting;*
> *Wind upon the heath, howling was and piping,*
> *On the heath and bog, black with many a snipe in;*
> *'Mid the bogs of black, silver pools were flashing*
> *Crows upon their sides picking were and splashing.*
> *Cockney on the car, closer folds his plaidy,*
> *Grumbling at the road leads to Limavaddy.*

From "The Irish Sketch Book 1842" by William Makepeace Thackeray

The family name McCausland goes back more than a thousand years to an intrepid member of the O'Cahan clan named Buey Anselan. Born in around AD 986, he was the son of Kyan, provincial king of southern Ulster, and was nicknamed 'The Fair' because of his pale complexion. Anselan would have enjoyed the company of his distant descendant, Conolly McCausland.

According to family legend, Anselan masterminded a daring attack on the Vikings in around 1013. The Danish oppressors at that time controlled large swathes of England and Ireland, and their leader Swein the Forkbeard ordered a feast to be held at their principal Irish garrison in Limerick to celebrate the birthday of his son, King Canute (he of the waves). Orders went out for a thousand beautiful daughters of the Irish nobility and gentry to be present at the festival to 'dally' with the lusty Danish officers, led by their general, Fergussin. The Irish were having none of it and made the Danes pay dearly for their lascivious ways. In what chroniclers called a 'memorable stratagem', a band of clear-complexioned Irish youths led by Anselan turned up at the feast disguised as women. They hid long Irish daggers called scains beneath their cloaks before going seductively to the bedchambers of their drunken hosts and massacring them with whoops and yells. Then they opened the castle gates to waiting compatriots who dispatched the rest of the Vikings with their swords.

A Danish army was sent to Ireland to exact revenge, but the princely Anselan, with a price on his head, was long gone, having escaped to Scotland with a band of followers in or around 1016. When Malcolm II of Scotland, a long-standing enemy of the Danes, heard of his exploits, he invited him to become his Master of Arms and enlisted his help in seeing off Viking marauders in Scotland. In return he bestowed on him 'ample lands in The Lennox' to the north of the present day city of Glasgow. Two years later, according to some accounts, Anselan married an heiress named Denniestoun and they had a son, John, born the following year. Anselan continued to prosper and was evidently a rich man when he died three decades later. His descendants – over the years the name became McAuslane – remained in the highlands of Scotland for more than half a millennium, flourishing on the shores of Loch Lomond and always playing their part in the bloody local wars of the time. One of them, Mac Beth, Baron Mac Auselane, who lived around the year 1400, was 'of great stature and uncommon strength' according to various traditional accounts.

A score or more generations on from Anselan, according to the historian Thesta Scogland, members of the family upped sticks and returned to their roots. She wrote that 'about 1600 one Baron McAuslane of Glenduglas went to Ireland' from Dumbartonshire and settled in County Tyrone near Strabane. The daredevil Anselan's descendants were back.

Twenty years later Baron McAuslane was followed to Ireland by his son Andrew, who settled there as part of the Plantation of Ulster under King James I. For the best part of a century, the Irish branch of the family prospered in Country Tyrone. Andrew's son Alexander remained in Strabane and was reportedly a 'prudent and active gentleman' who fought in civil wars. Then, in around 1711, Alexander's son, 33-year-old Colonel Robert McCausland, moved north to County Londonderry under the patronage of a wealthy relation, William Conolly, a lawyer and Speaker of the Irish Parliament.

Immensely rich, Conolly had made most of his fortune through shrewd land dealing, and by the 1720s he owned 100,000 acres in seven counties, giving him an income estimated at £25,000 a year. Legal documents of the time described him as a 'cunning, intriguing spark.' The Irish satirist Jonathan Swift calculated that if his half-yearly rents were collected in halfpennies it would require 250 horses to bring the money to his house. Some of Conolly's acreage was outside the market town of Limavady (then called Newtown Limavady), seventeen miles east of Derry. He had bought this land in 1697 from the debt-ridden descendants of Sir Thomas Phillips, a professional soldier who had been granted large tracts of Co Derry during the Ulster Plantation in the early 1600s. (Phillips, who had been given the land after his military exploits won him favour in royal circles, disparagingly referred to his *Limma Vaddy* estates as 'the horse pond'.)

As a major land-owner in the district, Conolly was elected a burgess of Limavady in 1701, but the town was a long way from his native Co. Kildare and he needed a trusted person on the spot to look after his interests. To his great sadness he and his wife Katherine were childless, but he was a generous benefactor to their relations, and one of these was Robert McCausland.

Exactly how they were related is unclear. It is possible that Robert was a nephew of Katherine Conolly, but a racier if unverifiable version of events has it that Robert's wife Hannah, born in about 1689, was Conolly's illegitimate daughter.

Whatever the nature of the link, Conolly leased some of his Limavady land to Robert in 1711, and subsequently made him his agent 'for the manor of Newtownlimavady.' The McCausland family's long association with Limavady and the Protestant cause had begun.

When Conolly died in Dublin 'of the apoplexy' (in modern parlance, a stroke) in October 1729, he was by common consent the richest man in Ireland. Robert McCausland was one of those who benefitted from his Will, inheriting a large parcel of land on the vast Limavady estates as an acknowledgement of 'the faithful services he has done me.' He put this land to good use, building on it one of the finest mansion-houses in the county. The property – which he called Fruithill - lay in the fertile valley of the River Roe surrounded by undulating parkland and woodlands - oak, beech, yew, cherry and sweet chestnut – dating back to the Plantation.

Limavady at that time was neat and well-ordered, a 'very clean English-like town', in the words of a visiting Irish physician Dr Thomas Molyneux, although he added discouragingly that the fourteen-mile journey to Coleraine took him four hours over 'dismal, wild, boggy mountains.' As well as a stocks, the town boasted a ducking stool on the banks of the Roe to control disorderly and nagging women, and anyone who left objects lying around in the street at night was liable to a fine of 3s 4d (17p). The Roe Valley was a Protestant stronghold, and Newtown Limavady, as befitted a strongly loyalist area in the Plantation heartland, would become a fertile recruiting ground for the Protestant militias that sprang up in Ulster later in the century.

Robert and Hannah had eight children – five girls followed by three boys. In honour of their wealthy benefactor they named the eldest boy Conolly, born in 1713. He was the first of many McCauslands to bear that name down the centuries. Conolly succeeded to Fruithill in 1734 at the age of twenty-one. Eight years later he married a twenty-four-year-old heiress, Elizabeth Gage, from the nearby estate of Bellarena, so adding to the family's already considerable wealth. Another lucrative union was formed when their son and heir - also Conolly, born in 1754 - married Theodosia Mahon from Strokestown House, Co. Roscommon, sister of the Irish politician and landowner Lord Hartland.

Like his father, the younger Conolly was twice made Provost of Limavady, a position equivalent to Mayor. A staunch unionist, he was a bitter opponent of the Society of United Irishmen, which was formed in the 1790s with the aim of uniting 'all the people of Ireland' over every religious persuasion. When a regiment of United Irishmen was formed in Limavady, Conolly and other 'gentlemen' resolved to take action against the rebels. Together with the Derry MP Sir George Hill, and the staunch loyalist Lord Cavan, he went on a sweep of the Roe valley accompanied by a troop of Derry cavalry and around a hundred militiamen. For ten solid hours they searched Dungiven, Gelvin, Bovevagh, Legavalan and Drummond, and confiscated ninety-five guns, seven bayonets and sundry pistols. The rebel movement petered out locally soon afterwards, boosting the resolve of those loyal to the Crown. In 1797, at their request, Conolly personally administered the Oath of Allegiance to more than six hundred people in the parish church at Magilligan.

A decade later a new threat to stability emerged in the shape of Napoleon Bonaparte, whose invasion plans for Great Britain included diversionary attacks in the north of Ireland. Conolly was seen as just the man to help thwart Boney's fiendish ambitions, and In 1809 he was empowered by the Lord Lieutenant of Ireland, the Duke of Richmond, to form the Balteagh Infantry, a local defence force of 107 men, including six sergeants and 'a trumpeter or drummer.' Armed with rifles, bayonets, blunderbusses and swords, they performed their duties with due solemnity, carrying out target practice, drill and military exercises in the fields at Fruit Hill.

By the standards of the day Fruithill was already an old-fashioned house as the 18th century drew to a close, and in 1796 Conolly added a spacious and well-proportioned drawing-room which made the property 'good and commodious.' Managing the estate was not all plain sailing, and he was constantly running into problems with land at Magilligan which he leased from Frederick Hervey, the Earl of Bristol and Bishop of Derry. Learning that the Bishop planned to up the rent, he complained to him: 'I fear I have been fined because of my own improvements. My demesne contains about 100 acres and above two thirds of it very bad land which at great expense I am scarce able to keep in decent order.' A decade later he again wrote to the Bishop telling him 'my bogs in Magilligan are much run out and consumed. The tenants of the land are daily murmuring and complaining because their cottages are not furnished to their satisfaction.'

In September 1802 some unknown problem required Conolly to sell his stock, crop and farming utensils at auction. The Londonderry Journal reported: 'The stock consists of 8 black coach horses, several saddle and work horses with a number of excellent milch cows and a very fine bull, some fat bullocks and heifers with a number of sheep, calves, pigs, goats etc etc. The crop consists of a large quantity of very fine oats, barley and wheat all nearly ripe with about 40 acres of excellent upland hay all tramped safe and about 6 acres of good potatoes.'

Whatever the reason for the sale, the family's finances were clearly on a firm footing by the time Conolly's heir, Marcus, succeeded to the estate in 1822. A.Atkinson Esquire, an English travel writer of the early nineteenth century, rhapsodised about Fruithill when he stopped there en route from Coleraine to Derry during Marcus's tenure, describing it as 'a distinguished feature of improvement in the very extensive and princely paradise of the See of Derry.'

His extravagant prose went on: 'The lodge stands like a snow-drop in the vale, surrounded by swelling lawns, richly cultivated fields, and sporting plantations, extending the attractions of their beauty to the neighbouring woods, and the distant outposts. The garden of Fruithill is in tolerably good keeping with the other features of this place. It embraces an area of nearly three English acres, walled in, well stocked with fruit-trees in full bearing, rather too well-stocked with apple-trees for the beauty of its appearance, and includes every class of vegetables necessary for the consumption of a house. The agricultural visitor will be gratified with the appearance of some very fine cattle of the Ayrshire breed, whose good cheer, and comely appearance, very plainly proved that the *lines had fallen to them in pleasant places.'*

Samuel Lewis, in his *Topographical History of Ireland,* written a decade or so later, was no less enthusiastic, declaring of Limavady: 'The scenery in various parts is highly interesting, the woods and plantations are thriving, and the country is ornamented with many handsome houses, of which the principal is the residence of Marcus McCausland, Esq.'

Marcus married Marianne Tyndall at St Michaels Church, Bristol, in 1815, and a childhood letter written by one of their daughters, also Marianne, though known to the family as 'Missy', provides another brief but charming glimpse of Fruithill in the early 1830s. 'My dear Mama, I hope you have completely recovered from your headache, your toothache and your earache, which I was sorry to hear you had very badly yesterday evening and the evening before. You cannot think what a beautiful little peachick we have got. Believe me dear Mama, your affectionate Marianne.'

(Poor Missy's adult life was far from happy. In 1845 she entered into a disastrous marriage with John Talbot, a wealthy landlord from County Roscommon. Witnesses said he treated her with 'coldness, indifference and unkindness,' particularly after the birth of their only child, Mary. In 1849 Missy allegedly began an affair with William Mullan, a stable hand on the Mount Talbot estate. Talbot duly obtained a divorce, and the salacious details of the 1856 Talbot v Talbot judgment gripped Irish society. Missy was banished to England and placed in a home for the 'unsound of mind,' but was later rescued by her sister and brother-in-law, Katherine and Thomas Paget, and lived with them at their Leicester villa until her death soon after her fortieth birthday).

Marcus was a generous local benefactor, and in 1832, at a cost of £70, he built a handsome brick schoolhouse for 'very poor children' on the road leading to Balteagh. The classroom was large enough to accommodate thirty pupils, and there was an adjoining bedroom for the schoolmistress who, in addition to her free lodging, was paid two shillings every Monday morning by Marcus's wife. On top of this the elder Marianne supported a small school in a lodge at Fruithill, where six girls from the estate were taught reading, writing and 'plain and fancy needlework' by the McCausland women.

Marcus's land at that time included the Rough Fort, a prehistoric defended farmstead or rath off the Ballykelly road to the west of Limavady, and he turned this into an early tourist attraction by building a fence round it and planting fir, sycamore, birch and a white thorn hedge on the site. It was donated by a later McCausland to the National Trust, and many of the trees he placed there stand to this day. According to 19th century Ordnance Survey records, he employed an 'aged man', known locally as Kane of the Fort, to look after the rath and keep the key to the gate. Keen to preserve Limavady's heritage, Marcus also took great care to protect the ruins of an old church on the estate, Drumachose, cultivating ivy on it as both an ornament and as means of keeping what remained of the building intact.

Marcus's philanthropy extended beyond supporting local schools and giving work to gnarled old men. Poverty was rife throughout Ireland, and before 1840 there was little general provision for those who could not cater for themselves. Government interference in society was neither normal nor considered appropriate. According to an Ordnance Survey report in 1833, paupers and beggars were 'very numerous' in Limavady. Marcus's workers would have been paid the standard wages of the time - 10d (4p) a day for labourers in the summer and 8d in the winter. Women and children were paid from 3d to 4d (approx 1.5p) a day for weeding or gathering potatoes. The Poor Law Union of Newtownlimavady was set up in October 1839 to tackle poverty, and Marcus was elected the first chairman of the Board of Guardians. Under his stewardship the union built a workhouse on the edge of the town capable of holding four hundred inmates. A contemporary newspaper report described him as 'one of those landlords who sought to make a numerous tenantry happy and contented; and to find for them constant employment.'

Like his father, Marcus belonged to the Derry militia, formed to serve the interests of Ireland's Protestant settlers and their survival. That meant, if necessary, taking up arms to protect the state from internal dissent and external threat. On the domestic front, he brought about the next big change to the estate. Fruithill was too small for his liking, even after the enlargements carried out by his father, and in 1825, three years after becoming head of the family, he commissioned a Dublin architect, John Hargrave, to design a new mansion to take its place.

The initial neo-Greek design for a house with six 'bed chambers', four dressing rooms and four reception rooms never got beyond the drawing board, and he had to wait eleven years to achieve his dream. In 1836 he pulled down Fruithill and replaced it with a new house built to the classic designs of the great 19th century architect Sir Charles Lanyon, at the time freshly appointed surveyor for the County of Antrim. It was Lanyon's first major commission, and the house was everything Marcus had hoped for, with a five-bay entrance front, a magnificent central hall with screens of fluted Corinthian columns and rich plasterwork ceilings in the hall, over the staircase and in the drawing-room. A dining room, morning room, library and saloon added to the grandeur downstairs. Upstairs, in the numerous bedrooms, large windows opened on to views of the Donegal hills and the Sperrin mountains. The stable court on the northern side of the house had space for six carriages, and the walled garden was one of the largest in Ireland. Building the new house cost Marcus the then colossal sum of £20,000, the equivalent of about £1.5m in 2013. The architectural historian Alistair Rowan wrote of Lanyon's design: 'He was never to be so chaste again or, one might add, so careful.'

Marcus called the house Drenagh, an ancient townland name originating from the Gaelic word draeighean (droigen in its old Irish form) meaning blackthorn or sloe bush, a shrub found in abundance on the estate and said by some to have mystical properties. The adjective form (draeighneach), signifying a place abounding in blackthorn or a field of sloes, appears in different forms in many Irish place names, as in Dreenagh, Drinagh, Driny and Drinaghan. Sloes, though beautiful, are as bitter as gall and their bushes have savage thorns.

The Drenagh estate during Marcus's time comprised nearly 13,000 acres, making it one of the largest in the county. The land descended to the Castle burn running to the south and to the Curly burn to the north and east. An Italianate high balustraded

Helen, Conolly and Eila at the wedding of Marianne Thompson-McCausland
September 1957

Drenagh – lithograph from the early 1800s .Vincent Brooks

Watercolour of the view from the front door by Geraldine McCausland 1904

Letter from Marianne McCausland to her mother circa 1830

Robert McCausland
died 1734

Conolly McCausland
1754 - 1827

Marcus McCausland
1787-1862
builder of the present Drenagh

Conolly Thomas
(1828-1902)
in cricket gear with Drenagh in background.

Conolly Thomas in old age

Maurice Marcus
(1872-1902)

Carving of McCausland names in Upper School at Eton

Maurice McCausland
and Eileen McCausland
(nee Ogilby)

Maurice above and Eileen with Helen, Conolly and Eila c. 1912

Sir Edward Carson (centre) at a rally at Drenagh

3. SIR GEORGE RICHARDSON, OFFICERS AND FRIENDS, 2nd BATTALION, NORTH DERRY REGIMENT,
AT THE UMBRA CAMP.

Maurice in the uniform of the 'B' Specials

SIGNING THE COVENANT, LIMAVADY

Maurice in uniform of His Majesty's Lieutenant for Co. Londonderry

Self Portrait by Helen sent to Lucius c.1928

Conolly's name carved in Upper School at Eton

Helen's identity card and permit to travel to Ireland 1918 (then still united) from school in Eastbourne for the summer holidays

Helen aged 18

Conolly in the family Bullnose Morris Cowley

Helen and Lucius' wedding day 30th April 1930

Drawing of Helen by Tharp

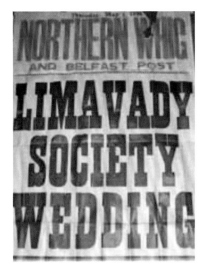

Billboard for
Helen & Lucius' wedding

The happy couple

Richard Edgcumbe 1680-1758. MP for
Plympton and served as Lord of the
Treasury under Sir Robert Walpole.
Painting by Kneller, courtesy of the
Mount Edgcumbe family.

Conolly and Margaret (Peggy) Edgcumbe
at Drenagh on their engagement.

Conolly and Peggy wedding 6th June 1932

terrace, with a commanding view point, overlooked an extensive Italian Garden. There were long meandering walks through beech woods and along the river banks. Through Marcus's mother, the McCauslands had acquired an additional 4,799 acres in County Roscommon, and as Queen Victoria began her long reign they could justifiably claim to be one of Ireland's foremost land-owning families.

Over the course of sixteen years, Marcus and Marianne produced nine children, of whom eight were girls, including the unfortunate Missy. To their great relief, in an age when producing a male heir was paramount; one was a boy. Born in 1828, Conolly Thomas McCausland was educated at Eton and Christ Church, Oxford, following which he spent brief spells in the Corps of Royal Engineers and in the diplomatic service before inheriting Drenagh in 1862 at the age of thirty-four. He threw himself into the running of the estate, and two years later won prizes at the Kennaught Farming Society's annual show for best mare, best two-year-old gelding or filly, best pure-bred Durham bull and best pen of pure-bred Leicester ewes.

As befitted the head of one of the county's leading Protestant families, he held numerous public offices, being a Justice of the Peace, Deputy Lieutenant of the county, High Sheriff and chairman of the Limavady Poor Law Union. A keen sportsman, he was a member of the Limavady Cricket Club and opened the batting in a match at Deerpark against a visiting team from Greenock in 1865. The Scottish visitors proved too strong for the local side and won by eight wickets. He travelled regularly to London where he kept an elegant town house in Gloucester Place, Marylebone, halfway between Hyde Park and Regent's Park, and convenient for Lord's. In keeping with his status he belonged to London's elite Carlton Club.

Like his father and grandfather he was a captain of the Derry Militia, and later in life he became a leading member of the

Ulster Defence Union – Protestant almost to a man - formed in the late 19th Century to protect Ireland's links with the United Kingdom. His name was among those of six hundred U.D.U. 'gentlemen' published by the *Belfast Weekly News* in October 1893 'for the satisfaction of Ulster Unionists.'

Conolly Thomas was still a bachelor when he inherited Drenagh, although like all McCausland men he had a healthy interest in the opposite sex. One of the Drenagh tenants in the late nineteenth century was a young woman called Sarah Tait, born in 1865, who lived just outside the main gate in one of the better cottages. In the opinion of some she had a great McCausland likeness, and it was said that Conolly Thomas knew the reason why.

In 1867, as he neared forty, Conolly Thomas married the Hon Laura St John, twenty-three-year-old younger daughter of the 14th Baron St John of Bletsoe. The wedding took place at Melchbourne in Bedfordshire, and was billed beforehand as 'Approaching Marriage in High Life' by the Northampton Mercury. 'Honoured Madam,' his old nanny, Sarah McAffery, wrote to Laura on Conolly's fortieth birthday the following year, 'I take the liberty of asking you to accept this little brooch as it contains the master's hair cut the day he was a year old. It was offered to me by the family, but I said no one should ever have it but his wife. So I hope you will keep it as a remembrance of an old and loving servant and also of the first birthday you have spent with him at Drenagh.'

Like Marcus and Marianne before them, Conolly Thomas and Laura had nine children, three boys and six girls. Drenagh was now at the height of its splendour. The library boasted shelf after shelf of gilt and tooled books – Sir Walter Scott's *Waverley Novels*, Macaulay's *Essays*, Malcolm's *Life of Lord Clive*, and dozens of bound volumes of the *Quarterly Review*. There was an Italian garden with a fountain inspired by one at the Villa d'Este near Rome, and filled with rhododendrons and rare plants collected in China. Around the Glen and the flower garden, and through the glorious woods, Drenagh offered some of the finest pheasant drives in the country. Guests arrived from all over Britain to let loose their guns as the birds flew between the ruins of ancient Drumachose church and the great Douglas firs.

In addition Conolly Thomas owned a grouse more on Sawel Mountain, more commonly known as Slieve Sawel, the highest peak in the Sperrins and straddling both County Londonderry and Country Tyrone. He was a stickler for the rules of sporting etiquette that governed pheasant and grouse shooting, and woe betide anyone who took away part of the bag without his permission. In the evenings his guests enjoyed dinner with an array of gleaming silver and crystal, and after the ladies had retired to the drawing-room, he entertained his male friends in the newly-created Billiard Room.

The Belfast News-Letter, reporting on a bazaar held at Drenagh in the summer of 1881 to raise funds for the renovation of the parish church in Limavady, provided a deliciously effusive description of the lawns and gardens at that time. 'No lovelier weather could have been wished for; no lovelier aspect than Drenagh demesne could have been selected. None, certainly, could have been offered with better grace that that which Mr C.T.McCausland, D.L. showed in placing his beautiful grounds at the disposal of the bazaar committee. It must be acknowledged that to him in great measure the enjoyableness of the day was due. The demesne, situated a short mile from the railway station, and reached by the cars of the neighbouring gentry, who had kindly lent them for the conveyance of visitors, contained some of the choicest possible bits of woodland scenery. The views on all sides from the lawn in front of Drenagh House, upon which the bazaar was held, were almost without parallel. In fact, the sight of a lovely valley on each side was probably regarded by the fair vendors as a drawback, for the temptation to stroll under richly-foliaged trees and along splendidly kept walks, which the view suggested, became in many instances too strong to be resisted. Certainly the paths, protected from the almost scorching rays of the sun, were calculated to make one entirely oblivious to bazaars, or, indeed, to anything else, except a dreamy feeling of thorough enjoyment. The splendid band of the 15th Regiment was present during the day.'

Not only bazaars were held on Drenagh's neatly-mown grass. There was also a cricket pitch where Conolly Thomas held an annual match between the town and the Drenagh estate. In 1885 he hosted an *Eleven Ladies of Derry v Eleven Ladies of Limavady* match, an event 'hitherto unknown in this part of Ireland' as the local paper reported excitedly, although it added with disdain that the bowling of the Limavady Ladies, who were soundly beaten, was 'very feeble.'

 Other McCausland activities as the century drew to a close included the fearsome mixed hockey matches which were all the rage in the winter months at a time when people thought nothing of bicycling twenty miles to play a match and afterwards cycle twenty miles home again in the dark. The matches were big social events, often enlivened by humorous touches, such as when the men played in skirts and wore hats with flowing feathers. Eileen Ogilby of Pellipar House near Dungiven, soon to marry into the family and become the mother of the Hero of Boulogne, wrote a poem about these matches – *Hockey Alphabet* – in which she noted that the McCauslands at the turn of the century 'all played like bricks.'

Another fine sight in Conolly Thomas's day was the coach and four which took the family on its travels. Drenagh's coachman in the latter part of the century was a steely-eyed perfectionist named Thomas Logan. His son Bob, who also worked on the estate, recalled years later in the *Coleraine Chronicle:* 'The four coach horses and the ladies' ponies had to be kept trim and neat, and many a bucket of sweat was lost in the process. But when you saw the luxurious coach and four prancing animals ready for a journey to another estate and the fine figure of my father in his immaculate rig and top hat, sitting high, the polished reins in his gloved hands, it was very compensating.' It was a golden age, although in 1895 the *Ballymoney Free Press* sensed the world was on the brink of change when it observed that while the bicycle was fast superseding the horse for riding purposes, 'the horseless carriage is destined to succeed both.'

Conolly Thomas was a tough customer, and did not hesitate to take anyone he thought had crossed him to court, as when he sued – unsuccessfully - a Londonderry fruit merchant who refused to take delivery of some Drenagh gooseberries which had deteriorated in the sun. His tenants found him difficult and crotchety, and many kept him at arm's length. One of these was S.M.Macrory of Ardmore Lodge, a miller and farmer who, like his father before him, rented land from the McCauslands in the parish of Balteagh. When S.M. installed new machinery at his Ardmore mills at his own expense, Conolly Thomas at once raised the rent on the grounds that the property was now more valuable. S.M. thought this was monstrously unfair, but when he took counsel's opinion he was advised that the law was on the landlord's side and that nothing could be done about it.

Given that Conolly Thomas's grandfather had suffered a similar experience at the hands of the Bishop of Derry a century earlier; he might have been expected to show some sympathy for S.M., but sympathy came there none. S.M.'s wife pleaded with Conolly Thomas, saying timidly: "Mr McCausland, we've never asked you for a favour before," to be told rather brutally: "Because you can't." Little sparks of fury would flash in S.M.'s eyes and he would mutter (without any known basis in fact) that the McCauslands had only got where they were because their ancestor had come over to Ulster as butler, chief bottle-washer and toady to William of Orange.

When Conolly Thomas died in 1902, his obituary in the Derry Sentinel said of him that 'belonging rather to the old school, he was a gentleman of the utmost courtesy.' Local worthies raised the then substantial sum of £114 to erect a window in his memory at Drumachose Parish Church, and one of those who was tapped for a contribution was S.M.Macrory who, rather magnanimously and perhaps through gritted teeth, handed over two guineas.

Chapter Three

The Young Master

Some people keep complaining that London isn't bright,
They should take a tip from Drenagh and install electric light.
If instead of 'midnight follies' a hockey team they'd run
Like the one we had last autumn, they would find it far more fun

From a poem about Drenagh by Eileen McCausland, c 1905

The man who set in train the events that would ultimately lead to the thirteen-year Drenagh dispute was the eldest of Conolly Thomas's three sons, Maurice Marcus McCausland. Born at his father's London town house on April 9 1872, he had the classic upbringing of one born to succeed to a great ancestral estate. Schooled initially by tutors at Drenagh, he was packed off to a boarding preparatory school in England – Cordwalles in Maidenhead – at around the age of ten. The school, founded to prepare boys for Public School or for the Royal Navy, placed a good deal of emphasis on physical exercise. Maurice thrived under the headmastership of the Rev Thomas Nunns and made full use of the ample space provided for sport.

From Cordwalles he went to Eton, just five miles away, arriving at Mr Cole's house in April 1885 during the week of his thirteenth birthday. He did not play in any school teams and was unable to boast any major academic prizes, but he evidently enjoyed his time there, and left the school in July 1891 when he was nineteen. Two months later he went up to Trinity Hall, Cambridge, to read classics.

A handful of surviving pages from a diary he kept in 1892 during his second term at Cambridge provide an intriguing glimpse of the 'young master's' privileged life. The picture they draw is of a hearty, pipe-smoking, sociable young man, not averse to a drop or two of whiskey, prone to eczema, and with a great love of the countryside. Highly proper and conventional, he went to church every Sunday, and each evening solemnly recorded in his diary both the weather conditions and great state events such as the funeral of the Duke of Clarence.

He took care to tip servants when appropriate, and maintained a keen interest in the welfare of Drenagh's employees, such as visiting the forester when he was ill and sending him tobacco as a get-well present. He had a healthy respect for old Conolly Thomas ('Father') and duly called on aged uncles and aunts when time permitted. Though never short of money, he made a careful note of his expenditure, jotting down each purchase and its cost, in practice perhaps for the day when he himself would have to supervise Drenagh's accounts. His greatest loves were beagling, shooting and fishing with his prized Hardy split cane rod, all of which took preference by a long way over reading books and writing essays.

And what a life he led. New Years Day 1892 found him taking part in a shoot in Castleblayney in County Monaghan. Once the guns were loaded, proceedings went forward with the dispatch of an eighteenth century amputation as he and eight others shot ninety-six pheasant, eighteen woodcock and eighteen rabbits before darkness forced them to head for home. They increased their tally the next day, and Maurice noted in his diary that he had 'never heard such banging before.' Of the first five rabbits he personally despatched, 'there was a black one, a white, a yellow, a silver grey and a brown.'

On January 4 the party rowed out to White Island in Lough Muckno (Maurice was stopped on his way to the jetty by a policeman who mistook him for a runaway youth from England) where he shot a snipe – 'the only snipe seen there for years' – and a widgeon. The following day he returned by train to Limavady, buying 'baccy' for his pipe and some neckties while he waited for his connection at Derry. There were still eight days left before he had to return to Cambridge for the start of term and, with the exception of the Sunday, when he walked to Drumachose parish church and back for the morning service, he spent all of them shooting at Drenagh with his father and his brother Pat. One night he stayed out until two a.m. shooting rats and rabbits by moonlight.

On arriving back at Cambridge with the then substantial sum of £20 spending money in his pocket, he quickly settled into an easy-going routine. 'Luckock came to lunch. Loafed about with Gosling afterwards' was his diary entry for Monday January 18. A dapper figure in his wing collar and spats, he just had time to listen to Canon Alfred Ainger preach the varsity sermon before he was off on his travels again, going to Wilbraham in the Cambridgeshire countryside to shoot pigeons and to Swaffham in Norfolk where he shot four hares and a brace of partridges.

Between January 25 and February 24 he went beagling or shooting on eleven separate occasions, joining shooting parties at Wilburton, Haddenham and Swaffham, and blasting pretty well anything that moved from the skies, including duck, water hen, pigeons and starlings. He went ferreting with relatives at Fulbourne, catching nine rabbits, four pigeons and a hawk, hunted with basset hounds at Waterbeach, and with beagles at Swaffham. All this, it should be noted, was in term time.

He mentioned in his diary that he 'worked in the evening' on February 2 and that on February 22 he attended a lecture at Swaffham on 'injurious insects', but other than that there is precious little evidence of any serious academic study. When he was not beagling or shooting, he liked to 'loaf about the town' with fellow students, dine with friends, play football, go to the theatre, play pills (a form of pocket billiards) or, for want of anything better, 'do absolutely nothing.' 'Felt very seedy and sleepy,' he wrote in his diary on arriving back at Cambridge on February 5 having spent three of the four previous days beagling and shooting. On one occasion he went with friends to see Corney Graine, a portly barrister-turned-comedian who performed musical sketches at the piano. Maurice was not impressed by songs like *The Masher King of Piccadilly,* and resented the 5s 6d (27p) he paid for the ticket and the shilling (5p) he forked out for a cab. 'For my part I did not want to see the silly old fool at all.'

With his interest in all matters avian, it was probably Maurice, while home for the summer vacation, who was responsible for a brief and curious item which appeared in *Naturalist's Note-Book* in the Cornishman newspaper in July 1892: 'Pigeon like to feed on small snails and slugs, when at hand. The other day one dropped dead at Drenagh, Limavady. Picked up, its crop was found packed with a hundred slugs. The slime of them had filled the throat and choked the gluttonous bird.'

Throughout his youth he was acutely aware of Ireland's political and religious divides. On April 8 1886, the night before Maurice's fourteenth birthday, the Prime Minister, William Gladstone, had introduced the Home Rule Bill, intended to transfer control of Ireland from London to Dublin. Driven by a genuine feeling of high moral purpose, Gladstone was convinced that Home Rule was the only realistic way to end centuries of turbulence. When the Bill was defeated in June, jubilant Protestants in Belfast left their work early to light bonfires and tar barrels and to sing and march with the Orange bands. As they did so, angry Catholics set fire to their chimneys, creating a thick pall of smoke over the city in an ominous foretaste of what was to come some nine decades later.

There was, of course, no question as to where young Maurice's own sympathies lay, and we can be sure that he too celebrated with his friends when he heard the news that the Bill had been defeated. More clearly now than at any time during the previous two centuries the people of Ulster seemed sharply divided into two ethnic groups with markedly different hopes and goals. It was almost as if Protestants and Catholics were separate nations. Protestants like the McCauslands considered themselves Anglo-Saxon with inbuilt virtues of thrift, capacity for hard work and respect for law and order. Nationalists emphasised their Gaelic origins, and laid claim to characteristics such as hospitality, passion and love of poetry. Fascinated by his own genealogy, Maurice set about drawing up a McCausland family tree, enlisting the help of his mother, Laura, to gather relevant information from elderly relations. He loved showing visitors round Drenagh and taking them up to the ruins of old Drumachose church where he would point out the reputed grave of Fin McQuillan, a tribal chieftain killed in battle with the MacDonnell clan centuries earlier.

In 1893, Ulster Unionists were appalled when the House of Commons passed a second Home Rule Bill, again instigated by Gladstone. Loyalist hatred of the Liberal Prime Minister knew no bounds, and it was rumoured that Conolly Thomas's great friend, Sir Thomas Lecky of Greystone Hall, had a china head of him affixed to the bottom of his chamber pot. Laura, encouraged by Conolly Thomas and their children, went into action and formed the Limavady branch of the Women's Unionist Association which, under her direction, amassed seventy-five members. At their first meeting they unanimously passed a resolution condemning the Bill as 'subversive of all the best interests of this country' and vowed to 'thwart the designs of selfish and wicked men.' Conolly Thomas had simultaneously become a leading light in the Ulster Defence Union, and once again there were celebrations at Drenagh when the House of Lords threw out the Bill by 419 votes to 41. It was said that only two Unionist peers were absent without valid excuse – one shooting lions in Somaliland, the other killing rats in Reigate.

It went without saying that Maurice would marry into a family with similar values to those of his parents, and there could be no more suitable bride than his childhood friend Eileen Ogilby of *Hockey Alphabet* fame. Like Maurice, Eileen was from an old planter family, and had been brought up at Pellipar House near Dungiven, eight miles or so from Drenagh. In her youth she enjoyed reading romantic novels, and attending balls and horse shows in Dublin where captivated young men called her 'The Star of the North.' For sheer wealth, her father, Capt Robert Ogilby, could more than match the McCauslands, owning as he did large tracts of land in both Dungiven and Woolwich. He was a Justice of the Peace, a Deputy Lieutenant for County Londonderry and, as a captain in the 4th King's Own Regiment, had distinguished himself in the Zulu war of 1879, the year Eileen was born. Old Conolly Thomas could not have been more delighted when Maurice and Eileen announced their engagement.

The couple were married on April 9 1902, Maurice's thirtieth birthday, in the eighteenth century St Georges Church in Hanover Square, London, but what should have been the happiest time of their lives was marred by tragedy. Earlier in the year Eileen's father had been diagnosed with cirrhosis of the liver, and he stayed on in London after the wedding to be treated by one of the country's most eminent doctors, Sir Francis Laking, physician to Queen Victoria, King Edward VII, and later to King George V. Unfortunately nothing could be done for Eileen's father, and within forty-eight hours of his daughter's marriage he had fallen into a coma. Three days later he died at the age of fifty-two. The distraught newly-weds had to cut short their honeymoon to attend his funeral at Dungiven on April 17, and years later Eileen recalled: 'Our honeymoon was no honeymoon and all sorrow.'

They had barely recovered from the shock when, in June, Conolly Thomas died of heart failure six weeks after his seventy-fourth birthday. There was no dower house on the estate and, as was the rather harsh custom of the day, his widow, Laura, though not yet sixty, had to leave Drenagh and find somewhere else to live. She moved initially to Devon before settling in the south of Ireland with her two unmarried daughters, Octavia (her eighth child) and Lettice. Sixty years later, Octavia, by then aged eighty-two, told Maurice's daughter, Helen, in a letter that leaving Drenagh was still 'vivid and heart-breaking in my memory.'

As the new head of the family, Maurice installed himself and his young bride in the large bedroom over the front of the house, and used the library next to the morning room as his office. He kept a close eye on the working of the estate, and took a keen interest in breeding short-horn cattle and black-faced sheep. A dog-lover, he also instituted annual retriever trials at Drenagh. One of his immediate problems was the payment of death duties, but Eileen was able to help with these and lent him enough money to avoid the need to sell off any of the estate.

The house boasted most modern creature comforts, with a turbine by the mill supplying electricity, a dumb waiter lift to carry food up to the nursery quarters and, in due course, a black daffodil of a telephone with the number Limavady 49. Lavatories were still few and far between, and boys and young men were expected to use an earth closet near the path that led to the Glen, something of an ordeal in bad weather, especially if the privy was already occupied when they got there.

Like his father, Maurice was a keen cricketer and an enthusiastic supporter of the Drummond Cricket Club, a mile from Drenagh on the road to Balteagh. Later he would be instrumental in setting up the National Trust in Northern Ireland. He had a stern, finely carved face, but the sternness disappeared with his eyes, which had a kind edge to them. Eileen, a great beauty, had a soft, low-pitched voice, but was capable of using it to good effect. Her calls for Maurice or her children, and more particularly the sound of her clearing her throat, echoed through the hall and up the stone staircase and made a lasting impression on all who heard them.

Maurice and Eileen set high standards, and many of their staff did not last the course, but an elderly and irascible butler with the splendidly Dickensian name of Grimes ensured the household ran as smoothly as possible. Born in Leicestershire in 1847, William Grimes claimed the McCauslands were 'near royalty', and was such an institution at Drenagh that a patch of land on the estate was named *Grimes' Plantation* in his honour, and was enshrined as such by the Ordnance Survey. Even when Maurice was advancing into late middle-age, the even older Grimes continued to call him 'Master Maurice.' Grimes was very particular about the silver and denounced anything he thought was not up to the mark in weight and quality as 'gingerbread.' He was a familiar sight on sunny afternoons, carrying a silver teapot on a silver tray out into the garden, followed by a maid carrying cakes and sandwiches. Head held imperiously high, he would stride across the grass to the 'Heather House,' a little summerhouse garlanded with heather, where the McCausland ladies at the turn of the century liked to read and do their needlework.

Maurice was already a magistrate when he took over the estate and, like his father, he would hold numerous other public offices, including that of His Majesty's Lieutenant of County Londonderry. As a staunch unionist and member of the Church of Ireland, he was as prepared as his father, grandfather and great-grandfather before him to take up arms to keep Ireland in the United Kingdom. He was a man of strong opinions, and enjoyed discussing religion and politics with his solicitor brother-in-law, Edward Boyle, another staunch unionist, whom he entertained to tea every Sunday afternoon. On September

28 1912, the two men, accompanied by Eileen, walked to Market Square in Limavady to sign the Ulster Covenant and Declaration in protest against the third Irish Home Rule Bill, which was yet another – and again ultimately failed - attempt by Westminster to provide self-government for Ireland. Following the lead of the Ulster Unionist leader, Sir Edward Carson, who was first to sign, nearly half a million men and women all over Ireland put their signatures to the Covenant and Declaration that famous Saturday. It was rumoured that some ultra-Loyalists did so in blood.

Every Sunday, without fail, Maurice led the family into Limavady to attend mattins at Drumachose Parish Church. The scene of many McCausland weddings and funerals, the church was 'guarded' by a 17th century cast iron cannon used by the Protestant defenders of Derry in 1688, and was invariably packed with friends and relatives who sang loudly and heartily. The family usually filled two pews and Maurice, as a pillar of both the Limavady and the Protestant community (he was a member of the Select Vestry of Drumachose, which represented and managed the concerns of the parish) usually read one of the lessons. On returning to his pew he kept a watchful eye on the rector to ensure his sermon was not too long. The simplicity of the services was very much to his liking. From an early age he disliked High Church and 'ritualistic' practices which he said 'smacked of Rome.'

Among the older members of the congregation there would have been those who remembered the so-called Limavady riots in 1854, when local Protestants took exception to a series of rallies held in the town by Redemptionist priests. According to a colourful if hardly impartial report in the Londonderry Sentinel: 'The townspeople regarded the influx of Roman Catholics with suspicion, thinking it intended as a menace, and as foreboding mischief to them. The demeanour of the Romanists, too, was calculated to strengthen this impression.

They strutted with an air of insolence and triumph through the streets; their language savoured of fanatical bigotry; and the tone and bearing of Roman Catholic servants and of the humbler class generally, was entirely altered towards their superiors who professed the Reformed faith.'

Matters reached a head when up to fifteen hundred Protestants held an impromptu rival rally outside Drumachose Parish Church at which the Rev George Scott of Balteagh endeavoured 'in a spirit of love and kindness' to explain to any listening Catholics 'how unscriptural it was to worship the Virgin Mary.' One of the Redemptionist priests, the Rev J Conway, responded by calling for 'Three Cheers for the Pope.' Several people were hurt in the inevitable uproar that followed, and Conway was arrested for allegedly firing a pistol at 'a respectable young Protestant woman.' The image of Protestant tolerance stretched beyond all reasonable bounds was not mirrored by the Catholic-supporting *Freeman's Journal*. While conceding that the Catholics had responded to the appeal for three cheers for the Pope with 'stentorian energy', it claimed they then 'retired peacefully' only to be set upon by 'cowardly' Protestant assailants armed with clubs, hammers and iron bars.

Although the trouble had taken place eighteen years before Maurice was born, he must have heard about the incident, and was probably rather proud of the fact that the magistrate who had the Rev J Conway thrown into jail that night was his father's cousin and close friend, William Gage. Times had changed since then, of course. Sectarian conflict on that scale would not be seen again in Limavady, and the town was now largely peaceful, even if deep-rooted prejudices remained close to the surface, not least among Maurice and many of his generation. In the meantime, having nurtured their estate for 170 years, the McCauslands found themselves at the dawn of the twentieth century enjoying unparalleled prosperity in their Roe Valley surroundings. No ghosts stalked Drenagh's acres.

Its inhabitants, having done their duty in one world, were presumably busy with their duty in the next.

Before many more years had passed, the future of Drenagh appeared to have been settled for yet another generation. Maurice and Eileen had three children. Two were girls - Helen, born in 1903, and Eila, born in 1910. The middle child was a boy, Conolly Robert McCausland, born in 1906, the future Guards officer and hero of Boulogne with his gun too hot to hold. As they celebrated the birth of their son, Maurice and Eileen assumed that he would eventually succeed to Drenagh himself and live out the rest of his days there – the seventh McCausland male in a row to do so. It turned out to be dramatically more complicated than that.

Chapter Four

Home Fun

The winter sun upon the larch
Turning their branches brown to rose,
the glow,
Reflects the willows on the water's edge,
So that one leans to see the beauty
of its bough –
A heron on majestic wings
With leisured grace glides slowly out of sight.
Three swans upon the lake...
What sudden things
Create a rapture in the soul,
A rapture...and an ache –

'The Lake – Drenagh' by Helen McCausland, January 1929

Conolly Robert McCausland was born on July 11, 1906. The cries of the peacocks that strutted across the Drenagh lawns, descendants perhaps of the 'beautiful little peachick' Marianne 'Missy' McCausland had written about so charmingly eight decades earlier, were among the first sounds to be imprinted on his mind. So were the cawing of the rooks that lived in the great beech trees where the long drive finally bent towards the house, and the crack of guns during the pheasant shoots each autumn and winter.

Although Drenagh was by now past its heyday (under the Irish Land Act of 1903 – usually known as the Wyndham Act – three quarters of the estate was compulsory purchased by the Government and passed on to the tenants at highly advantageous terms) he enjoyed a comfortable and privileged upbringing. No fewer than eight servants lived in the house during his childhood – two nursemaids, two housemaids, a cook, a kitchen maid, a footman and a groom. The senior nursemaid was Elizabeth King, a middle-aged widow from County Sligo, whose influence on her young charges was profound. Known to all as 'Nanny King', she remained close to the family for the rest of her life, and at the time of her death in 1954 was still living with the widowed Eileen two miles from Drenagh at Ardnargle.

Almost as soon as he was out of his pram Conolly was expected to walk with the grown-ups every Sunday to Drumachose Parish Church, often hand in hand with his adored sister Helen, who was three years his senior. The prayers the young Conolly said were not confined to Sundays and to church. Nanny King, purse-lipped and holy-minded, also insisted on prayers when the children sat down to eat, and she once refused to let one of Conolly's young cousins, Denis Gibbs, have strawberries at breakfast because he had failed to thank God for what he was about to receive. Deep down Nanny King had a heart of gold, but she could instil fear in any child.

Soon there were journeys further afield. Perched on the wooden benches of a horse-drawn wagonette, the family would head off to the wild and magnificent Atlantic coast some twelve miles away. One destination was the Umbra at Magilligan, several acres set back from the beach where they owned the Red Cottage, a corrugated iron and pitch pine affair with four bedrooms. Another was Magilligan Point on The Foyle estuary where the short ferry crossing to Greencastle in County Donegal was made all the more exciting because, in the absence of a quay, the boatmen carried their passengers to the waiting boats on their backs.

The spectacular stretch of coast became an integral part of Conolly's childhood. The Irish poet Louis MacNeice, born one year after him, visited Magilligan at about the same time

41

and in his unfinished autobiography, *The Strings Are False,* he described seeing the strand for the first time as one of the greatest experience of his childhood. 'Magilligan Strand – not that I then knew its name – is one of the longest and smoothest strands in Ireland...we suddenly came round a corner and there it was, unbelievable but palpably there. Once again, as with my first sight of the Atlantic, I had the sense of infinite possibility, which implied, I think, a sense of eternity. Magilligan Strand was like falling in love...'

At Magilligan Point, Conolly and Helen, and later their younger sister Eila, explored the great sandstone Martello Tower built in 1812 in response to the threat of a French invasion, and played in the huge sand dunes bearded with marram grass and rare wild flowers. Under the protective gaze of the adults they learned to swim in the choppy waters at Downhill and the Umbra. 'We all had a lovely bathe – except Nurse, she had to paddle in to bathe Baby,' nine-year-old Helen wrote to her mother after a trip to Magilligan in the summer of 1912. 'Conolly dug away the sand and made a kind of well which looked like a flood.'

The railway line was accessible from the beach at Downhill and they could place halfpennies on the rails which, when the train had passed, would be hot to the touch and miraculously flattened to the size of a penny. Always on these outings there were crowds of people and sumptuous picnics, especially if it was someone's birthday. Sometimes there were picnics up on Keady mountain, with its glorious views of the Roe valley, or further afield near Benbradagh in the Sperrin Mountains where the McCauslands owned a large acreage for sheep grazing and grouse shooting, the latter being a popular sport in Northern Ireland until the 1920s. The ancient oak woodlands of Banagher Glen beyond Dungiven were another favourite destination. Occasionally there were trips to Portrush, where Conolly and his sisters would clamber on board the tramway to the Giant's

Causeway, hailed at its opening in 1883 as the 'first long electric tramway in the world.'

On the way home they would gaze across Lough Foyle at the port of Moville on the Inishowen peninsula and, if they were in luck, see one of the great liners steaming in from Glasgow to pick up passengers who hoped to make their fortune in the New World. "There's nothing between there and America," the grown-ups would tell them. Conolly's imagination was stirred by these ocean-going vessels. In 1912 he painted a picture of a large four-funnelled passenger liner with a frightened-looking woman standing on the deck. His artistic endeavour was perhaps inspired by the Titanic, the Belfast-built leviathan which notoriously foundered that spring with huge loss of life during her maiden voyage across the Atlantic.

The children were not over-indulged. They went on paper chases, climbed trees, and enjoyed inventing their own games, such as a home-made version of Happy Families which featured their immediate family and close relations. 'Have you got Master Gibbs?' 'No, but have *you* got Miss Ogilby?' They had a collection of bears for which they built homes and provided tea, and were the proud possessors of a magnificent white rocking horse, complete with saddle and bridle. Their imaginations worked overtime, and Helen and Conolly conjured up numerous adventures with a make-believe winged friend called Perseus who, they fancied, flew regularly to Drenagh to visit them, perching at night in the great beech tree on the lawn.

All three enjoyed bird nesting, which at that time was considered a respectable hobby provided one did not take more than one egg from the nest. They spent as much time outdoors as the weather permitted and, like all children, had their fair share of scrapes and tumbles. In one four-week period in the spring of 1916, Conolly sprained his hand and needed a sling after he fell off a see-saw, Eila slipped on the gravel and cut open her knee, and both Conolly and Eila were hurt when they fell into drainage ditches. They succumbed to the usual childhood illnesses and Conolly was proud of the fact that he was 'never sick once' when he caught whooping cough. When all three caught measles at the same time, tiny Eila horrified the nurse by running around naked shouting for roast 'potater.'

Limavady Station was a particular source of excitement in their young lives, for there seemed to be a constant flow of Drenagh guests arriving or departing by steam train. The single-track branch line from the town stretched three and a quarter miles along oil-stained timber and gravel to Limavady Junction, where travellers could pick up the Derry-Belfast express. By tradition, Drenagh's departing guests were seen off from the platform by those still staying at the house, the latter waving and cheering as the little train with its three carriages picked up speed, sending up clouds of whitish fiery smoke with short, emphatic puffs. A couple of miles away, when the train steamed past the home of Eileen's mother at Ardnargle, she and her own guests would wave their handkerchiefs from the terrace, which overlooked the track, so giving the passengers a second send-off.

The trains were manned by three men – a driver, fireman and guard – and were so punctual as they chugged to and fro across the Roe valley that labourers in the fields would set their watches by them. 'Sit, sit, sit for Dungiven,' the Guard would shout on the south-bound train when it arrived at Limavady. Drenagh's guests invariably used the first-class compartments, which were richly upholstered in navy blue and had spotlessly white antimacassars on the backs of the seats. There were no corridors, but one compartment had a little private lavatory, and people who found themselves in that compartment made a point of using it whether they needed to or not. If Mr Connolly, the stocky, spade-bearded station-master, saw a Drenagh guest accidentally head for a third-class compartment (there was no second class), with their racks of varnished pine and gobbets of spit on the floor, he would rush forward in his dark blue frock coat and kepi with a horrified shout of "Yez cann't go in there; come on in here."

The most celebrated guest to stay at Drenagh in those pre-war years was the brilliant lawyer Sir Edward Carson, the revered Unionist leader and hero of loyalist families like the McCauslands. Carson had risen to prominence in 1895 when as a young QC he ruthlessly cross-examined Oscar Wilde in the famous libel action brought by the playwright against the Marquess of Queensbury. He was at the centre of another celebrated case when he cleared the name of a 13-year-old naval cadet, George Archer-Shee (the Archer-Shees were friends of the McCauslands), who had been falsely accused of stealing a postal order. The trial became the basis for *The Winslow Boy,* the award-winning play by Terence Rattigan.

Tall, lean and angular, Carson was venerated in his native Ireland for more than his legal brilliance. It was his championship of the Ulster loyalists in their determination to remain part of the United Kingdom that won him iconic status. In 1910, after eighteen years in Parliament, he became leader of the Ulster Unionists in the House of Commons. Declaring his resistance to the jurisdiction of a Dublin Parliament over Ulster, he had vowed to defeat 'the most nefarious conspiracy that has ever been hatched against a free people.' A Belfast clergyman inspecting a local boys' school at around that time asked the class: 'Can you tell me who is the Supreme Being?' A united shout of 'Carson' was the reply. Even his Republican enemies admired him. 'Carson the Prod,' they said, 'was the only man in Ireland with bollocks.'

The McCauslands put themselves at Carson's disposal, and in 1914 Maurice played a significant role in a well-planned operation, inspired by Carson, to smuggle some twenty-four thousand Mauser rifles and three million rounds of ammunition into Larne and Bangor. The weapons were distributed by car to prepared dumps throughout Ulster – including one at Drenagh - to protect the province. Carson wanted to maintain the Union of Britain and All-Ireland peacefully, but he believed that preparing for war was the way to achieve this. Maurice was proud to have taken part in the gun-running enterprise and to demonstrate his unswerving loyalty to 'The Big Man', he named a plot of land on the Drenagh demesne *Carson's Croft*.

In April 1914 Carson made his only known appearance in Limavady. A committee of local worthies, including Maurice and his brother-in-law Edward Boyle, spent months preparing for the visit, and huge crowds turned out on a fine Thursday afternoon to greet their hero. Arches above the streets displayed such messages as 'We choose death before dishonour' and 'We prepare for defence but not for defiance.' The local paper reported: 'The visit of a prince could not have been characterised with a greater wave of enthusiasm.'

The climax of the afternoon was a visit by Carson to Drenagh. Here he inspected 4,000 men of the North Derry contingent of the Ulster Volunteer Force, who were under Maurice's command. The UVF – Protestant to a man - was in effect Carson's private army and was pledged to fight any attempt to sever or dilute Ulster's attachment to the United Kingdom. "Please God," thundered Carson from a makeshift saluting stand in the Drenagh fields, "if the worst comes to the worst, you will show yourselves worthy sons of worthy ancestors, and you will make history as they did with the motto of 'No Surrender.'"

To his lasting excitement, seven-year-old Conolly was allowed a grandstand view of the proceedings, standing next to Carson himself as the volunteers marched past. He wrote to a friend nearly half a century later: 'The great review here is of course quite indelibly printed on my mind. The thrill of standing beside the great Sir Edward on the farm wagon which formed the saluting base and of seeing the march past – these are things I shall never forget.'

When the review was over, Carson was driven to Protestant Street, where Maurice presented him with a key to the new UVF drill hall. Then he returned to Drenagh under the protection of a motorcycle escort to spend the night. Throughout his stay forty hand-picked men from the UVF, attired in khaki, great-coats, caps, puttees, bandoliers and haversacks, guarded the house and patrolled the grounds. They were armed to the teeth with service rifles, bayonets and fifty rounds of ammunition each, a precaution which some Limavady residents privately felt was excessive. The room Carson slept in was christened the Carson Room, later to be renamed the Orange Room by Eileen.

While at Drenagh, the 'Supreme Being' sat down with three-year-old Eila and taught her to recite a poem, *No Surrender*, which was popular at the time with children throughout the North of Ireland.

> *Edward Carson had a cat,*
> *He sat it on the fender,*
> *And every time it caught a mouse,*
> *It shouted 'No Surrender!'*

The next morning, as he left the house to catch the 8.10 a.m. train from Limavady, he walked beneath an arch of union jacks made especially for the occasion by Conolly and Helen. Much to Conolly's embarrassment, but to everyone else's amusement, he banged his head on the arch as he shook Conolly's hand.

Afterwards Carson sent a letter from Mountstewart in Co Down to 'Miss Helen, Master Conolly and Miss Baby McCausland.' He wrote: 'My dear young friends. I was very pleased to receive your nice letter today. I am so sorry I had to leave Drenagh without seeing all the nice things you desired to show me but I hope the next time I pay you a visit I will have time to see everything. Baby must never forget her 'No Surrender' poem, and she will understand better every day what it means. I hope you are having a happy day full of sunshine as it is here. With affectionate regards, yr friend and leader, Edward Carson.'

At an early age Conolly's name was put down for Eton - his father's old school - and in September 1916, a month after his tenth birthday and at the height of the Great War, he was despatched to Edgborough, a small, privately-owned boarding school in Guildford, Surrey. At the beginning of his first term he was accompanied to England by Maurice and Eileen, who treated him to an indulgent week in London before delivering him to the school. The weary travellers arrived late after the long journey and went into the dining-room to find the other boys already having their supper of milk and *Fancy Lunch* biscuits. Conolly had rarely, if ever, set foot outside Ireland before and had to struggle to hide his trepidation. It helped that a fellow pupil was his first cousin Denis Gibbs (he of banned strawberries fame) who by an ancestral quirk was also his third cousin and who was tasked with keeping a protective eye on his slightly younger relative.

When he was older Conolly would often make at least part of the journey by himself, travelling backwards and forwards three times a year on one or other of the various sea routes. With his tuck box and trunk, he would set off by train from Limavady Junction to Belfast's York Street station. From there his usual option was to take a cab and catch either the Larne-Stranraer ferry or the Belfast-Liverpool ferry, the latter route entailing a night in a double cabin which in those days cost five shillings (25p) for the crossing, with an early morning cup of tea thrown in for an extra shilling. Often on these war-time journeys he felt a frisson of fear, for German U-Boats patrolled the Irish Sea and passenger ships were not off-limits. In 1918 more than 500 people drowned when a U-Boat sunk the steamship *Leinster* in Dublin Bay. Death was never far away, and Conolly and Helen were devastated when a young Drenagh footman whom they both adored went off to fight the Germans and was killed in the trenches. Closer to home, though nothing to do with the war, both were upset when the body of the old Drenagh woodman, McCun, was found one March morning in 1916 in the River Roe.

As Conolly progressed through Edgborough, he proved increasingly resistant to discipline and often displayed a fiery temperament. To the concern of the headmaster, Mr James, he regularly provoked fights with other boys, particularly if they came from the south of Ireland. The year he arrived at the school, Irish republicans staged the infamous Easter rising in Dublin aimed at ending British rule. Taking a leaf out of his father's loyalist book, not to mention that of the great Carson, Conolly thought the Nationalists who wanted to break away from England were a Bad Lot, and the Sinn Feiners were beyond the pale. 'Dirty Shinner' was one of the worst insults he could hurl at anyone. One boy, in particular, Somerset Stopford-Brooke, the son of a Unitarian minister from the south, became his sworn enemy. Conolly would yell 'Rebel' at him, and Stopford-Brooke would shout back that Conolly was a 'Scot', a sneering reference to Drenagh's Plantation forebears. Conolly's cousin Denis would try to break up their fights but with little success.

Returning home to Drenagh for the holidays was always a joy, particularly when the war ended and the sea crossing no longer presented any danger. For a boy entering his teenage years, the estate was a thrilling place. By 1919 Drenagh boasted two motor cars, an open Talbot Darracq tourer and a Venus saloon. As yet there were no petrol pumps in Limavady, and the only way to purchase fuel was in two-gallon cans until Hutchinson's Motor

Services in Catherine Street acquired a single Pratt's pump in 1922. Collecting petrol was the job of Drenagh's concertina-playing chauffeur, Mercer, who always drove as fast as he could. If he saw flocks of chickens on the road – and there were often chickens wandering around – he would put his foot down and make straight for them, causing Eileen to shriek "MERCER, slow DOWN." The Talbot had to be hand-cranked, and on at least one occasion Mercer badly strained his back trying to start it, forcing the family to cancel a trip to the new-fangled *cinematograph* in Derry.

During that summer of 1919 the Gibbs cousins came to stay at Drenagh, and Conolly and Denis devoted many blissful weeks to boyish pursuits. A favourite pastime was to go into the yard and rubbish areas with their air guns and pot rats, of which there were a great many. Another was to go down to the Curly burn, where weathered snags split the water like broken, grey teeth, and hurl great sods of earth at the wasps' nests in the bank before running for dear life. Sometimes the angry wasps managed to retaliate and the boys would run home rubbing their backsides, to the distress of their mothers but to Nanny King's undisguised delight. The 'Jolly Boat', a canvas affair with small oars which was kept on a lake on the estate, also kept them busy, as did setting night lines over the burn to catch eels.

On one never-to-be-forgotten occasion they went to the Ulster Motorcycle Championships at Downhill and watched in awe as the machines raced along the hard sand beneath the Mussenden Temple at what seemed like impossible speeds, the harsh burr of their two-stroke petrol engines temporarily drowning out the percussion of the waves on the beach. There would not be excitement like it until Alan Cobham's Air Circus arrived at Limavady in 1933, thrilling the crowds in a field outside the town with daredevil displays of aeronautical wizardry.

Of the two boys, Conolly – rather crudely nicknamed 'Scales' by his siblings because of a skin condition inherited from his father - was the naughtiest, and he often led his cousin astray, as when they crept up on the Drenagh peacocks and removed some of their feathers. There was an inventive streak to Conolly's mischievousness. His father was interested in archaeology and antiquarian research. He kept an impressive collection of old flints and arrow-heads in the Drenagh stables, and was a member of the Ancient Monuments' Advisory Committee. As a young man he had been fascinated by the discovery by a ploughman in a field near Drenagh of the so-called Broighter Hoard, a remarkable cache of Iron Age gold objects including an exquisitely worked model boat and a bowl of beaten golden. A large grey stone standing by itself in one of the Drenagh fields gave Conolly an idea, and with a hammer and chisel he fashioned it into the shape of a primitive throne with a seat and foot-rest. Maurice was thrilled by the discovery of this 'prehistoric' artefact and invited a professional archaeologist to view it. Could it be a discovery on a par with the Broighter Hoard? Might it become known by historians as the Drenagh Throne? Conolly eventually let on that he and not Stone Age man had crafted the object, but not before he had enjoyed a megalithic laugh at his father's expense.

The food at Drenagh was always excellent. With its powerful scent of fruit and flowers, the large walled garden was a veritable wonderland to the children, with the beds of strawberries along the west wall proving a particularly strong magnet. There were large greenhouses and vine houses, and a solitary bay tree standing in their midst. Beyond the wall were numerous frames, which contained another cornucopia of garden produce.

In the large kitchen Mrs Aylward the cook ruled her culinary kingdom with iron discipline, presiding over a well-scrubbed refectory table which stretched out beneath gleaming copper saucepans like a sleeping monster. The children were always intrigued by the great bowls of cream and pails of butter-milk in the dairy, the mountains of soda bread piled on the table, and the jars of brandy cherries that jostled for space on the shelves with tins of tapioca and sago. When Helen was tiny, Mrs Aylward allowed her to choose lunch on her birthday – April 6. Helen had to write down what she wanted on the kitchen slate and on more than one occasion she plumped for hotpot, chiefly because she knew how to spell it.

The excitements and discoveries on the Drenagh demesne, with its box hedges and lush meadows, seemed endless. There were fascinating people to meet, like the shepherd, Bob Dickson, up on the mountain with his flock, and old Sally Scott in her little cottage with its large turf fire going straight up through the roof, causing the children's eyes to sting with smoke. Sometimes they came across Gregg the steward, who was not always happy to see small boys on the loose on the estate, but who could usually be softened up by Conolly's wit and charm. The house itself always seemed to be full of people, young and old in equal numbers, not to mention numerous cats and the occasional stray peacock. Dogs sprawled across the floor dreaming rabbits, while old tennis racquets and bits of outdoor games equipment stood in a corner by the umbrella stand in the outer hall.

Being close friends, Conolly and Denis shared a room next to Maurice's dressing-room. Some of their talk was about girls, in whom both were beginning to show a lively interest. They were particularly taken with their cousin Gladys Boyle, a regular visitor to Drenagh. With her bare feet and slightly fey, gypsy appearance, she struck them as the most beautiful and exotic creature they had ever seen. (Sadly she would fall ill and die soon after her 21st birthday). Her only rival at that time was Conolly's sister Helen, whom her cousins found beautiful in a very natural way. Once, while hiding behind the great beech tree on the lawn, Denis watched his elder brother Michael walk over and give Helen a playful kiss as she reclined in a hammock, a gesture which she accepted with good grace.

Conolly was unusually devout for a boy of his age, and spent long periods on his knees in prayer before climbing into bed. He was, his family had observed, 'always searching for something.' Denis's prayers were shorter than Conolly's and he was invariably in bed before his cousin. It was then usual for Conolly to come and sit on Denis's bed and keep him awake talking. Sometimes he did this after Denis had already gone to sleep, waking him with a start. One evening this habit of Conolly's caused pandemonium. Denis woke from a nightmare just as Conolly sat on his bed, and he ran screaming in terror towards the door. This deeply disturbed Conolly and he too shrieked in alarm. For a minute or so the two screeching boys stood there, Denis with his back to the door and clutching the handle, and Conolly facing him.

The noise caused the grown-ups to stream up from the dining-room, fearing some terrible disaster. Denis was taken to his mother's bedroom down the passage and Conolly went back to his own bed. Denis's father, the Rev Reginald Gibbs, then Vicar of Clifton Hampden, near Oxford, (he was married to Maurice's sister Lucia) sat with Conolly for some time and soothed away his fears. The two had always got on well and found it easy to talk to one another. Several days passed before Denis felt able to sleep in Conolly's room again. Conolly assured him: "You know, Denis, there's nothing to be frightened of any more. I've got nothing on my mind now and I shall not be coming along to sit on your bed after you've gone to sleep. Uncle Reggie has calmed me down completely."

Uncle Reggie's calming influence included lending Conolly a family prayer book. Conolly was touched by the gesture and learned some of the prayers by heart, a feat not appreciated by

Maurice. Although fond of Reggie, he privately complained that the behaviour of the Gibbs family at morning services was 'high church' and he dismissed it as 'rubbish.'

Not long after the episode in the bedroom Conolly returned to Edgborough to take his Common Entrance exam. Maurice was naturally anxious for his son to succeed academically, although it seems he did not have high expectations. He wrote to him hopefully: 'I wonder how you got on with the exam papers. Even if you could not manage them this time you can always have more attempts, and we shall also have longer time in which to prepare.' In the formal style of the day, he ended with the words: 'I remain your very affectionate father, M.M.McCausland.'

Maurice need not have worried. In due course Conolly secured his place at Eton, arriving there in April 1920. He found himself in illustrious company. Among his contemporaries at the school were the future novelists Anthony Powell, George Orwell and Ian Fleming, and the future Prime Minister, Alec Douglas-Home. Conolly's house master was Francis Wellesley Dobbs, a 50-year-old maths 'beak' who, as an Ulsterman with roots in County Antrim, went out of his way to make his young charge feel at home.

Tailcoats and top hats, a benign fagging system and not infrequent beatings were the order of the day, the most common charge being 'cheek to Senior Election.' Interested in current affairs, Conolly was elected a member of the house Debating Society, but his time at Eton was not characterised by pyrotechnic displays in the form-room, and his sole academic honour was to win a prize in the class exams (known as Trials) at the end of his first term. At sport he fared better. He earned his house colours for shooting and football, and made a minor name for himself in rowing, reaching the semi-finals of the Novice Pulling in 1924. The following year he rowed in his house four, and again in *Hibernia* in the Procession of Boats on the Fourth of June.

Religion was a solemn business at Eton, and Conolly enjoyed singing hymns with six hundred other boys in the magnificent 15th century chapel. Over the centuries many members of the McCausland clan had made their living in the church, and it is more than possible that Conolly, while also interested in an army career, began considering such a path for himself. He was confirmed at Eton by the Bishop of Oxford, the Rt Rev Hubert Burge. Maurice travelled from Ireland for the occasion, adding a dissonant note by making it plain he did not approve of the Bishop because 'he indulged in ritualistic High Church practices.' It was a criticism which the young Conolly, already defensive of High Church rituals, did not think was fair.

Chapter Five

Ninety Fateful Words

It is old but it is beautiful, and its colours they are fine
It was worn at Derry, Aughrim, Enniskillen and the Boyne.
My father wore it as a youth in bygone days of yore,
And on the Twelfth I love to wear the sash my father wore.

From the ballad The Sash My Father Wore, popular among
Ulster loyalists and invariably played by Orangemen as they
marched through Limavady every July 12.

Back home in Ireland the political temperature was rising.
The year after Conolly arrived at Eton, (1921) Ireland
was partitioned under Lloyd George's Government of
Ireland Act, and Protestants in the North prepared for civil war.
Helen wrote to her mother from Paris: 'It is too sickening that
all these troubles have started again, all through that traitor
Lloyd George, but I think people in England are having their
eyes opened at last. I read Lord Carson's speech in the House
of Lords several days ago. It was splendid.' (Carson had said
of the Treaty between London and Dublin: 'I never thought I
should live to see the day of such abject humiliation for Great
Britain.')

Determined to protect his beloved Ulster to the last, Maurice
organised a recruiting drive to help form a local contingent
of the Ulster Special Constabulary, whose most famous
component was the 'B' Specials. The Specials - formed in
October 1920 - were an armed corps, organised partially on
military lines, to be called out in times of emergency, such as
war or insurgency. The force was almost exclusively Protestant
and unionist and as a result was viewed with great mistrust
by Catholics and nationalists. The potential recruits from the
Limavady area refused to be deterred by Maurice's dramatic

peroration when he addressed them at Drenagh. '"Well, lads, there it is," he said. "I suppose that by this time next year we'll all be pushing up the daisies."

The following year, as a district commandant of the 'B' Specials, Maurice was kept busy during the first elections for the Northern Irish Parliament, posting his men at polling booths in Limavady and the surrounding area to guard against surprise attacks by Sinn Feiners who, it was rumoured, planned to bring time bombs into the booths and drop acid into the ballot boxes.

Perhaps it was the sight of these serried ranks of uniformed men parading on the lawns of Drenagh that finally decided Conolly on a military career. Soldiery, he decided, was a profession for a young buck who wanted a bite at the wonders of the world, and within two months of leaving Eton in July 1925 he had begun an officer training course at Sandhurst with the aim of joining the Irish Guards. Maurice, while approving of his son's choice of career, would have preferred him to have picked another regiment, his reason being that he would be unable to match the large allowances many young Guards officers received from their parents. An unstated reason was possibly that the Irish Guards traditionally had a strong Roman Catholic affiliation.

Conolly's days were long, with Reveille at 6.30 a.m., followed by intensive sessions of drill, weapon training, P.T., tactics and riding until lights out at 10.30 p.m. The work was harder than he had expected, but he quickly got to grips with the regimented routine, writing to his mother: 'I think it is doing me a lot of good and I have a terrific appetite and feel very fit. Altogether it is a good life and very healthy.' In a letter to Maurice, he added: 'We have all got sore shoulders and split fingers as a result of sloping arms.'

On his rare days off he travelled by bus to towns like Aldershot, Windsor and Guildford, or went to the cinema at Camberley with 'a rowdy party' of Sandhurst friends. A keen rugby player, he was popular with the other cadets and respected his superiors. He especially liked his Sergeant Major, '...an Irish Guardsman from Tipperary with a beautiful southern brogue, frightfully smart and most awfully nice...if anybody does anything wrong he appeals to Holy Jasus or Shainted Mhary.'

His expenses, met by Maurice, came to around £200 a year. This included his Mess food (four shillings, or 20p a day) and an allowance for beer and cider. As he told his father: 'One feels pretty thirsty after all that drill and running about.' During his first term Maurice sent him a supplementary cheque for £6 to enable him to buy a bicycle and wrist watch. Conscious that he remained a financial burden on his parents, he constantly assured them he was being frugal and that the cost of supporting him through Sandhurst would reap dividends. 'I am determined to try and become something high up here because the standard required for officers in the Guards is very high and if they don't think you good enough you can get chucked out which is a good thing as it stops gadding about all the time... everyone here thinks very highly of the Irish Guards. There is always a chance of a very good job as adjutant to some of the government jobs in India or somewhere, which is very well paid.'

By the following year he was doing well enough at Sandhurst to be made the commandant's orderly, and he duly passed out with flying colours in February 1927. The next time he arrived at Drenagh it was as 2nd Lieutenant Conolly McCausland of the Irish Guards. His immaculate appearance impressed his family. They also noticed that far from blunting his spiritual side, the army had if anything accentuated his High Church leanings. Irish Guards officers were often drawn from British Roman Catholic public schools such as Ampleforth, Downside and

Stoneyhurst. This made the regiment's Catholic padres highly influential, and two of them - Fathers Julian Stonor and Joe Murphy - were to have a strong influence on Conolly's life.

Both were colourful characters. Stonor, a Cambridge graduate, had previously been a Benedictine monk at Downside Abbey. He was a tall aesthetic-looking man with a mystical air. To the surprise of his congregations, he was apt to go into a trance during morning communion, and a lot of embarrassed coughing would ensue before he 'came back' and continued the service. He claimed that ghosts regularly approached him in private houses to ask about their friends and relatives. Since he did not always know they were ghosts, these encounters could be confusing, and he described them afterwards with great jollity. In years to come, Stonor would be present with Conolly and his men at the Battle of Boulogne in 1940, showing no fear as he tended the wounded yards from the front line.

Father Murphy, a Redemptionist priest from County Clare, was a very different character, small with twinkling eyes and a great sense of humour. Like Stonor he would become a life-long friend of Conolly and a regular guest at Drenagh. The army's Catholic padres were sometimes said to be more effective than their Church of England counterparts at dealing with the men's spiritual problems. Non-Catholics – Conolly included - would often confide in them and seek their advice.

Though not yet twenty-one, Conolly was showing an interest in many religions. He had toyed with Buddhism, studied meditation with a swami, and had investigated the beliefs of the Plymouth Brethren. However, it was his growing attraction to Catholicism that now began to worry his parents. Protestantism and political union with the United Kingdom went side by side, and Maurice and Eileen were fervent upholders of both. They tolerated Catholicism, and indeed employed several Roman Catholics at Drenagh, including the head gardener Peter

Gibbons, and the groom Denis Deighan. Grimes the butler, himself a Protestant, was married to a Catholic, though he tended not to advertise the fact.

But Maurice and Eileen were only prepared to take their tolerance so far and, like almost everyone else in their social circle, they believed the Roman Catholic religion should be kept at arm's length. Eileen's friend, Inez Macrory, who lived in The Chalet at Balteagh, typified the majority Protestant view. Describing the young maid who did her housework, she once said conspiratorially: 'She does quite a good job for a Catholic.' Inez's mother-in-law, Frances Macrory, went further: 'Cook wanted; active; obliging; must be Protestant,' read a notice she placed in the Belfast News-Letter. Maurice thought 'candles on the altar,' as he put it, were 'nonsense', and he felt saddened when two of his sisters – Lettice and Eleanor – converted to Catholicism as adults, the latter when she married an army officer from Dublin, Walter Hackett, in 1907. Although he never had any deep theological arguments with Conolly, he repeatedly made it clear that he disliked High Church views. Much as he loved his son and wanted him to succeed to Drenagh, he could not countenance the thought of the estate falling into Catholic hands.

Another example of his sectarian prejudice occurred when the National Trust became interested in acquiring the prehistoric Rough Fort, which lay on McCausland land outside Limavady. Maurice was happy to hand it over, and suggested forming a provincial committee for the National Trust. 'There's only one condition,' he told the Trust. 'The committee must all be Protestants.' Embarrassed by being drawn into religious controversy, the Trust eventually wrung a modest compromise out of him whereby one of the six committee members would be a Roman Catholic. Thus was established the National Trust in Northern Ireland.

Eileen's views on Catholicism were well illustrated by a brief conversation she had many years later with a Sister Murphy who had arrived to nurse her during an illness. 'Which are you?' asked Eileen, despite her weakened state. 'Protestant,' replied Sister Murphy. 'Thank God…' muttered Eileen, and fell into a peaceful sleep. She undoubtedly agreed whole-heartedly with Helen's description of attending 'High Mass' with Roman Catholic friends in Paris in 1922: 'Nobody could hear a word of what was going on. Bells rang every now and again to let the people know when to kneel and when to stand etc. What struck me most was having to pay for our seats, such a beastly idea. There were no hymns or anything for the people to join in - everyone was deadly silent the whole time. There were various funny old men dressed as admirals who walked up and down continually tapping sticks on the floor and saying things in Latin. I didn't feel I'd been to church – far more like a theatre.'

Whether Maurice believed there was any real danger of Conolly converting we shall never know (years later Conolly would tell the High Court that although he had no intention of converting in 1927 he could not rule out the possibility) but that summer Maurice resolved to take a simple if drastic precaution, no doubt encouraged by Eileen. Since the previous century, Drenagh had been 'entailed' and the property was held at the time under an 1897 deed of re-settlement under which Maurice was tenant for life, and Conolly was 'tenant in remainder'. Entailment was a legal device, feudal in origin, designed to prevent a landed property from being broken up as it passed down the generations. Recognising the threat of sub-division among daughters, it generally limited succession to elder sons. The practice was for a resettlement to be made when the eldest son reached 21, under which the land would be settled on his father for life, while the son, as 'remainderman', was guaranteed a future interest.

In July 1927 Maurice travelled to England to celebrate Conolly's twenty-first birthday with him, and while there he told him the property would have to be re-settled now that he had come of age. He added that the new deed of settlement was a 'matter of form' and that it had been 'done by his father before him.' What he failed to tell him was that he had asked Alexander Ingram, the family solicitor, to include a provision in the new deed that would disinherit any successor if he or she became a Roman Catholic. Significantly, the instructions to Ingram came from Maurice alone even though they were in his and Conolly's names. Conolly was evidently in the dark at this stage about his father's plan.

Draconian provisions in respect of Drenagh were nothing new. Old Conolly Thomas, for instance, had stipulated in his Will that any daughter of his who inherited Drenagh, whether married or not, should at all times use the McCausland name, as should her present or future husband by obtaining a Royal Licence. Failure to do so within a year would result in immediate forfeiture of the estate. Maurice, however, had entered uncharted territory with his controversial new provision. That he appeared to have neglected to tell his son about it, either then or later, is perhaps understandable if difficult to justify. He was fifty-four years of age and must have hoped it would be a good many years before the succession to Drenagh became an issue, by which time, fingers crossed, Conolly's youthful flirtation with Catholicism would surely be a distant memory. In the meantime he could avoid ruffling Conolly's sensitive feathers and risk a family rift by saying nothing, reckoning that if there was any explaining to do it could and should be left to Ingram. Almost certainly he viewed the provision as a nothing more than a deterrent, and not as a device which would ever actually have to be used.

Ingram, as instructed, asked a conveyancing barrister called Longfield to draw up the provision. Longfield did so, although in a prophetic warning he told Ingram that he was rather against such provisions *'as they often lead to costly litigation'*. Now came the lighting of a long fuse. Longfield drew up the provision in such a way that if any successor became a Catholic, not only he but also his heirs would be disinherited, even if the heirs were not themselves Catholic. The relevant clause – Clause Fifteen of the resettlement – was labyrinthine in its wording, and almost any layman trying to work out its meaning could have been confused. It stated:

> 'If any person hereby made tenant for life or tenant in tail by purchase of the settled freeholds shall become a Roman Catholic or profess that he or she is of the Roman Catholic religion then and so often as the same shall happen the settled freeholds shall go and remain to the uses upon the trusts and subject to the powers and provisions to upon and subject to which the same would have stood limited and settled by virtue of these presents if such person were dead without issue.'

Did Longfield really mean to include Conolly's heirs in those ninety fateful words? Apparently not. He wrote to Ingram that the clause he had drafted 'was designed to prevent a person who is or becomes a Catholic from enjoying the settled property.' He made no mention of heirs, yet he managed by his opaque wording to include them. Equally, what were Maurice's true intentions? Did he mean Clause Fifteen to apply to both Conolly and his heirs? More than two decades later the Appeal Court decided he meant it to apply to Conolly alone. Yet Edward Brown, a partner of Alexander Ingram ('Wee Brown' as the family called him) thought differently. Long afterwards, in a letter to Conolly's sister, Helen, he said Maurice knew exactly what he was doing.

At the heart of the subsequent costly confusion was the family solicitor, Ingram. He failed to tell Maurice about Longfield's reservations and he did not mention Clause Fifteen to Conolly, possibly because he suspected he would refuse to put his name to the resettlement deed if he fully understood its implications. He wrote to Conolly only once about the resettlement, explaining some of the detail and telling him it followed the general lines of the 1897 deed, adding that he should sign it quickly to avoid stamp duty. There was no word in his letter about the forfeiture clause, despite its enormous significance.

So what was Ingram playing at? Long after his death, an Appeal Court judge, Lord Justice Babington, said 'the most charitable view' was that he and Maurice each thought the other had explained Clause Fifteen to Conolly. Conolly's wife, Peggy, was blunter, and more inclined to suspect impropriety. She would say that Ingram – himself a staunch Protestant - had 'maliciously misled' her husband.

One way or another, it was a significant lapse on Ingram's part. It meant that when Conolly signed the resettlement deed soon after his twenty-first birthday, he had little idea what he was letting himself in for. Indeed, having struggled through the first two pages of complexity, he evidently gave up reading the document and never spotted the fateful clause. He would testify years later that had he known about it he would never have signed the resettlement deed. And if he had not signed the deed he would have not – as the courts later ruled – have been bound by it. Consequently he would have succeeded to Drenagh outright on Maurice's death without any of the subsequent complications.

That Maurice's action in having the forfeiture clause drawn up was highly unusual is beyond doubt. Indeed, it is possible that Clause Fifteen was unique in the annals of the law. Saint Anne Line, an English martyr executed during the reign of Elizabeth I, was disinherited together with her brother William for converting to Catholicism in the 16th century. So was Elizabeth Ann Bayley, the first native-born citizen of the United States to be canonised by the Roman Catholic Church. In both cases, however, they were disinherited by their families retrospectively and without prior warning. There was no 16th century equivalent of Clause Fifteen.

In the same vein, Oscar Wilde's father, a non-practising Protestant and mason, warned his young son he would disinherit him if he pursued his interest in the Roman Catholic faith, but never had to carry out the threat. Closer to home was the case of Billy Clonmore, the only child of the 7th Earl of Wicklow and a contemporary of Conolly at Eton. Clonmore converted to Roman Catholicism in 1932 and was disinherited by his father as a result. He was also banished from the family home – the palatial Shelton Abbey - on Sundays because he was thought to be an embarrassment on account of his attending Mass with the Catholic servants.

In Conolly's case, the turmoil that would ensue was still years away, but the scene was now set for a momentous and divisive court case that would impinge on every immediate member of the family. 'A countryman between two lawyers is like a fish between two cats,' wrote Benjamin Franklin in 1737. His words could easily have applied to the Drenagh dispute.

Chapter Six

A Fine Romance

So, my beloved, each season of your life
New beauty still unfolds to me, and I
Your lover still, love your maturity,
Sweetheart become my bride, and hide my wife

From a sonnet written by Lucius Thompson in 1941 to celebrate eleven years of marriage to Helen

In the mid-1920s, Conolly's elder sister Helen fell passionately in love with a gifted Cambridge student, Lucius Perronet Thompson, her third cousin and one of the most talented economists of his generation. He was as smitten with her as she was with him, more so if anything, but there was one big stumbling block. Maurice and Eileen – Eileen in particular – did not at first approve of the match thinking them both too young.

Helen was a home-loving girl who immersed herself in life at Drenagh and in the Limavady community as a whole. Among her many artistic accomplishments was mastery of the tin whistle - *Tea for Two and Fight the Good Fight* being high up on her musical repertoire. In 1924, in her role as Brown Owl, she accompanied the Limavady Brownie Pack when they sang *Off for the Holidays* and *Three Little Pigs* at a packed charity evening in the local Orange Hall. Her sister Eila also took part in the entertainment, playing Countess Highfly in 'The Lost Temper', billed by the organisers as a morality play in two scenes. The evening was attended by a proud Maurice and Eileen, and raised a handsome sum for both blinded soldiers and the Girl Guides. As the local paper reported: 'On the motion of Mr M M McCausland, thanks were accorded to all who had assisted towards the success of the evening, and the entertainment terminated with the National Anthem.'

From her childhood onwards Helen was especially close to Conolly. Their abiding love for one another possibly sprang from the Drenagh nursery where Nanny King tended to favour Eila, so pushing the two older children into an unbreakable alliance. As a small girl during the reign of King Edward VII, she was educated by governesses in the 'school room' at Drenagh before being sent to England to board at Queenwood Ladies' College in Eastbourne, an establishment with a reputation for health, bracing air and sea breezes, and where one of her contemporaries was the future stage and movie actress Martita Hunt, famed for her role as Miss Havisham in David Lean's 1946 screen version of *Great Expectations*.

Helen did not enjoy Queenwood and pined for home. Ever the doting younger brother, Conolly wrote regularly to her from his school in Surrey to keep up her spirits. One of his letters, written during the First World War when he was eleven years old, went: 'Dear old Hell. I hope you are well. (How is that for a rhyme?). Poor old kid. I hope you don't feel home-sick at all. After all, the time is going jolly quick although you wouldn't think so. We must pack up your troubles in our old kit bags and smile smile smile. So smile away. With love from your affectionate Conolly.'

On leaving Queenwood, Helen continued her education in Paris before joining her cousin, Joanna Gibbs, at the Byam Shaw School of Art in Kensington, and her long, loving letters to her family in Northern Ireland were one manifestation of her homesickness. A poem she wrote on the death of her friend Kate Roper in 1935 illustrated her joy at having grown up at Drenagh.

In memory of April days
Of primroses, the Tavern,
The sun glinting on the burn,
The Spring that shone on all our ways –

The wishing seat, and all thereon
We wished – the glen and moss-grown paths
Of bare legs, and books and trees,
Picnics with the swans – and cream –
The unaccountable joy
Of overflowing baths
And uncontrolled laughter –
Of birds, and light, and song – a dream
To hallow passing years – and after.

There were no driving tests in those days, and at an early age
Helen learned to motor around the narrow country lanes,
although these expeditions were not without their drama. On
one occasion, in driving rain, she ran over and killed a goose
on the mountain road between Garvagh and Limavady. Within
seconds she was surrounded by three villainous looking men,
their eyes black nubs of anthracite, and several gaunt women
wearing men's caps who bewailed the loss of the goose and
roundly cursed Helen, her car and all motorists. With jabbing
fingers, they claimed they had encountered her car before and
that it had killed more of their livestock than any other. The
angrier they became, the higher they put the value of the goose.
Eventually Helen gave them a £1 note, threw the goose in the
back of the car and sped away, with the imprecations of the
bereaved women ringing through the damp air behind her.

Helen was in her early twenties when she lost her heart to
Lucius, who was one year her junior and still a student when
their romance began to blossom after a Cambridge May Ball
in 1924. That summer Lucius and his sister Lalage stayed at
Drenagh, enabling the attachment to grow and flourish. Helen
first felt she was falling in love after a game of ping pong at the
home of mutual friends, although in her first letter to him she
was coy about her feelings, and signed herself unromantically
'Your affect. cousin Helen McC.' There were few opportunities

to be alone, and they got to know each other mainly through letters and by slipping out of dances and talking earnestly and at length about literature, art, architecture and music in Lucius's car. She regarded him as a rock in her life, and felt his absence keenly when, as frequently happened, they were parted for long periods. 'It is odd,' she told her *owne true knighte* in an early love letter, 'but I hardly ever dream of you, and when I do it's always that you are not there, such as awful nightmares about thunderstorms and things, and I can't find you anywhere to cling to.'

Lucius had been born in Simla in 1904, the second child of Sir John Thompson, the Chief Commissioner of Delhi, and his wife Lucia, known as Shuffie. (Their first child, a girl, had also been born in Simla and died there as an infant). In 1912 he was packed off to the South of Ireland – his maternal grandfather, Robert Tyrrell, had been Regius Professor of Greek and Professor of Ancient History at Trinity College, Dublin, and was acclaimed in the world of academia for having edited Cicero's correspondence. Lucius spent much of the rest of his childhood in his aunt's and later his grandmother's matriarchal households, where the cold, damp surroundings were a stark contrast to the warmth and bright colours of India.

A letter his father sent to him from India in September 1913, when Lucius, then eight, was beginning his first term at a boarding prep school in Ireland, urged him to be guided always by Polonius's last piece of advice to his son Laertes in *Hamlet*:

> *To thine own self be true,*
> *And it must follow, as the night the day,*
> *Thou canst not then be false to any man.*

Lucius's father went on: 'Every time you play or work you must try to do better than you did before. You know every properly brought up little boy has a little friend inside his own mind, whom he never sees but who often talks to him and tells him what he thinks of him. He is a very clever little friend too and never tells lies. He knows at once whether you are telling the truth or playing a game well or working your best or behaving like a little gentleman, and he doesn't hesitate to tell you. And if you find he says 'All right – you've done your best', that is better praise than anyone can give you. I want my dear dear boy to keep this letter and read it before he goes back to school every term, because as long as I live I can never give him better advice. And it will be a terribly long time before I can see him and talk to him myself.'

Lucius was mature for his age, and highly perceptive, being more of a surrogate parent than a brother to his four younger siblings. At the age of ten, when he returned to Ireland after a visit to India, his father – known to the children as 'The Buster' - handed him a note putting him in charge of Gerald and John, a task he undertook diligently and conscientiously. The over-riding sense of duty which characterised much of his life probably had its roots in the responsibilities placed on him by his absentee parents. Gerald and John continued to regard him as the voice of authority even when one became Chairman of Kleinworts and the other an Admiral.

The school to which Lucius had been despatched in 1913 was Mourne Grange, a Spartan boarding establishment in Co Down run by Allen Sausmarez Carey, a terrifying, cane-wielding disciplinarian. Proverbs 23 13-14 was the school's creed: 'Withhold not correction from the child. Thou shalt beat him with the rod, and shalt deliver his soul from hell.'

Remembering his father's advice, Lucius set himself high standards and expected others to follow suit. During the war there was an epidemic of chickenpox at Mourne Grange, and Lucius and three other boys were confined to the sanatorium with nothing to do. Eventually they came up with the ingenious idea of turning a precious sugar lump into a dice by drawing numbers on it with ink. Dreaming up various games that could be played with a single dice, they passed the time quite happily until one of the boys gave way to temptation and ate the sugar lump. Lucius was outraged and for the rest of his life he held up the episode as an example of 'caddish' behaviour.

Never one to confine his eyes to the narrow ground beneath his feet, he excelled in the classroom and on the sports field. Latin was taught for an hour a day six days a week, and his flair for the ancient language ensured he escaped the worst of Carey's wrath. Despite the harsh conditions, and the occasional attack of asthma, he won a scholarship to Eton, a colossal achievement even by Mourne Grange's formidable benchmark. In the event, some hemming and hawing by his father prevented him from becoming an Etonian contemporary of Conolly. The 'Buster' decided to send him to Repton instead, having been told it was an excellent school, but changed his mind on being advised that Eton was even better. He telegraphed Shuffie from India telling her of the about-turn, but she had by now bought the Repton uniform, and Lucius's name-tapes had been sewn on to his clothes. She was 'damned' if she was going to have them sewn on to another set of clothes, and so Repton won the day. Although the school did not quite have Eton's cachet, Lucius prospered there under the headmastership of Geoffrey Fisher, a future Archbishop of Canterbury, and was an exact contemporary and good friend of another future *Cantuar,* Michael Ramsay, from whom he snatched the First Prize in Classics.

From Repton, Lucius won a classics scholarship to Kings College, Cambridge in 1923. With little money to spare, he acquired good pieces of furniture and interesting artefacts for his Cambridge rooms. He loved his time there and flourished in the beautiful surroundings and invigorating male company. University contemporaries noted that 'being fair, fresh-faced, debonair, elegant, a keen oarsman and already a connoisseur of beautiful objects, he was widely assumed to be an Etonian.' He enjoyed the academic company and, as well as coming into the orbit of the celebrated economist Maynard Keynes, he was a contemporary of Kim Cobbold, the future Governor of the Bank of England. Both men would have an important influence on his career. He had a certain *hauteur,* and when the College Council sent round a circular deploring the scribbling of graffiti on a lavatory wall, Lucius loftily returned his to the bursar, Hugh Durnford, with a note saying he presumed it had been sent to him in error.

Innately ordered, he had a chivalrous and delicate manner that earned him male as well as female admirers. During a student trip to Paris he complained to Helen in a letter: 'Every morning queues of filthy men accost one with the most foul suggestions. However, it annoys me to be taken for that sort of young man or to have these stinkers talking to me, so they usually don't stay long. Even if I were inclined that way – which luckily I never have been – the memory of you would be the most complete armour against them.'

He was politically as well as socially conservative, having little time for either the emergent Labour Party or for workers who downed tools. During the General Strike of 1926 he travelled to the London docks with fellow students and spent several back-breaking days unloading flour and other foodstuffs from strike-bound ships.

Brilliant with a majuscule and magisterial B, he was expected like his forebears to achieve a double first in classics, and this he duly did in 1927, although he received no response from his father when he sent him a telegram informing him of his triumph. This may have been due to nothing more than the vagaries of the international postal system but he was understandably hurt by the lack of even an acknowledgement.

Helen, by contrast, sent him a telegram saying: 'Millions of congratulations – I knew you would', and wrote the same day in a letter: 'My darling, darling – how grand of you to do so brilliantly. I'm simply bursting with pride.'

With his classical education, Lucius had a tendency to trot out a Greek or Latin quotation whenever a suitable occasion arose. He even persuaded Helen to dabble in the language of Homer and Aristotle, teaching her to write her name in Greek (for the rest of her life she signed her letters to him in Greek characters) and encouraging her to read *The Odyssey*. He had what today would be called a 'social conscience', and was proud to be the great-great grandson of Thomas Thompson, a radical reformer and associate of the anti-slavery campaigner William Wilberforce.

About religion he was in two minds. 'I think Christianity itself is good,' he told Helen in an early letter. 'It is the church's representation of it that I am not sure about.' While staying at Drenagh in 1925, the highlight of his visits to the parish church in Limavady were the surreptitious glances he cast in Helen's direction during Sunday mattins because she 'looked so frightfully beautiful.'

Unfortunately, his achievements did not so far impress Maurice and Eileen, who thought that he and Helen were too young to be embarking on a serious romance. For a time they even tried to stop the two from writing to each other, and prevented Lucius from paying any further visits to Drenagh. They felt a better candidate for Helen's affections was William Lenox-Conyngham, the illness-prone heir to the 350-acre Springhill estate in Moneymore, Co Derry, or perhaps one of the Ritter or Beasley boys who came from 'good families' in Limavady. Helen was having none of it. She gently rebuffed Lenox-Conyngham's tentative advances, and the spurned and sickly suitor remained a bachelor for the rest of his life. The Ritter and Beasley boys were non-runners from the outset.

Helen realised, however, that Lucius's comparative youth and poverty would be frowned upon by her family. As early as 1925 she wrote to him: 'I do sometimes wonder if my love for you is strong enough to face all that would have to be faced… sweetheart, don't please *don't* love me too much, as I couldn't bear you to have a heartache ever.'

Matters reached a head in 1926 when Eileen confronted Helen about what she perceived to be Lucius's shortcomings and listed six reasons why she thought he was undeserving of her daughter's hand in marriage. Helen reported her peppery observations to Lucius in a letter, telling him: 'You see, darling, Mum is an unmitigated snob, there is really no other word for it, and if you were a budding peer or else tremendously rich and owned an ancestral mansion (thank goodness you don't) I think half the difficulties would vanish away. I will tell you all the objections quite ruthlessly, as you wanted to know, but don't be hurt dear, or too much annoyed.'

The six reasons, as catalogued in Helen's letter, were: 'You have no great name. You do not have what she considers nearly enough money. You are frightfully effeminate. You come of an irreligious and eccentric family. You are much too weak-minded and would have no authority. We are related.' Helen added: 'Darling, have you blown up with rage yet? Don't.'

She then proceeded to counter each of Eileen's objections, with the exception of their kinship, which involved nothing more contentious than shared great-great grandparents. Starting with Lucius's 'name' and financial situation, she said that having no name and money 'means that you haven't got some horrid old barrack of a place crawling with ghosts and stuffed away in some Godforsaken part of the world…when I see Ma in a state of complete exasperation over servants and things, I want to say "from all larders and storerooms, from all kitchens and cooks, from all servants and their wiles, from all the bothers and worries connected with a house, Good Lord deliver us."'

On the question of effeminacy, a word which had fewer connotations then than it does now, Helen conceded that her mother might have a point. 'This is true to an extent,' she wrote, 'but then it can hardly be used as an argument against, as it concerns me and only me, and I have chosen it because I like it beyond any other type of character, and I would love my 'true knight' more than any disgusting 'cave man' or strong and silent bully! I suppose most women like being dragged about by the hair – there is certainly a bit of the brute in most men, but why any sign of gentleness or chivalry in the male nature should be put down as effeminate, and therefore a thing to be despised, I can't think.'

She went on to dismiss the notion that Lucius was eccentric, although she did wonder if there might be a problem with religion. 'It is the only stumbling block so far, in the general sense that I don't think you are religious. I am because I have been brought up to be.' As for weak-mindedness, she declared this to be utterly untrue. 'Mum's idea is that you have been ruled by women and you would never restrain me from *my mad projects.* Therefore we should just drift along like jellyfish.' In fact, she went on, Lucius was anything but weak. His refusal to modify the number of letters he wrote to her, for instance, was 'terribly grand, most awfully grown-up and strong.'

She added: 'Parents are extraordinarily selfish about their children and always think they are getting the worst of everything. She (Eileen) hasn't considered what an ignoramus of a wife you might have, with just a smattering of education, and who would be much too ignorant to assist you in any way.'

In another letter she warmed to an age-old theme: 'There does seem to be an unbridgeable gulf between the older and younger generation, and I suppose it is almost impossible for them to see things from our point of view. They are so frightfully busy condemning and disapproving that they don't realise how completely different everything is now. Their youth was so padded and protected compared to ours, and all the *not quite nice* things so carefully kept out of their way. Consequently they didn't grow up as quickly as we have through more or less fending for ourselves and seeing things as they are. They, poor darlings, have given us the rope, and they hold up their hands in amazement and disgust when some of us occasionally hang ourselves.'

To add to the difficulties, Eileen was not alone in waxing indignant about Lucius. Helen's sister, Eila, by now in her last year at Crofton Grange School in Orpington, Kent, also took against him, though for different reasons. Eila's antipathy stemmed mainly from her devotion to Helen and a dog-in-the-manger dislike of her being involved with anyone who might take her away from Drenagh. On one notorious occasion she looked with disdain at a wooden tea caddy which Lucius had given to Helen and promptly spat in it.

Helen told Lucius: 'As for Eila she is only an exceedingly ignorant child and obstinate to boot – so her opinion goes for nothing, though I wish she wouldn't be such an ass. I'm afraid all the arguing in the world won't turn you into a peer my love, or make you a millionaire, nor will it stop mum thinking (idiotically) that if I marry you I will have thrown myself utterly away, or Eila from enlarging on the fact that because you are not the type she would have chosen, that no one else should!' (In fact, Eila later came close to marrying Lucius's brother, John).

As for Maurice, his attitude to the romance was summed up by Helen in a single sentence: 'Much too young, no money, quite impossible, run off and play tennis – I must get on with my letters.'

Of all the family only Conolly was wholly supportive, an oasis of understanding in a Saharan drought, and he agreed not to let on when, as occasionally happened, Helen and Lucius managed to meet clandestinely. The payback, wrote Helen, was that 'he wants to know exactly how many times you've kissed me – as if I know!!' Despite her great love for Conolly, she sometimes found him too hearty for her liking, and blamed this in part on Eton. 'Repton (School) sounds lovely,' she told Lucius in a letter, 'and your sons will certainly go there. This is if by any chance they are mine too!! Anyhow, mine will not go to Eton, whosoever they are.' (In this prediction she proved to be quite wrong).

Lucius's response to the shafts of criticism from Eileen and Eila was immediate and robust. He wrote to Helen from his rooms at Cambridge: 'I haven't got a job now but presumably I will get one of sorts in two years time; and with any luck a fairly good one. Unless it really makes you miserable to receive my letters, I refuse to modify their number. My aching for you is quite inexpressible. I love, love, love, love you. I take it that the position with Cousin Eileen is that she thinks it all ridiculous in the extreme and also rather regrettable as I am not nearly good enough for you – in which I quite agree with her. Money is of course a filthy snag, but lots and lots of other people get on without having millions in the bank, and I think you and I, my darling, are rather of the ones who don't fight terribly because we haven't a Rolls Royce to dash about in…if it is any comfort to you, you know I love you more than all the world.

'I am furious rather than sad about it all. Darling one, you are being bullied badly and there is only one remedy for that, and that is to take a strong line. Guerilla warfare is awful; it is wearing to both sides and leads nowhere. A row is unpleasant but it clears the air, and after it one knows how one stands. So, my darling, I really think, as you suggested, you must have it out in a real argument. You will be fighting for reason and all the winged victories of the Greeks will be on your side. You MUST MUST MUST refuse to be bullied and remember that no one on earth has a right to tell you what you have got to do. That is what must be done – the sorting out of Cousin Eileen's theories, which at present are nothing but a vague tangle of hostility.'

Strong though she wanted to be, Helen baulked at the idea of having it out with her mother. She became increasingly ground down by criticism and began to wonder if she and Lucius should call it a day, or at the very least, as she put it, 'go into hibernation.' Forced to keep their love affair secret from all but a few trusted intimates, they could not even hold hands in public, and during one long-awaited weekend tryst in Cambridge, their only physical contact was a stolen kiss in the back of a taxi. Begging Lucius not to carry out a threat to send a letter of complaint about the situation to Maurice and Eileen, she wrote: 'It would only make things fifty times worse and would gain us nothing.' Later she wrote: 'I've rather lost the thread. Dearest, I'm awfully muddled over it all and can't think a bit clearly.'

Lucius at that time harboured ambitions to join the Foreign Office after he left Cambridge at a starting salary of £325 a year. Helen was less worried by the relatively low salary (she knew her allowance would help them to live comfortably) than by a convention that diplomats should not marry until they were thirty. 'I am beginning to realise how ghastly it would be to go on missing you for practically nine years,' she said. 'I don't want you to think so much about me, or anything to do with the future.' She added that for the time-being 'we should be no more than cousinly in every respect' and suggested they should write to each other only once a fortnight. To avoid upsetting her parents she asked Lucius to send letters from Cambridge by the morning post, so that they would arrive the following afternoon and not provocatively 'under the noses' of the family at breakfast.

Her attempt to lift the drawbridge a little, if not pull it right up, plunged the normally equitable Lucius into despair and he accused his *Madonna* of 'trying to fall out of love' with him. He said writing once a fortnight would be 'too awful' and that they should at least communicate on a weekly basis. 'I simply hate the thought of us not being together always,' he told her. It did not help that Lucius's mother also thought her son too young to be forming a serious attachment.

To add to Lucius's woes, Helen's letters to him frequently described dances she had attended all over Co Derry in his absence. Like a Roman soothsayer pronouncing on the runes, he scrutinised her words for signs that she was not looking after herself properly and – worse still – that her affection for him might be waning. 'My beloved angel,' he told her, 'I am going to scold you badly as I am very angry with you. A letter came from Eila saying you were looking like a sheet and yet would persist in dancing and dashing around. Please, my ownest, take care of yourself terribly well for me. When you have as much beauty and charm as you, it is your duty to take great care of it, and not to go squandering it on wretched little dances and rags. Besides I am jealous of you wasting it away from me.' At the back of his mind was possibly the haunting thought that Helen might transfer her affections to the debilitated William Lenox-Conyngham, who was still lurking dotingly in the background. 'If you find him nicer than me, you must admit it to yourself and me, angel one,' he wrote.

But Lucius was the gold standard by which all other prospective suitors were measured, and Helen quickly softened her tone, sending him a self-portrait of herself to cheer him up.

She wrote of it: 'Have just done this with a new charcoal pencil that I invested in yesterday. Don't hesitate to burn it if you don't like it. The tilt of the head is all wrong – it ought to be a little sideways – but it's frightfully hard to get. The eyes are a fiasco! I wish they were more like that! No, it isn't a scrap like me – still I'll send it to amuse you.'

At the same time the two made plans to meet in England before Christmas. They had the opportunity to stay at the house of Lucius's Aunt Kitty in Kensington (she was champion of the young and something of a rebel) and they agonised over whether it would be sensible to spend the night under the same roof. Fearing she would be 'overwhelmed with romance', Helen wrote: 'You see, darling, I think we might both be terribly unsettled by a long and intimate meeting like that – at the moment we are in a fairly placid rut, and not finding life too much a nightmare! But if we meet each other under those circumstances, and find that we cannot bear it without each other, what in the world are we going to do? We would of course miss each other after any sort of meeting, as you say – but after one of that sort it would be twice as bad and I really think would make us too miserable afterwards to have been worth it. It really comes down to this – do you think about twenty hours enjoyment is worth a blank and aimless twenty days? Or perhaps twenty weeks?

'And another thing, sweetheart, suppose (only suppose) we fell 'out of love' and married other people, or even didn't, how would we feel about it, I mean having been like that with each other? I really don't know what to say, and it would be distinctly unpleasant if the parents got wind of it. But I am wavering terribly. I think, sweetheart, I will think about it till tomorrow morning and tell you my decision at the end of this letter.'

In the morning she added a postscript: 'Darling, I think no – really. I dreamt that we had met, and woke up with a violent yes. But it has given way to a fairly definite no. Sweetheart, I really do think it would be bad, especially for you. Once we begin meeting 'unbeknownst' in that way it would be hard not to go on, and until we are more certain of each other it would be terribly unsatisfying.'

By Christmas 1926 their relationship was back on a more even keel, although Helen felt obliged to return a brooch Lucius sent her because it was 'far too big a present.' Instead she asked him to safeguard it until they were officially engaged. By now they were at least able to joke about their difficulties, and Helen suggested she make Lucius a pin-cushion – 'a great big man's one of course, not at all effeminate and frilly. Or would you like a strong silent boot bag?'

Now and again there were upsets, as when Lucius admitted to some minor indiscretion over the New Year, provoking a furious response from Helen. 'I am seriously annoyed with you. At least, not seriously – in fact on thinking it over I'm not annoyed at all – only thoroughly revolted and disgusted. How *could* you behave like that with that filthy drunk woman? I do think it's nauseating, odious and thoroughly common to say the least of it. As for being of a good Irish family – pish, tosh. And anyhow, if she is, she ought to be all the more ashamed of herself. Very laudable morals too, *husband in China...New Years invitation* etc etc. And you swallowed every word of it, innocent weakling...and kissing her, the vile creature – ugh! I suppose it's an experience, and rather dashing – at least, it isn't really dashing a bit as it's easy enough to find people of that type who make those sort of advances. Oh darling, what ever possessed you? Were you *as tight as an owl too*? Thank goodness I wasn't there anyhow – I'm not jealous, as of course I've no right to be, not being engaged to you. By Jove, if I was tho...! Neither of course can I judge you, as I suppose you were being

81

gallant, and perhaps could not get out of kissing her…anyway I just hate, loathe and detest it, and if you're going to carry on gallivanting to that extreme, ie traipsing about after fat old drunkards…however, perhaps that's enough on the subject. Do write back and tell me you don't care what I think if you want to – I shan't mind a bit.'

In a subsequent letter Helen was more sanguine, although the incident still rankled. 'I'm not going to be jealous of you being gallant to nice people, but I do hate to think of you wasting yourself on drunken vamps. You are so precious to me, you see.' Meanwhile there were signs that Eileen was changing her mind about Lucius. At the end of February 1927, after Lucius had rowed to victory during the Lent Head of the River races on the Cam, Helen was able to report: 'I told Mama what an athletic genius you were and I think she was duly impressed! I think she is taking a much more lenient view, which is grand.'

But the road ahead remained long and tortuous. In April Helen wrote: 'Mum is calming down splendidly about things, though I know she hates us meeting. According to Eila she is quite confident that it will all blow over if we don't see each other much; so, darling, I'm afraid you are never going to be asked here again, at least not for ages.'

In August there appeared to be a breakthrough when Eileen, her prickles temporarily in abeyance, agreed to let Lucius stay at Drenagh, but at the last minute she changed her mind. Helen told Lucius: 'I can hardly hold the pen I'm in such a rage. I'm most unspeakably disappointed and could weep buckets. It's disgusting.' Her only consolation came from the words of a fortune teller at a local fete: 'A few tears over a guest to the house, disappointment, disagreement with a member of your family…tears, more tears, a lull, a certain amount of dullness, then great happiness.'

The fortune teller was spot on. Despite the soul-searching and the long periods apart, Helen and Lucius persisted with their romance, and Maurice and Eileen's objections gave way to approval. Lucius was allowed to spend the following New Year at Drenagh and was so overcome with emotion when he departed on January 7 1928 that he wept openly in front of the family. On the way back to Belfast docks he could not even bring himself to look out of the train window at Downhill and the Mussenden Temple because they brought back such poignant memories of seaside picnics with Helen, and of the time he had raced along the sand to retrieve a brown knitted coat she had left by the railway bridge.

His visit did much to soften Eileen's attitude and she told Helen later in the month that she 'liked Lucius a lot.' By the following summer the couple were officially engaged and had begun collecting furniture and household items for their first home, a £1,700 house in Bayswater, London. 'It will be thrilling coming to see you in your own house,' Helen's friend Kitty Roper wrote to her. 'Oh Helen, my dear, will you ever be able to housekeep? Think of those nauseous chops at the Umbra. Remember meat must never be kept more than twenty-four hours in hot weather!' Even now, the couple behaved with the utmost discretion in front of Maurice and Eileen, confining any intimacy to private corners of the house. A Drenagh maid once excitedly confided to the other servants that she had 'caught them in a clinch in the hot-press.'

Despite Helen's earlier protestations in a letter that he should not settle for a desk job, Lucius was by now working for Helbert Wagg and Co, a leading stock broking firm founded in 1823. 'I should loathe to think of you swarming about the city among the masses, wasting your brain and energy, having miserable lunches at a filthy Lyons and being choked up in gloomy offices all day,' she had told him. 'Even if it is interesting it will be unhealthy and no occupation for a healthy young man.' Lucius had been asked to stay on at Cambridge as a don, a position much more to Helen's liking, but on this rare occasion he ignored her pleas. From Helbert Wagg he moved to Brendan Bracken's *Financial News* as a £3-a-week financial journalist, while conceding a nod towards academia by teaching English at the Working Men's College in Camden Town in his spare time. A dazzling career with the Bank of England lay ahead.

Their wedding took place on April 30 1930 and was remembered in Limavady for years afterwards. Some three hundred guests arrived at Drenagh, which was misleadingly if strictly speaking accurately described in the *Derry Journal's* account of the occasion as a 'terraced' house. More than four hundred presents were on display in the downstairs rooms, including a four-piece silver coffee set presented the previous night by the estate's employees, some of whom asked in their wonderment if the crystal bowls given to the couple were for 'broth.' Other gifts included a vase from Drenagh's distinguished pre-war visitor, Edward Carson, and a silver salver and a bound copy of Mrs Beaton's *Household Management* from Lucius's colleagues at the *Financial News*. Lucius's gift to Helen was a Regency brooch, and hers to him a gold hunter watch and chain. All in all, there was enough silver, vases, plates, jugs, cutlery and cut-glass to kit out the first-class dining saloon of an ocean-going liner, although Lucius's brother Gerald observed mischievously in a letter to his other brother John that 'there was a certain amount of junk.'

Ironically, given Maurice and Eileen's initial opposition to the romance, it was Lucius's parents who were absent on the Big Day. Not long before the wedding some four hundred people had died when British troops opened fire on demonstrators in Peshawar, triggering protests across the subcontinent. 'Owing to the unrest in India, Sir John Perronet Thompson and Lady Thompson were unable to leave the country to be present at the wedding ceremony of their son,' reported the *Irish Times*. Gerald wrote to his brother, who was also absent serving at sea: 'There wasn't a single episode (at the wedding) which didn't cry aloud for The Buster and Mother. Blast the navy and the Government of India.'

The day of the 'Limavady Society Wedding,' as the *Northern Whig and Belfast Post* billed it, was warm and sunny. As the couple emerged from Drumachose parish church, the Limavady Brownies strewed primroses from the Glen at Drenagh in their path. 'I have never seen two people look so radiant as you and Lucius coming out of church,' Conolly wrote to Helen afterwards. Maurice ensured spirits were high in the huge marquee on the lawn by laying on eighteen dozen bottles of champagne. "Isn't Miss Helen just lovely?" said a guest, Mary Irwin, as the 27-year-old bride glided past in her satin dress. "She looks like something come down from Heaven." The Dean of Derry, in proposing the toast, said: "During her whole life she has been a messenger of brightness in her home."

Clouds of confetti and rose leaves filled the air as the newly-weds set off from Limavady Station at the start of their honeymoon armed with forty-two congratulatory telegrams to read on the train. The station-master, Mr Woods, had gone to great trouble to decorate the station, and a huge crowd – both guests and non-guests – gathered on the platform to see them off. As the bridal train steamed out of the station to the accompaniment of cheers, whistles and copious rice-throwing, a large boot attached to the guard's van clattered along behind it. At Limavady Junction the couple were given the run of an entire carriage reserved for them by the Belfast and Northern Counties Railway. Yet another carriage, reeking of new paint, was waiting for their exclusive use at Ballymena when they boarded the connecting train to Belfast.

Back in Limavady the fun continued long after the train had gone. Someone seized the hat off the stout Mr Woods and plumped it on Conolly, while Denis Gibbs rammed another guest's topper on Mr Woods, eclipsing his head like a candle snuffer. The bewildered and embarrassed Mr Woods, beetroot in countenance, was then hoisted shoulder high and cheered heartily for his efforts.

Before the crowd departed, Conolly gave a speech of thanks and raised three cheers for Limavady's senior police constable, who was there to keep an eye on things. The constable was also hoisted up by the merry-makers to loud applause, and he in turn called for three cheers for the Irish Guards. Since no one wanted the day to end, Conolly invited everyone present – guests and townspeople – to join him for a drink at the Alexander Arms in Main Street. (It was rumoured afterwards that Maurice was not best pleased to receive the bar bill). A procession of cars then headed back to Drenagh, where Denis Gibbs managed to crash Maurice's Cowley saloon into the gates, damaging an axle. This did not stop him, Conolly, Eila and some of the younger guests from driving thirty miles to Strabane with bottles of champagne for more partying. Conolly wrote afterwards to Helen: 'All Limavady was in a wild state of excitement. You never saw anything like it – never.'

The next day thirty local shopkeepers and tradespeople – 'the butcher and baker' as Eileen called them - came to view the wedding presents and walk round Drenagh's garden. In the house itself most of the occupants were feeling, as Conolly put it, 'morning afterish', but the faithful Grimes, now in his eighty-fourth year, mixed them a cider cup which, since half the mixture was brandy, perked everyone up enough to play an energetic round of charades after dinner. Even Eila, who at times during the previous forty-eight hours had been visibly distraught over 'losing' her beloved sister, joined energetically in the fun.

Two days after the wedding, having over-nighted on the sleeper train from Paris, Helen and Lucius arrived in the South of France where for a fortnight they toured cathedrals, museums, chapels, monasteries and Roman ruins in Cassis, Arles and Nimes. At Frejus they spent two nights at a hotel-pension called Bellevue which turned out, in Helen's words, to be 'kept by the foulest old woman in France and her rather fouler daughter, who were determined to extract their pound of flesh' (which as it happened amounted to just 25 francs a day, or 20p). In one of the sheltered inlets at Cassis, Lucius took the opportunity to go swimming, hiring a racy red swimming costume for the occasion.

Helen and Lucius's marriage had got off to the happiest of starts, a joyful exclamation mark after years of courtship, and they would remain devoted to one another for the rest of their lives. Their serenity matched that of Drenagh itself, which was enjoying a period of unprecedented stability. No one could have foreseen the trouble that lay ahead, but the seeds of the future difficulties had already been sown and most of the key players in the looming legal dispute were now in place. Another was about to arrive on the scene.

Chapter Seven

A Jewel of a Bride

Beauty is not rare; in the land of Paddy;
Fair; beyond compare, is Peg of Limavady

From "The Irish Sketch Book 1842" by William Makepeace
Thackeray

Helen and Lucius were not the only ones in love. The
year they married, Conolly became smitten too. His
uncle, Reginald Gibbs, the kindly clergyman who had
calmed him down after his 'funny turn' at Drenagh as a boy,
had by now become the vicar of St John the Baptist Church in
Aldenham, Hertfordshire, a parish in the gift of his cousin Lord
Aldenham. This made it relatively easy for Conolly to visit his
Gibbs relations from the Irish Guards depot in Surrey or from
their HQ at Wellington Barracks near Buckingham Palace.
During one such visit he met Margaret Louisa Edgcumbe -
Peggy - beautiful daughter of Kenelm Edgcumbe, the future 6th
Earl of Mount Edgcumbe.

The third of four children (she had two older sisters and a
younger brother) Peggy had been brought up in Hertfordshire,
first at Holwell Court in Essendon, and later at Aldenham
Grange, close to Uncle Reggie's vicarage. She had been
schooled at home by governesses, and had emerged from these
confined surroundings with a limited understanding of the
ways of the world. Be that as it may, Conolly was immediately
smitten by her intelligence, good looks, energy and artistic
temperament. "She is a jewel!" was how one of his envious
friends described her to him.

There must have been times when Conolly recalled the ditty
reproduced at the head of this chapter. Though written by

William Makepeace Thackeray about a Limavady innkeeper's daughter he met during a tour of Ireland in 1842, in Conolly's love-struck eyes the words could have applied equally to his own Peg of Limavady, as she was soon to be. He enjoyed telling the story of how, despite not wanting to venture out one evening, she reluctantly agreed to accompany him to a party and proceeded to dazzle every man in the room. The proud suitor proposed to her in the 'Heather House' – the heather-clad summer house in the Drenagh garden – where they immediately celebrated their betrothal with tea and cake brought to them by the ever-attentive Grimes.

Peggy's arrival on the scene was a relief to his family, who had not always approved of Conolly's girlfriends. One, Flora Harvey, (not to be confused with her sisters Nora, Laura and Dora) from Malin Hall in Donegal, with whom he was 'thick' in the mid-1920s, was disliked by Maurice and despised by Eileen, who thought she was a 'modern minx.' Helen described her privately as a 'worthless creature' and a 'dirty little viper.' Unlike Lucius, she was not banned from Drenagh, but she was made to feel unwelcome there, and Conolly sometimes despaired of his parents' hostility towards her.

Peggy was in an altogether different league from Flora. As far as Maurice and Eileen were concerned, her aristocratic credentials and easy grace made her the perfect match for their son. Like the McCauslands, she came from an ancient land-owning family with a rich and colourful history. Her fifteenth century ancestor, Richard Edgcumbe, (grandson of William de Edgcumbe and his wife Hilaria, the heiress of Cotehele in Cornwall), played a pivotal role in securing the Crown of England for the Tudors. By siding with the Earl of Richmond (the future Henry VII), Edgcumbe incurred the wrath of Richard III, who ordered a Cornish landowner, Sir Henry Bodrugan, to seize him. A chronicler of the time wrote: 'He was so hotly pursued and narrowly searched for, that he was forced to hide himself in his thick woods at Cuttail (Cotehele). Here extremity taught him a sudden policy, to put a stone in his cap and tumble the same into the water, whilst those rangers were fast at his heels; who, looking down after the noise, and seeing his cap swinging thereon, supposed that he had desperately drowned himself; and, deluded by this honest fraud, gave over their further pursuit, leaving him at liberty to escape.'

Edgcumbe subsequently joined forces with Henry and fought side by side with him on Bosworth Field, placing a crown on Henry's head after King Richard was killed in the battle. Henry rewarded him with a knighthood on the field and gifted him Totnes Castle. Now it was Edgcumbe's turn to hunt down Sir Henry Bodrugan. The latter escaped by jumping over a cliff near his home at Mevagissey – still known as Bodrugan's Leap – and seeking refuge in France, but not before he had roundly cursed Sir Richard from the boat that took him to safety. Piers Edgcumbe, Sir Richard's son, inherited his father's courage and intellect, and received a knighthood on the field from Henry VIII at the Battle of the Spurs in 1513, when English troops routed a body of French cavalry. (More than four centuries later, Peggy's brother and youngest son would both be named Piers.)

The lives of the Edgcumbe women were no less rich in drama. In 1588, after the family had moved to Mount Edgcumbe, overlooking Plymouth Sound, the then Lady Edgcumbe entertained a dozen Spaniards from the wrecked armada to a lavish dinner before having them hanged the next morning. A century or more later, another Lady Edgcumbe succumbed to illness and was interred in the family vault. The sexton, noticing she was wearing a valuable ring, returned to the vault by night, opened the coffin, and endeavoured to remove it from her finger. The ring would not come off, and as he pressed, pinched and pulled at it, the 'corpse' sat bolt upright and opened its eyes. Not surprisingly the sexton fled in terror. The revived Lady Edgcumbe took the lantern he had conveniently dropped and returned to the house, much to the delight and amazement of her grieving husband. She made a full recovery from her premature burial and gave birth five years later to Richard, the first Baron Edgcumbe.

For sheer eccentricity, Emma Gilbert, who became Countess of Mt Edgcumbe in 1761, eclipsed all the other Edgcumbe women. The daughter of the Archbishop of York, Dr John Gilbert - and Peggy's four times great-aunt – she treated her beloved pet pig Cupid with the kind of solicitude that gave a new resonance to the expression 'live like pigs.' Wherever the countess went, Cupid trotted faithfully behind her on a golden lead, joining her at meals and accompanying her in her carriage on trips to London. The grief of the countess when her cherished companion died in 1768 was satirised by the coarse West Country poet Dr John Wolcot, who wrote a 'consolatory stanza' about the pig's demise.

> O dry that tear so round and big,
> Nor waste in sighs your precious wind.
> Death only takes a single pig –
> Your Lord and son are left behind

The countess was oblivious to such mockery. She built a 30ft stone obelisk resembling Cleopatra's Needle in memory of Cupid (it stands to this day) and had him buried beneath it in a gold casket. King George III, visiting Mount Edgcumbe in 1789, pointed out the pig obelisk to Queen Charlotte and chortled: "It's the family vault, Charley! The family vault!"

Emma's diminutive father-in-law, Richard, described by Horace Walpole as 'one of the honestest and steadiest men in the world,' was equally prone to animal adulation. He spent a large sum on a Doric temple at Mount Edgcumbe in which to place the skeleton of his favourite dog, a large hound which was said to haunt the grounds for years afterwards. The skeleton remained there until well into the twentieth century before being buried by the sixth earl – Peggy's father – because it was falling to pieces.

Invitations to dine at Mount Edgcumbe were never turned down lightly, and during the nineteenth century the hospitality offered there was legendary. The Morning Post wrote of a New Year Ball at Mount Edgcumbe in 1820: 'The festivities at this noble mansion were of the most splendid and magnificent description, and were attended by all the rank and fashion in the neighbourhood. About thirty persons sat down to a sumptuous dinner; this was followed by a ball. The saloon was most brilliantly lighted; and, in short, the *coup d'oeil* was such as is seldom seen. The supper, consisting of every delicacy of the season, was laid out on two tables in the gallery, and had a very pleasing effect. On Saturday morning, before the departure of the guests, they partook of an elegant *dejeune*, which, it is scarcely necessary to add, was equally sumptuous with the former part of this magnificent *fete*.'

Even Queen Victoria dropped in one day. The diary of Frances Lady Shelley records that on August 24 1852 Her Majesty disembarked from the royal yacht at Cremyll at seven o'clock in the morning and walked up to the stables at Mount Edgcumbe, where Peggy's newly-awoken great-grandmother rushed down to greet her. 'Her Majesty playfully quizzed Lady Mount Edgcumbe, and called her a *lazy, lay-a-bed*,' reported Lady Shelley gleefully.

With their shared wealth of colourful family history and huge circle of friends, Conolly and Peggy began planning their wedding, but first they had to attend to various formalities. One of these was putting their signatures to a McCausland marriage settlement. This was not an uncommon procedure among wealthy families at that time, and generations of McCausland men and women and their betrothed had done the same before them. Conolly and Peggy's marriage settlement was on much the same lines as earlier documents but crucially contained the new forfeiture clause drawn up five years previously at Maurice's request.

Was Conolly aware that he was again signing up to the clause he had unwittingly agreed to in 1927? Before the wedding, he went to the office of the family solicitor, Alexander Ingram, in Catherine Street, Limavady, to discuss the settlement. He was given a document which referred to the clause, although he would testify years later that he did not notice the crucial ninety words. He had also been told about the clause by his brother-in-law: Lucius and Helen had agreed to the same forfeiture clause when they signed their own marriage settlement in 1930, and Lucius took the opportunity to warn Conolly of its possible consequences when they met in England before the wedding. As would become apparent later, Conolly either failed to listen to him properly or chose to forget.

Certainly the clause was far from his mind when he and Peggy were married at Aldenham on June 6 1932. Reggie Gibbs himself conducted the service, assisted by J.J.O'Mally, the chaplain of the Brigade of Guards. Conolly's great friend, Maxwell 'Mac' Stronge, one day to become his other brother-in-law, was best man. It was the biggest and grandest event in the village in living memory, and Maurice and Eileen were in their element. The medieval church teemed with the rich and titled – four viscounts, three earls, five lords and more than twenty knights of the realm, as well as high-ranking figures in politics, the armed services, the church and the law. Villagers crowded every vantage point in the churchyard and in the lane outside to catch a glimpse of the twenty-year-old bride, while local children strewed the path in front of her with flowers.

The Herts and St Albans Times noted breathlessly: 'The whole of Aldenham was en fete for the occasion, for the wedding was an event of interest and importance unrivalled in the village for years. Tall and slim, and wearing a beautiful gown of oyster-coloured satin, the bride was a picture of typical English girlhood as she entered the church on the arm of her father. Not for many a day has a ceremony of such colourful and picturesque charm been solemnised with the walls of Aldenham Parish Church. The scene was as glowing with richness and beauty as that outside, for masses of white lilac and laburnum beautifully adorned the picturesque old building.'

The ceremony was full of Irish touches. The organist played *Londonderry Air*, the choir sang *St Patrick's Breastplate* – said to have been written by St Patrick in the fifth century - and Peggy wore a veil of old Irish lace borrowed from Eileen, and worn by all the family brides up to and including the 21st century. Warrant Officers of the Irish Guards formed a guard of honour, and the groom beamed with pride beneath his trim moustache as four pipers in saffron kilts piped the couple out of the church. Of the scores of gifts they received, one of the most touching and valued was an inscribed ashet from Drenagh's employees.

One of the Northern Irish guests at the wedding was the family solicitor, Alexander Ingram, one of the three trustees of the Drenagh settlement. At this stage he was still one of the very few people to know of the existence of the forfeiture clause which would deprive Conolly of Drenagh if he became a Roman Catholic. As the happy couple exchanged their vows, he could hardly have envisaged the turmoil that would result from his handling of the issue. But all this was still many years away...

Conolly and Peggy honeymooned in northern France, bathing at the fashionable costal resort of Deauville, where international stars like Josephine Baker and Buster Keaton liked to spend their vacations, and relaxing on Cabourg beach where Peggy amused Conolly by building a 'sand botty'. They dined at restaurants where it was possible to eat chicken at two francs a plate. Perhaps, as the sun went down, there was a little discreet skinny dipping, for Conolly – like his brother-in-law Lucius - was a great believer in going into the sea *a la nature* as he put it. 'It is funny how it is so much nicer to bathe this way, isn't it?' he wrote to Peggy some years later.

Conolly's army career meant that most of the couple's early married life was spent in England, but his love of home frequently brought them back to Ireland. It was during one of these visits that Conolly took a closer look at his marriage settlement and, as he would admit in court years later, read Clause Fifteen properly for the first time. Even then its full significance passed him by. To a layman like Conolly, the clause might as well have been written in ancient Coptic for all its clarity, and he was not prepared to go the trouble of finding out what it meant. He would claim later that while he understood it to mean his father would cut him off if he became a Catholic, he 'didn't think it had anything to do with my wife or children.'

One way or another he did not lose any sleep over the matter. Maurice was only sixty and any problems that might arise from the forfeiture clause must have seemed some way off. Besides, for the time-being at any rate, it was all academic because Conolly was not a Catholic. And supposing he converted, the very worst it seemed might happen would be that the succession skipped a generation and Drenagh went to his eldest son. Full of the joys of marriage and imminent fatherhood (Peggy gave birth to their first child, Marcus Edgcumbe McCausland, fifteen months after the wedding) he had better things to think about than some dry legal document.

He had little doubt that Drenagh would one day be his and, during his trips to Ireland, he was full of imaginative ideas for improving the estate. He loved fishing, and one of Peggy's first gifts to him was a greenheart fishing rod which he treasured for years until, to his great sadness, it was lost from Drenagh during the war, no doubt 'requisitioned' by one of the many servicemen who were stationed there. Hatching a plan to stock trout in a lough in the hills above the estate, he prepared a number of shallow ponds in the Drenagh woods in which to place young fish and grow them there until they were large enough to be transferred to their final home.

He obtained his initial stock from the mill pond at Ardmore Lodge, two miles away, which was drained and cleared of mud every summer. In 1932 Conolly and his friends collected a large number of small wriggling fish from the shallows, placed them in buckets of water and drove them in relays to Drenagh. It soon became apparent that even this short journey was too much for the tiny fish and they began to show signs of distress and turn belly upwards. The remedy was cunning and effective. Conolly enlisted several barefoot country boys to accompany the trout to Drenagh, which they did with delight since to travel in a car was a rare thrill. Each bucket had an attendant small lad who, when the little fish started to flag, pumped furiously into the water with a bicycle pump until the oxygen revived them.

Conolly had worked out an ingenious plan for feeding the fish while they were in the stew ponds. The Drenagh woods were infested with cats, domestic animals run wild, which were a constant threat to the pheasants and their young, and so of a summer evening he and his house guests would go down and pot the miscreants with .22 rifles and then suspend the corpses on ropes stretched across the fish ponds. After a few days it was only necessary to jiggle the rope and a shower of nutritious maggots would cascade into the pond, to the great delight of the trout. On this diet they quickly put on weight and grew to a great size but it turned them into confirmed bottom-feeders so that when they were transferred to their mountain lough not one of them ever rose to a fly.

One of Conolly's close friends at that time was Pat Macrory, four years his junior, who lived at Ardmore Lodge with his parents and two sisters. Despite the frosty relationship of their respective grandparents half a century earlier, Macrory had a great affection for Conolly. Their affinity had been cemented in the final days of 1929 after Macrory's fifteen-year-old cousin, Molly, died two days before Christmas following an operation intended to cure her of a persistent throat infection. Macrory was one of the four pall-bearers at the funeral in the little church at Balteagh and helped to carry Molly to her resting place in the churchyard. As he passed through the church gate he had a dreadful feeling that the coffin was slipping from his shoulder but Conolly, standing outside the church, saw his difficulty and at once sprang forward to put his shoulder beneath the coffin. It was a spontaneous act of help and friendship that Macrory never forgot.

Conolly loved acting (to the hilarity of the audience he played a large-bosomed Mrs Sinbad in the *Limavady Revue* in January 1930) and in 1932 – just after his marriage – he and Macrory resolved to stage a Sherlock Holmes play at Limavady Town Hall in aid of local charities. Macrory adapted two of Conan Doyle's stories into a three-act play called *Murder at Midnight* and wrote in his diary that Conolly was 'over-joyed' when he read it. With Macrory as the great detective, Conolly as the murderous villain and Helen's lovesick admirer William Lenox-Conyngham as Dr Watson, they performed the play during the Christmas holidays to packed matinee and evening audiences. The local paper gave them an enthusiastic write-up and described their performances as 'crisp and convincing.' The only hitch occurred when Macrory appeared on stage with his trousers accidentally unbuttoned. Maurice, who was sitting in the front row, sent a note back-stage saying: 'Pat's flies are undone. Is this part of the play?'

Afterwards they drank heartily to their thespian triumph, for alcohol was never in short supply at Drenagh. During one of

Macrory's visits there, Conolly found a bottle of poteen in the cellars with a handwritten label dated 1865, a relic of the early days of Conolly Thomas. Macrory recalled afterwards that the two of them 'drank it neat with plain water, a clear translucent liquid with just the faintest hint of blue in it, a pink gin turned into a blue gin as it were. It was velvet smooth on the tongue, our heads retained a bell-like clarity and our conversation became sparklingly brilliant. Then we tried to stand up and fell flat on our faces.'

There were many other forms of entertainment in those pre-television days. In 1931 Conolly and his sisters clubbed together to buy Maurice a radio gramophone for Christmas, then the ultimate gift for an indulged parent. 'The machine works off the electric light so there is no bother with batteries or accumulators,' Conolly told Helen and Eila. To be able to listen to concerts and symphonies, and hear the latest records by artists like Mildred Bailey, Noel Coward and Louis Armstrong in the comfort of their home, must have been an extraordinary experience for Maurice and Eileen, let alone for any servants in the room, most of whom had probably never been to a concert in their lives.

When the weather permitted, there were endless outdoor pursuits, including riding, roller-skating, paper chases, helping out at the annual Drenagh Retriever Trials, and going to the races at Ballyarnett. Every summer Conolly hosted numerous tennis tournaments, or took his house guests to play at the homes of friends. 'The party from Drenagh arrived for tennis,' wrote Macrory in his diary on August 25 1932. 'The general standard of play was appalling but very funny. We howled with mirth at some of the most absurd shots.' Hockey remained another popular sport, and was sometimes enlivened with appearances by the bachelor rector of Limavady, Canon Thompson, whose ferocious play earned him the nickname of Thompsonius Pugnax. Short and stocky, the perfect shape to be fired from a cannon, he would charge down the field like a tank, head down and stick whirling, ruthlessly butting away all who stood in his path, men, women and small children alike.

After tennis and hockey there might be flag games in the Glen, Prisoner's Base being a favourite. In the evenings Conolly and his guests often played the famous Drenagh *Passage Game*, an exciting and rumbustious variant of Hide and Seek which came to a sudden end on one occasion when Eila tripped on some steps and broke her nose. Like his father, Conolly enjoyed shooting, and his diary entries echoed those of Maurice nearly half a century earlier. On January 22 1936, for example, he recorded a bag of sixty-three pheasant, three woodcock, three pigeon and three 'various.' On a gentler note, he enjoyed going to whist drives, playing billiards, and taking part in family parlour games like *Famous Men*.

The tradition of family picnics by the sea lived on, although now some of the trips to the coast took place at the romantic hour of midnight, with car headlights illuminating the choppy waters at Magilligan and Downhill, and sandwiches being eaten by torchlight. Drenagh by now boasted no fewer than three cars – a Cowley, an Austin and Conolly's Morris Minor - an impressive number at a time when to own just one was still extremely rare. During the winter months the family regularly travelled to fashionable resorts in Europe where they skied, skated, tobogganed and went to fancy dress parties. Few years were complete without visits to friends and relations in Scotland and England.

Cinema outings were another popular pastime. In the early 1930s silent movies were shown in Limavady Town Hall, with an elderly spinster gallantly pounding out 'Turkish Patrol' on a tinny piano, or the 'Eton Boating Song' if and when water featured in the story. The manager of the Town Hall cinema was the ever-cheerful Frank Coghlan, who kept the family well-briefed about forthcoming attractions. "No need to book for this one," he would tell the McCauslands. "It's one of them historical films and there'll not be many at it. It's the smell of a costume that keeps them away, you know, the smell of a costume." Coghlan had a rooted objection to paying entertainment tax and evaded it by the simple means of never tearing the tickets in half, but simply using the same tickets over and over again. For this offence he was prosecuted from time to time, but he was one of Maurice's fellow magistrates on the local Bench and he would say with a knowing grin that with any luck his colleagues would give him the benefit of the Probation of Offenders Act.

With the advent of talking films the Town Hall was abandoned and a local businessman, James Hunter, opened two real cinemas in the town, the Regal in Catherine Street and the Roe in Main Street, the latter being opened by Eileen in a grandiose ceremony. Seats in the front row cost 1/6d (7.5p) and since both cinemas had three different programmes a week it was possible if one so wished to see six different films a week for a total cost of nine shillings (45p). The Limavady audiences could be noisy and rowdy if a film was not to their liking, but they always stood in respectful silence for the National Anthem, which was played at the end of every evening performance. Eileen's patronage of the Roe meant that any visiting McCauslands were assured of prime seats in the balcony, far above the madding crowd.

As the years went by, Conolly involved himself increasingly with the local community. In 1934, at the age of twenty-eight, he became - like his father and grandfather before him - a Justice of the Peace, and in 1935 he joined the Limavady Branch of the British Legion. Two years later he was made a Deputy Lieutenant of Londonderry. He was also appointed High Sheriff of Londonderry, a job which required him to attend judges at Assizes.

The first time he did this, at Londonderry County Assizes in March 1937, Peggy and a kilted four-year-old Marcus watched proudly from the public gallery with the Drenagh nurse. As the Derry Journal reported the next day, the solemn proceedings were 'interrupted by a cry from a little kilted boy sitting between his mother and nurse. When he saw his father in the uniform of a guards' officer take his seat on the Bench beside Mr Justice Brown he became very excited. The child made his voice heard during the reading by the Clerk of the Commission. The nurse promptly hustled him out of court. When the Clerk had finished, the Judge smilingly called up to the gallery: "Bring back that little child, or he will be disappointed."' Thus was Marcus's introduction to public life. Exactly thirty years later he himself was also made High Sheriff.

That same year Conolly resigned from the Irish Guards and moved back to Ireland. Maurice was becoming increasingly frail and he felt he should be nearby. He and Peggy settled into Cumber House, a large Victorian property outside the village of Claudy, fourteen miles from Limavady. Their second child, Fania, had been born in 1936, and their life there was happy and tranquil. In preparation for taking over Drenagh, Conolly spent a term at Oxford studying agriculture and practical farming, and immersed himself in the business of running a large estate.

As for his young bride, she had ambivalent feelings about Northern Ireland. Although Peggy glided into her role as future chatelaine with grace and charm, there were times when she positively disliked the rain-swept province with its political and religious divides. Her father-in-law had suffered from chronic rheumatism since his early fifties and was often bent double and needed sticks to walk. Her mother-in-law was regularly bed-ridden with bronchitis. No doubt Peggy wondered if the unforgiving climate would one day play similar havoc with her own bones and lungs.

Nor can she have viewed the prospect of running a big house like Drenagh with undiluted relish. Conolly's younger sister, Eila, graphically described some of the problems of managing servants in the 1930s in a letter to Helen: 'For the first time in my life I had the household brawls to cope with when Mammy was away. Needless to say, they (the servants) fought like cats and dogs, and came to me with their petty little stories. I tried to unravel them the best way I could and delivered lectures all round to those concerned. It began on March 1st when both Doris and the under housemaid gave me notice. I discovered Doris was at the bottom of everything so let her go, and persuaded Annie the underling to remain on. She's a good little creature and does her best – it's a pity about Doris because she is an excellent upper housemaid but unfortunately has a tongue of abnormal length.'

Compared to middle-class Aldenham, just fifteen miles from London, rural Ulster was primitive and unsophisticated, and Peggy often felt like - and was seen as - an outsider. Several years younger than Conolly, her comparative youth added to her occasional feelings of isolation. In particular, she sometimes found it hard to deal with Conolly and Helen's great affinity.

Those who knew Peggy and Conolly well felt that while they undoubtedly loved one another, there had never been for either of them the coup de foudre, the lightning bolt that seizes people in a whip crack of electricity and shakes them by the hair. Lucius made this point in a letter to Helen when Peggy was in her late twenties, saying he agreed with a friend who described her as 'a girl full of energy, intelligence and possibilities, but quite undeveloped, as if she had never had a love affair.'

For Conolly's sake Peggy tried to put on a brave face and, like every previous generation, she would leave her stamp on Drenagh. She was highly artistic, with a gift for painting and drawing, and in due course she would embellish the botanical beauty of the estate with an all-white 'moon' garden, but she would never love Drenagh the way Conolly did. 'You have to be careful,' she told her daughter-in-law, June, years later. 'This house is like a ship's anchor. It can pull you down.' To Conolly the 'anchor' suggested security and stability, but to Peggy it implied a stifling restraint.

Nonetheless, there was little to trouble the young McCausland family during those halcyon days in the mid-1930s, and their future seemed secure in every respect but one. Conolly could feel a pull like thin wire through his bloodstream, not leaving him alone, drawing him towards Catholicism. A visit to the exquisite thirteenth century cathedral at Chartres, one of the finest examples of the French high Gothic style, had pulled him in further, and it perhaps dawned on him that sooner or later his attraction to Catholicism would lead to trouble.

But all this was still far away. In the meantime, the hazards of life in Ireland were not without their funny side. Shortly after her marriage Peggy was driving home to Limavady from Derry with her foot hard down on the accelerator, for it was a good straight main road with no other traffic. Suddenly, without warning, a battered old jalopy shot out across her path from a side lane and turned towards Limavady. Peggy, steaming up behind it, braked hard but could not avoid hitting it hard astern, at which it leapt forward but kept going. Peggy, alarmed and angry, overtook and signalled the driver to stop, which he obediently did. A cheerful red bucolic face with a broad grin was thrust out of the driver's window. "Have you ever driven a car in your life?" demanded Peggy furiously. The totally disarming answer was a simple 'No!"

Chapter Eight

The Approaching Storm

At Christmas we'd a time of it with parties night and day
There were so many dances that we really felt quite gay
It was a sight to see the local ladies 'take the floor'
Dressed in the 'chic creations' made by 'Mademoiselle Amour.'

From a poem about Drenagh by Eileen McCausland c 1905

The first of Helen and Lucius's six children – a son– was born at their home in West London in February 1931, ten months after their wedding. Both parents had made elaborate preparations for the event. Helen, though suspecting she was carrying a boy, trimmed the cot in pink in advance because she thought it 'a softer and more becoming baby colour.' She also accumulated a large collection of baby clothes from well-wishing friends, and interviewed and hired a nurse – Miss Phillips – months in advance of the birth. Lucius, ever on the lookout for a bargain, managed to acquire a sumptuous 25-guinea Leveson pram for just £5 from a woman who no longer needed it, and built a shed in the back yard to house it. 'She has separated from her rich but odious husband and so won't be having any more urchins,' he explained to his mother in a letter.

During the first moments of his life the new baby was unnaturally quiet, causing some concern to both Lucius and Eileen, who were waiting anxiously downstairs. 'We heard him give one cry and then he was silent,' Lucius wrote to his mother. 'I persuaded Eileen it was a cat.' Lucius went upstairs to investigate, and feared the worst when he saw the nurse's worried demeanour and heard her urgent request for brandy. But all was well. 'After ten anxious minutes we heard a healthy howl,' wrote Lucius. 'Having decided that life was preferable, even under a Labour government, *(Ramsay Macdonald had become Labour Prime Minister twenty months earlier)* he took up his duties with vigour and has since devoted himself to a scholarly study of his fists. Cousin Eileen was a very good companion to wait with and answered a very large number of questions I asked her about the process.'

The baby's full name was Marcus McCausland Perronet Thompson, who after the birth of Conolly's son became known as Mark, and among his Godparents was his doting Uncle Conolly. As Maurice toasted his first grandchild's health at Drenagh, no one could possibly have foreseen that the new baby would have a pivotal role in the family turmoil that lay ahead.

Strong and healthy, Mark made his first trip across the Irish Sea that August, accompanied by Helen and a nanny. 'On the journey over The Hogget was singing and talking and stretching the sides of his shoes,' Helen told Lucius in a letter. 'He sat on his nanny's knee and chewed crusts of toast which he threw down after a bite or two, so the floor got rather strewn with urchin manure.' 'The Hogget' was the first of several nicknames Helen and Lucius bestowed on Mark.

Their private language included several nicknames for each other, 'My Duck' and 'My Drake' being top of the list, with regular references to duck anatomy such as bills and webbed feet. When apart, as they frequently were, the Duck and the Drake wrote long letters to each other on an almost daily basis, their love for one another shining through on every page. 'Almost continuously I miss you in one way or other, but now and then it becomes so sharp as to advance right into the foreground of my mind,' Lucius wrote to Helen two years after their marriage. On another occasion, when he left Helen at Drenagh to return to London after a family holiday, he wrote:

'A perfect moon at the full is filling me with longing for you…
may God's blessing be on you my only love.' Helen wrote from
Drenagh: 'When I woke this morning I instinctively turned
round to see if you were awake, and it was horrid to find no
monster in the bed. Darling, are you missing me in bed too?'
They often slept with their letters to one another under their
pillows.

When together, they loved walking, visiting friends and going
to parties. Any small squabbles were quickly smoothed over.
'Came back slightly disgruntled, which was remedied later,'
Helen wrote enigmatically in her diary after a Sunday walk
with Lucius.

Other coded words in their repertoire included 'The McClocks'
and 'Hogs' for their children, while any addition to the family
was referred to as a 'New Hog', sometimes delicately shortened
to 'NH.' In September 1932 a New Hog arrived on the scene
in the shape of Marianne ('My darling Helen,' wrote Conolly
on hearing of the birth, 'how simply grand – more power and
many blessings to you and Lucius') to be followed by Dominick
in 1936, and Benedict in 1938. There would be two further
additions – Teressa (Tessa) and Virginia, known jointly as the
'Skirts' - in 1939 and 1942.

As Lucius's career continued on its sharply upward curve, the
family moved out of London to a spacious late 18th century
house – Amwell Grove – in Great Amwell, Hertfordshire,
twenty miles north of London. The house overlooked the New
River, an artificial waterway built in 1613 to supply London
with fresh drinking water, and among those who had fished
its water was the village's most celebrated resident, the angler
Izaak Walton. The Thompsons were able to afford two retainers,
Mr and Mrs Taylor, who cooked and gardened respectively
and lived in a cottage in the grounds. They were known by the
family as the 'Jolly Olds', later shortened to 'J.O.' for her and

'Joey' for him. With its large garden and rural surroundings Amwell Grove was the perfect place to bring up children (Lucius extended the house by building a nursery wing above the dining room) but throughout the 1930s the highlight of each year was the great trek to Northern Ireland. Helen's devotion to Drenagh and all that it stood for had passed as if by osmosis to her children. All grew up with a deep love and respect for the home of seven generations of their forebears, and they never ceased to look forward to their annual visits.

Every summer before the war trunks were loaded into Lucius's capacious old Sunbeam (later followed by a Lagonda and an Alvis) and the children were squeezed into the back with their Nurse for the journey to Liverpool, with various stops on the way to be sick and have picnics. In those pre-dual carriageway, pre-motorway days, it was a journey of many long hours. Their route took them through the newly-built Mersey Tunnel and on into the bustling port where the children gazed in awe at the Liver Birds and listened with fascination to the ships' sirens echoing across the water. This was before the days of roll-on roll-off ferries and the motor car had to be placed in a sling and hoisted by crane on to one of the Belfast Steamship Company's three new acquisitions, the Ulster Monarch, the Ulster Prince and the Ulster Queen.

Once on board, the family were shown to their cabins by forelock-tugging stewards. These were cramped cubes with neatly made bunk beds, mahogany furniture and discreetly positioned cuspidors which passengers were invited to use if they wanted to be sick. Then they made their way down low corridors to the dining saloon where waiters in starched white uniforms served them their evening meal. Many of their fellow passengers had brought on board fishing rods, dogs and – unthinkable four decades later – guns. As dusk fell, the ship set off on the 150-mile crossing to Belfast, herring gulls and guillemots whirling in her wake and alighting in screechy unison on the deck rails. Lucius was a poor sailor and always carried a pocket flask of brandy to settle his stomach. To the children's surprise, he sometimes invited them to take a swig as well.

Walking down the gangway at Belfast early the next morning was like stepping into another world, utterly different from their peaceful life in rural Hertfordshire. The commercial bustle of the docks was already in full swing as shouting men unloaded the ships, and large horses plodded the cobbles pulling heavily-laden carts with iron-rimmed wheels. Trams trundled along the streets, and the smell of creosote, tar and kippers filled the air. No matter that a lashing rain laden with salt was usually sweeping in from the sea, dropping a grey curtain over the city and causing the tram-lines and cobbles to glisten like fish scales. This was Ireland, and as they headed out of Belfast towards the distant Sperrin Mountains and Limavady, the rain was all part and parcel of 'a grand soft day.'

On they went, never failing to be enchanted by the whitewashed cottages, the moorland hills, and the vividly green stone walled fields. At last, after a couple of hours or so, the great Drenagh wall came into view, overhung by a canopy of trees - sweet chestnut, oak, birch and ash. As they turned in through the gates, their excitement mounted. The surface of the thousand-yard-long driveway – built by their great-great grandfather Marcus in 1830 to replace an earlier entrance to the north of the estate - was not tarmaced in those days, and Lucius drove along it at a sedate pace. 'Never go down a gentleman's drive at more than 20 m.p.h.' was one of his rules of motoring.

'There's the house,' Helen would say as they rounded a bend in the drive. First the rhododendrons came into view, and then the shallow flight of stone steps leading to the balustraded terrace. Off to their right was the great beech tree where Conolly and Helen's imaginary friend Perseus had once lived, and on which family initials carved in the bark in the 1880s were (and still are) visible.

The house was a place of wonder. On one wall in the outer hall hung a decorative display of rifles, blunderbusses, swords and bayonets, relics of the Balteagh Infantry set up by an earlier Conolly in 1809 to help repel the French in case of invasion. One of these rifles, it was said, had been manufactured by the same gunsmith – Henry Deringer - who made the pistol that shot Abraham Lincoln. In the vast inner hallway, adorned with bowls of sweet peas, the children's feet rang hollowly on the stone floor. Precious paintings hung on the walls, including one of a horse by the renowned equine artist John Herring. On the floor sat the great gong which summoned them to meals. In the dining-room, Grimes the butler (he lived and worked at Drenagh until shortly before his ninetieth birthday in 1937) had applied so much beeswax to the table over the years that its surface had acquired a kind of crocodile skin effect, and the children enjoyed the sensation of digging their fingernails into the wax in the moulding round the table's edge.

The sounds of Drenagh were a constant source of pleasure and intrigue, whether it was the yard bell calling the men to work at the start of the day, the gardeners tramping into the house with fresh plants, the peacock descendants of the 'little peachick' strutting around the lawn calling to each other, or Eileen clearing her throat in the hall, a sound which echoed up the wide stone staircase and into the night nursery. The smells were equally evocative – burnt toast wafting up the back stairs, the porridge which Nanny King, now approaching seventy, carried up for breakfast, and the malted milk she brought them at bed-time. The harness room, which housed many different kinds and styles of saddle, had another special smell all of its own. So did the apple room where Peter Gibbon, the head gardener, would take them to choose an apple each. Outside, the sweet and sodden smell of the Glen pricked their nostrils, as did the magnolia grandiflora in the walled garden, and the peaches, nectarines, grapes, figs and tomatoes in the greenhouses. At bath-time they loved sinking into the peaty brown water, although its smell was not always a pleasant one if it was the season for retting the flax.

Colourful characters abounded on the estate. One, John Anderson, was in charge of the Curly Burn generator which produced power for the electric bar fires in Drenagh's bedrooms. On one occasion a flash flood in the burn caused the generator to become red hot. This so alarmed Anderson that he jammed all the levers to 'off' and cycled frantically up the lower drive to the lawn, where he dismounted, ran breathlessly up to the house and turned off all the electricity. Finding Eileen, he blurted out that the generator was running red hot, so he had come as fast as he could to turn everything off - "and I got here just in time, before the electricity."

There were endless places for the children to explore. In a passage that ran round the courtyard at the side of the building, where the servants were housed, they made their acquaintance with the old rocking horse which Helen, Conolly and Eila had played with as children, although by now it no longer had a tail or mane, and possessed only the remnants of a saddle and bridle. Here too they played the famed Passage Game so enjoyed by generations of McCauslands.

One side of the stables housed different kinds of covered horse-drawn carriages, their leather upholstery musty and mouldering, so that climbing into one carried with it the risk of disturbing a rat. One open-wheeled conveyance was known as the Yellow Bounder, and was sometimes harnessed to a pony so that Helen could travel around the estate and visit the family retainers. One of these retainers was a man named Jimmy Meeghan who filled two churns with spring water from the glen every morning and carried them up to the house on a wooden yoke, a taxing task for he was stiff and lame from a childhood illness. He and his black-skirted mother lived with her other children in a cottage with an earthen floor near the main gate. The younger ones, huddled and shapeless, had no shoes and wore cut-off adult trousers held up at the waist with string.

Superstition abounded, and the Thompson children loved hearing about the ancient legends and folklore. Country people in County Derry still believed in the brooneys, invisible creatures who appeared by night and threshed the corn for their favourites. Tales were told of the 'little people' who tended hawthorn bushes in the fields, and there were stories of farmers who had been spirited up into the night air by fairy folk. It was said that if you were brave enough to sleep under a bush at the Rough Fort, once owned by old Marcus McCausland, on Midsummer Eve, a voice would whisper in your ear and tell you the name of the person you would marry. Few took the chance for it was supposedly just as likely to tell you the date of your death, if it so fancied.

Stories were also told of the legendary Irish giant Finn MacCool, who was said to have built the Giant's Causeway, and whose 'thumb' - a rocky promontory on Binevenagh Mountain to the north of Drenagh - always fascinated the children. At Banagher Glen, one of the family's favourite picnic spots, a monstrous snake was said to live in a deep pool on the Crooked Burn - the only one that St Patrick had failed to kill. The avenue leading to the Ritter family's home at Roe Park was reputedly haunted by a black dog, the sight of which was said to mean death within a year. And anyone with an ounce of sense treated a large stone up by old Drumachose Church with the greatest respect, for it was said that something terrible would happen if it was moved.

Drummond Corner, just beyond Drenagh's main gate, was reputedly haunted by the ghost of a local taxi driver who had been killed when he failed to negotiate the bend. It was claimed that he would leap on the running boards of passing cars and try to wrest the steering wheels from their drivers' hands so that they should suffer the same fate. Even those who laughed off the story as nonsense had to suppress a prickle of fear if they drove past the spot alone at night. Just as they did if they passed Black Maggie's cottage near the little humpback bridge close to Streeve Hill, which was said to have a curse on it and had been struck by lightning on the day old Maggie died.

A mile or so north of Drenagh, and no less scary on a dark night, was the Murder Hole Road, where the infamous eighteenth century cut-throat and highwayman, Cushy Glen, had preyed upon travellers making their way between Limavady and Coleraine and buried their bodies on the bleak moorland. Eventually he was killed himself by one of his would-be victims, but it was said that his ghost still haunted the lonely stretch of road.

Another mysterious spot was the Dogleap on the river Roe, the site of pre-Plantation Limavady. In medieval times a dog reputedly jumped across the river at this spot to warn the O'Cahan clan of an impending attack, so giving the settlement its name. ('Limavady' is Gaelic for 'The Leap of the Dog.') At the beginning of the twentieth century the Dogleap land was owned by the Robertson family, who were friends of the McCauslands. Some time before the First World War, Max Robertson, then in his twenties, decided to look for the O'Cahan treasure, which was said to be hidden in a shaft beneath a great boulder high above the river, and was reputedly protected by a supernatural guardian, powerful and malignant. Max and two farm hands loosened the bolder with crowbars and began heaving it away with ropes. As they did so, Max reported afterwards, a huge blast of wind roared through the trees, lifted them off their feet and dropped them thirty yards away in a cow pond. The attempt was immediately abandoned.

'Max knew when to take a hint,' his sister Dorothy told the McCauslands.

Helen told the children about another old superstition that the wishes of those who bowed three times to the new moon would come true. Not long before her marriage she had written a nonsense poem about this belief:

> Tonight, to bow to the moon
> I went out alone in the dew,
> I went with my wishes three
> To where the linden tree
> Stretches her boughs to the moon
>
> But beauty in her flight
> Swept me into the night
> Smothered me with her wings
> Touched on intangible strings
> That made of the night a tune
>
> Under the new-born moon,
> Standing alone in the dew
> In the shade of the linden tree
> I forgot my wishes three,
> Forgot to bow to the moon

Few days were complete without a visit to the sea, where Lucius would plunge into the sea in a torso-covering swimming costume while the children paddled, built sand castles and dug holes on the beach. Thompson family holidays at Drenagh usually coincided with those of their McCausland cousins, and Marcus and Fania often joined them on these outings. Mark and Marianne thought of Marcus as more like a younger brother than a cousin, although they could not help noticing that the future heir to Drenagh commanded at least as much if not more attention from Maurice and Eileen as they did, a fact which occasionally left them feeling a little hard done by.

They greatly enjoyed the company of their uncle and aunt. Peggy, assured, cheery and energetic, was full of ideas for games and activities in which none of the rules and restrictions that bound them in England seemed to apply. Marianne was particularly struck by an image of her coming down the stairs, and recalled decades later: "She was wearing a kilt which swung from side to side as she descended. Her handsomeness, self-confidence and vigour hit me like a wave." Conolly complemented Peggy perfectly, a mischievous and kindly uncle with a pronounced sense of humour. Based as he was in England, he was also a regular visitor to Great Amwell, and could usually be relied upon to dream up some subversive fun.

He demonstrated this in May 1939 when he drove Mark and Marianne to visit their Gibbs cousins in Aldenham. On reaching the vicarage driveway, Conolly gave eight-year-old Mark a hasty lesson in working the pedals of his trusty Fiat Topolino before plumping him behind the steering wheel. Then, with six-year-old Marianne sitting in the back seat, Conolly crouched down out of sight next to her and told Mark to proceed down the driveway. When a waiting Denis Gibbs stepped forward to greet his visitors he was more than a little surprised to find the two children seemingly alone in the Topolino, having apparently driven the fifteen miles from Amwell by themselves.

Both at home and in the wider world the halcyon days of the early and mid-1930s became clouded and unsettled as the decade neared its end, and Helen and Lucius were struck by tragedy. In 1937 Mark, Marianne and Dominick all became desperately ill with an unknown disease, and Dominick succumbed to it on Easter Day, Helen's thirty-fourth birthday. He was just six months old. In a telegram to Drenagh, Helen wrote: 'Little Dominick's struggle ended at four o'clock this morning. Do not think of us as unhappy.' Later she told Maurice: 'We thought we might be going to lose Mark, and we prayed long and hard then that if one of them had to go we should be left our first-born. Then the valiant little man *(Dominick)* rallied and we did so hope he would stay with us too, but the poison had got too deeply into his system. Such a splendid spirit he had and oh so brave. We were proud of him.' The inscription on Dominick's headstone read:

> *Over the grave of their little son DOMINIC JOHN PERRONET*
> *Lucius and Helen Thompson have placed this stone. He was born*
> *on October 7th 1936. On April 4th 1937 an unknown infection*
> *took him. But his brother and sister recovered. For him taken and*
> *for them left their parents thank GOD.*

Of the scores of letters Helen and Lucius received, one of the most touching was from Eila. 'My lovely sister,' she wrote. 'I have always loved you for your gaiety of heart, but now I think I love you even more for your quiet and lovely courage in the face of adversity and soreness of heart. You were the white candle whose bright flame never once flickered or grew dim, but shone bravely on through the darkness of your night. I knew that you were brave, but how brave I did not know and could not conceive till now. How tremendously proud I feel of you. God has indeed blessed me in giving me such a sister, and Lucius such a wife.'

One by one the countries of Europe were sucked into the war. Drenagh too was about to face great upheaval. As the decade drew to a close Conolly prepared to take the first steps in a chain of events that would test the family's cohesion to its limits.

Chapter Nine

The Die is Cast

Your father left the Protestant tradition
And you were Catholics –
A private matter of faith and conviction
But there is no such thing in Ulster.
You are labelled one way or another
Even by your own eyes

From 'In memory of Marcus McCausland' by Penny Mander, 1984

In 1936 Maurice was made a member of the Privy Council of Northern Ireland, a body created fourteen years earlier in the wake of partition. The council rarely met and was largely ceremonial, but for Maurice it was a fitting honour after a lifetime of public service, and meant that his name was now prefixed with the prized adjectives *Right Honourable*. In this exalted position he and Eileen were invited to the coronation of King George VI in Westminster Abbey in May 1937. With seats above the peers in the South Transept, they had a birds-eye view of the Royal Family, including the future Queen Elizabeth. 'The two little princesses were sweet in their long frocks and trains,' wrote Eileen to a relation. 'Princess Elizabeth was very sedate but Margaret Rose had a good look round. The service was beautiful, with such a wealth of colour and pageantry that it almost took one's breath away, and one felt thankful for a good King and Queen and such an empire.'

In December 1937, at the age of sixty-five, Maurice's health began to fail and he underwent an operation in London. He appeared at first to make a good recovery, but the following month he developed acute appendicitis and needed a second operation. When he died in a London nursing home soon afterwards (in a sad twist of fate his death occurred on Eileen's fifty-ninth birthday in January 1938) it was in the secure belief that the forfeiture clause had done its job and that Conolly had put Drenagh before religious conviction. In fact it was the start of an extraordinary family saga that would see all his plans and wishes unravel at enormous cost to the family.

Maurice was buried on January 18 at Drumachose parish church in Limavady, where many McCauslands had been buried before him and where he had read countless lessons over the previous four decades. His oak coffin, draped with black crepe, was drawn on a farm cart from Drenagh to the church by estate workers, and afterwards borne to the graveside. More than 150 wreaths were laid on his grave. Helen, who was heavily pregnant in London with her fourth child, Benedict Maurice Perronet, (Benedict, meaning 'Blessed', was in thanks for a healthy boy following the tragedy of Dominick's death, and Maurice after his grandfather) was unable to attend, but Conolly sent her a vivid description. He wrote: 'Dearest Daddy – it was a real Triumphal Procession rather than a funeral. The triumph of a sweet, humble and unselfish life. It just seemed to prove the truth of the words - 'Blessed are the pure in heart' – which you suggested should be his epitaph. The service was just one shout of triumph and thankfulness…it was wonderful in every way. How great a strength he was to me and all of us.'

Prayers were said for Maurice again the following Sunday when the congregation thanked God 'for his devotion to duty, for his manifold interests and joy in life, for the youth that was ever in his heart, for the perfect companionship of his married life, for the love of his children and grandchildren…' An obituary in The Belfast Telegraph noted that he was a staunch Unionist and described him as 'the premier resident of Limavady, a public benefactor, a firm friend of the townspeople, and was ever found in the forefront of any movement for the welfare of the community.'

Initially there was no outward sign of trouble over the succession to Drenagh. On his father's death Conolly became tenant for life, and young Marcus, then aged five, became the 'remainderman'. Father, mother, son and baby daughter moved into Drenagh from Cumber House, and once again the sound of small children echoed through the old ancestral home. The Drenagh estate at that time comprised three thousand acres and was worth about £75,000. In addition there were investments valued at £70,000 or so. The total in today's money would be more than £5 million. If Conolly was toying with the idea of converting, he must surely have known there was a lot at stake. Yet even now he had only a hazy understanding of the forfeiture clause, and probably did not realise he could be putting his tenancy of Drenagh in jeopardy, let alone that of Marcus.

Peggy was prepared to go along with his wish to become a Catholic, even to the extent of allowing the children to convert as well, but she made it clear from the start that she herself would never go down the same path. Not religious herself, she was no respecter of the Roman Catholic or any other church.

Eileen, whose deep dislike of Catholicism remained undimmed, became increasingly apprehensive about her son's intentions and even now, after all these years, she clearly hoped he would 'see sense' and not do anything drastic. Early in 1939 she travelled to Africa and spent several weeks with her nephew Michael Gibbs, an Anglican priest in what was then Rhodesia (now Zimbabwe), and who later became Dean of Johannesburg. In a letter to Conolly in February she made clear her feelings about 'duty', holding up Maurice as a shining example of what it meant to be the head of a family like the McCauslands.

She wrote: 'I know you thought of me on my sad (sixtieth) birthday and of your beloved father. His is indeed a lovely memory and his life of service a great example to follow. I know

Happy Days: Summer 1934 at Drenagh. The Thompson and McCausland families enjoying the puppies. L to R. Conolly Marcus, Peggy. Lucius and Mark standing, Helen and Marianne seated.

MARTIN, KING, FRENCH & INGRAM,
SOLICITORS & LAND AGENTS.

W.A. INGRAM.
J.-R. YOUNG.
E.G.C. BROWN.

OFFICES:
LIMAVADY & DUNGIVEN.

ALSO AT
11, LOMBARD ST, BELFAST.
AND
7, ST STEPHEN'S GREEN, DUBLIN.

TELEGRAMS: "INGRAM, LIMAVADY".
TELEPHONE: Nº 7 LIMAVADY.

Limavady,
Co. Londonderry,

3rd October 19 40.

McCausland Trusts

Dear Helen,

I was much surprised and distressed to receive a letter from Conolly yesterday telling me that he had been received into the R.C. Church on 3rd May last. Enclosed is a copy of the Religion Clause in the Re-Settlement of 1927 under which he has by this action irrevocably forfeited for himself and his family all interest in Drenagh and the rest of the settled property; of which you are now the owner as tenant for life, subject to the Name & Arms Clause a copy of which is also enclosed.

We shall place all dividends and rents henceforth received to credit of an account in your name and await your instructions as to the Demesne and other property of which Conolly is in occupation. He mentioned that he had some talk with you about an indemnity to his Trustees but nothing of this kind is feasible.

It will be a matter for you to decide whether you ought to join with your brother in seeking to defeat your Father's wishes by installing a R.C. at Drenagh than which, as I am sure you know, nothing would have given him greater pain and which he had done everything possible to prevent by provisions in which Conolly con-curred. You would be entitledto claim repayment of a part of the

The first intimation that Conolly had changed religion.
Letter to Helen from family Solicitors Martin, King, French & Ingram.

Irish Guards awaiting embarkation.
Conolly on left.

A corner of the Communal cemetery at
Outreau where 16 Irish Guards and 3 Royal
Artillery are buried.

Conolly at Amwell Grove on his
return from Boulogne May 1940

Amwell Grove in Hertfordshire home of Lucius and Helen (showing the first floor
Nursery wing added by Lucius)

To Helen, eleven years married.

When first I loved you it was as the dawn
Of some May morning, so surpassing fair
That no succeeding noontide could compare
For loveliness. Yet, now the noon comes on,
Though morn's delightful prime is passed away,
This hour is with a deeper fragrance filled,
The sweetness of the early dews distilled
To the full nectar of a summer's day.
So, my beloved, each season of your life
New beauty still unfolds to me, and I,
Your lover still, love your maturity,
Sweetheart become my bride, & bride my wife.
And when day sets, one love, a star, shall
rise
To light not earthly but eternal skies.

Poem from Lucius to Helen on their 11th wedding anniversary

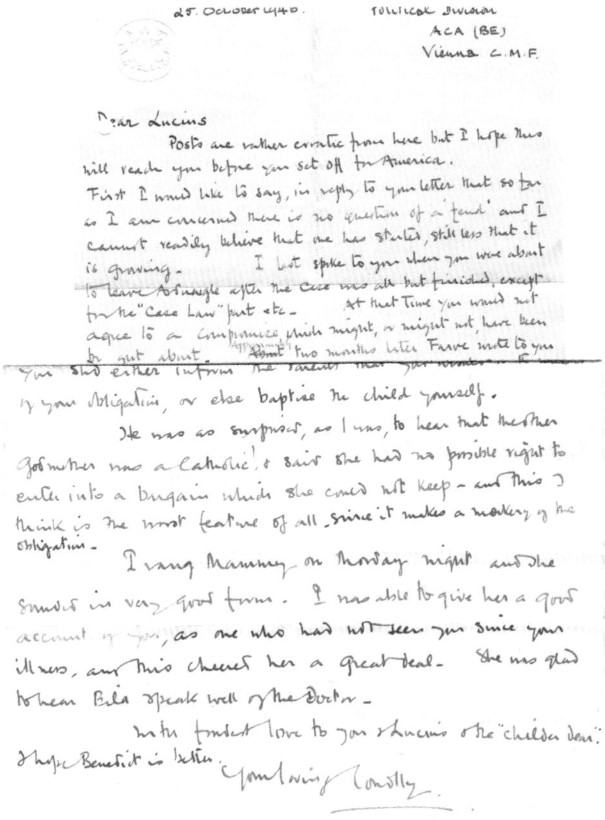

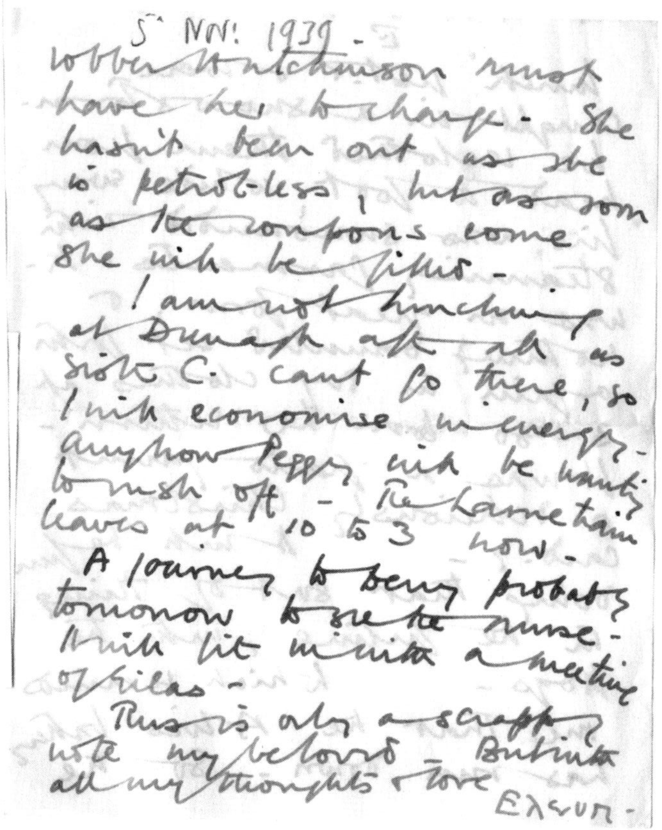

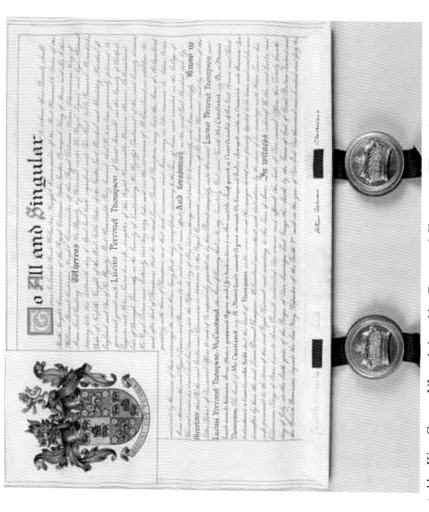

Royal Licence granted by King George VI, and signed by Garter and Clarenceux Kings of Arms, giving Lucius and Helen and their children the surname of Thompson-McCausland

Lucius Thompson-McCausland

Mark Thompson-McCausland

Thompson coat of arms: azure with a
golden lion "passant guardant" and a
golden lion "rampant" on top

Thompson quartered with the Mc-
Causland coat of arms of an azure
boar's head on gold with three
"azure boars passant".

Wedding of Eila McCausland
and Maxwell Stronge 1945

The Grand Jury of Derry. Conolly as a member is front row left with his son Marcus
beside him as High Sherriff.

Conolly

A group outside the door at Ardnargle 1952.
L to R: Peggy McC, Fania McC, Eileen McC
with James Stronge, Betty Boyle, Denis Gibbs,
'Nannie' King, Lucius and Helen T-McC and Eila
Stronge.

View down from the edge of Benevenagh over Magilligan, with the Umbra in foreground and level crossing bottom left. Top left can be seen Magilligan Point and Lough Foyle with Inishowen beyond. The Red Cottage, beloved by generations of the family for its isolation, can be seen clearly just right of centre.(photo c. 1954)

Rifles of the Balteagh Infantry (1809)in the outer hall at Drenagh. These were removed for safety reasons in the recent Troubles.

Drenagh: view through the outer hall and front door

Drenagh from the north west

Drenagh from the air

Epcombs, home of the Thompson-McCauslands

Family tradition continues in Upper School Eton

Helen seated at her desk at Epcombs
and Lucius (taken at the Treasury)

Conolly's coffin in the Saloon at Drenagh. (Lucius & Helen in the Hall beyond)

Conolly leaves his beloved Drenagh for the last time to be drawn on a farm trailer to Limavady: a piper and escort from the Irish Guards followed with the family

Marcus going shooting

Marcus – portrait by Derek Hill

you do try to follow as a good and loving son and pray always that you may be helped along the road of duty which is not always easy, but right. You have seen and know how everyone loved and respected him and looked up to him though he thought so little of himself and was *lowly in his own eyes*. It is wonderful how everyone feels the goodness of a really good person - even the toughest and most pagan. Michael (Gibbs) is another example of that, for everyone out here likes and admires him and loves him and speaks so warmly of him, though I know he, poor dear, is a bit discouraged by all he has to face and struggle with - but he is helped along the road as we all are and we cannot be too thankful for the blessings and mercies that surround us. I know that I can never be thankful enough for Daddy and my three precious children, and the love of those I love.'

Eileen's gentle hints were in vain, and by August 1939 Conolly's mind was nearly made up. During a trip to London he visited Lucius at the Bank of England, where the latter had recently begun work after a spell running the London office of a large American concern, Moody's Economic Services. Conolly had always enjoyed his brother-in-law's company and felt able to confide in him about deeply personal matters. 'I have come to love and admire him more and more…how great a strength and help he was to me and all of us,' he had written about Lucius in a letter to Helen after Maurice's funeral. There and then, in Lucius's office above Threadneedle Street, he revealed that he was close to converting.

Lucius understood and sympathised with Conolly's spiritual needs, and took the news in his stride. He had no idea that in the ensuing drama he, Helen and their young son Mark would have central roles. He did, however, have an important piece of advice to impart to Conolly. He reminded him of the religious forfeiture clause they were both bound by and about which he had warned him seven years earlier. As he understood it,

Conolly risked losing Drenagh if he converted, and the estate would pass to Marcus. In Conolly's own best interests, he said, it would be wise for him to take a close look at it.

It did not occur to Lucius at this stage that Marcus and his siblings might be barred from the succession too and that Helen, as Conolly's elder sister, would then become next in line to succeed. Still less did it enter his head that as a consequence of this the Thompson children would replace their young McCausland cousins in the order of succession.

Certainly the potential for a massive family upheaval was lost on Conolly. A month after his meeting with Lucius at the Bank, Britain declared war on Germany and he at once rejoined the Irish Guards. At no point, by his own admission long afterwards, did he check up on the forfeiture clause, as Lucius has recommended. One possible reason for this lapse was that he already knew precisely what it said, but this seems unlikely. As the High Court was to conclude years later, the probable explanation was that he was in such an 'unsettled state' that Lucius's 'wise and sensible advice just simply failed to sink in.'

Meanwhile he embraced Catholicism ever tighter. As a prelude to conversion, he regularly attended Mass at Roman Catholic churches. One of these occasions was while he was staying with Lucius in Hertfordshire (Helen was in Ireland awaiting the birth of their fifth child, Teressa). Conolly and Lucius's brother, Gerald, already a Roman Catholic convert, drove to Ware and worshipped together in the Church of the Sacred Heart of Jesus and St. Joseph. Conolly told Helen in a letter: 'The old priest seems a dear old boy (some name very like macaroni!); a nice little church but very small of course – however it was full which is always cheerful.' Though his tone was light-hearted, the effect of his words was dramatic.

Helen was staying with Eileen at Ardnargle (Eileen and Eila had settled there after Maurice's death) when she received his letter. Deeply spiritual herself, she disliked High Church 'trappings.' Back in 1929 she had vividly expressed her views on religion in a letter to Lucius when he left Cambridge. 'Oh darling, I just can't imagine your room at Kings empty and dingy – and still less with a crucifix in it. How nauseating. Why must people create symbols for themselves (and hang them up) of a thing that is so grand and beautiful and broad that it can never be caught and held down? One might as well try to hang up the North Wind.' On another occasion she told him: 'Roman Catholics are dependent for their faith upon others i.e. the Priest, the Pope, images, and cannot do without them…it is one of the few parts of Roman Catholicism I could not fit in with.'

Despite her issues with Catholicism, Helen was broadly sympathetic to Conolly's wishes, on the basis that it was his life and he should be free to do what he wanted. Eileen, by contrast, was distraught. Earlier that month she had told Helen in a letter: 'I need not tell you I feel Conolly's desertion of his church very deeply and perhaps bitterly, though I try to keep the latter feeling out of it.' On her arrival in Ireland, Helen had found her mother in low spirits, not helped by the fact that she had been suffering from bronchitis and had been refusing to take her medicines, which included a foul-tasting tincture containing strychnine. Too ill to leave the house, Eileen had been spending much of her time brooding about her son.

Rightly or wrongly, Helen showed her the latest letter from Conolly. She wrote to Lucius shortly afterwards: 'Mammy, having heard of Conolly's excursion to the 'mass' on Sunday, is plunged into gloom this morning. Poor darling, it is hard to know whether to show her letters that may make her miserable, or to withhold them, which would make her feel left out. I, knowing which course I would prefer, showed her Conolly's this morning and wish to goodness I hadn't. The controversy has started afresh. We had so much hoped it had died down. Conolly most unfortunately gave her some pamphlet to read in which Mammy discovered that not only is the Pope infallible (which always sticks in her gullet) but that the 'Bench of Bishops' are too. I must say that takes a bit of swallowing but to her it is vinegar and gall. She feels that Conolly is quite lost to her. I wish she was easier to talk to, but she won't open her heart, and resolutely refuses to accept what help we can give, and with a fearful 'no surrender' air has decided that she must bear this alone.'

A night or two later there was a heated family argument about Catholicism, with Eileen on the one side, emitting clouds of doctrinal squid ink, and Helen and Eila on the other, trying to persuade her that Catholicism was not as malignant a force as she believed. Peggy, who had driven over from Drenagh for supper (Conolly was with his battalion in England), was also drawn into the exchange, which lasted for a full ninety minutes. Helen told Lucius later: 'The discussion rose and fell till twelve o'clock, all of us getting hotter than we meant to, leaving, as always seems to happen, Mammy feeling that we are against her. It is so distressing, because really we are all fundamentally agreed, but because we contradict one or two of her really bigoted ideas (there is no other word) against the R.C. doctrine in a vain hope of helping her to see what one believes to be their reason, in a flash one has embarked on a course of attack and defence. I feel exhausted and shattered and it is so useless. We simmered by degrees. But how stupid and useless to lose sleep over a point of dogma. Poor Peggy - driving home alone to a lonely house and bed.'

Meanwhile Christmas came and went with Lucius kept in England and Helen, Mark Marianne and Benedict living at Ardnargle. The joyful arrival of Eileen Teressa, 'our beloved fifth', on 30th December cheered all the family. By April 1940 Eileen appeared more relaxed about the Conolly situation. She and Conolly enjoyed each other's company when he stayed at Drenagh while on leave from his regiment a month before his conversion. One evening he drove over to Ardnargle with some blossoms for Eileen from one of the Tibet rhododendrons growing in the Drenagh gardens…'a lovely white one with loose-hanging bells tinted with pink, which has never bloomed before,' Eileen told Helen. 'How Daddy would have admired it.'

Another four weeks passed before Conolly finally walked into the little chapel at Ascot on May 3 and completed the religious journey he had begun more than a decade earlier, emerging into the spring sunshine an hour or so later as a Roman Catholic. The die was cast. [1] The timing was possibly connected with the deployment to Norway of his sister battalion, the 1st Irish Guards, three weeks earlier (they suffered heavy casualties) and the sobering knowledge that the 2nd Battalion's turn to dice with death could not be far away. By converting when he did, he had his faith to sustain him during his two gruelling and bloody expeditions across the Channel shortly afterwards.

Another possible clue to the timing was a brief and enigmatic paragraph in a letter from Helen to Lucius at the end of January 1940. 'Conolly wrote such a sad worried letter to Mammy. He said he was *sick at heart* at what Peggy had told him. You will have heard I am sure, but it must be left as it is, I am convinced. One has got to trust people. You will have consoled him, darling, I know.' Helen's letter contained no further details but the import of her words suggests Conolly was feeling vulnerable on more than one front in the spring of 1940. Only a few weeks earlier he himself had referred to his *soucis* (worries) in a letter to Helen, and implied that they centred on Peggy. It is probably significant that he did not tell Peggy beforehand about his conversion. That he failed to inform her in advance about

[1] In recent years (21st century) it has become received family wisdom that his battlefield experiences were the deciding factor in his conversion, but this perception is wrong. The action he saw at the Hook of Holland and in Boulogne came after not before his conversion.

such an important moment in his life suggests a substantial level of estrangement between them during the early part of the war.

To begin with the news of his conversion was kept mainly within the family and caused few ripples. Eileen was among the first to be told and evidently sent him a supportive letter, for he replied to her on May 17: 'I was so happy to get your sweet letter. There is nothing between you and me Darling Mammy and never will be.' Helen and Lucius were also sanguine about the news, and were among the first people Conolly visited on his return from Boulogne. (Lucius's essential war-time work for the Bank of England had kept him in England). Over tea on the lawn at Amwell Grove, Conolly recited Captain John Marnon's ballad about the Battle of Boulogne to the family. There was much hilarity, especially when he explained that 'Geld fur marmalade' was cod German for 'money for jam.' Conolly then joined them in taking young Mark to his new school. He told Eileen in a letter: 'I came back to supper with H & L and we had long talks and great cracks on every subject you can think of.'

As far as the majority of the family was concerned, the most exciting news about Conolly that spring was the announcement that he had been awarded the Military Cross. Helen wrote to Eileen: 'Isn't it glorious about his M.C.? Everyone here is so sweet and interested and he might be a brother to any of the immediate neighbours too, they were so delighted with us!' Back home in Limavady, where news of the religious conversion had yet to filter out, Conolly was hailed a hero, and was particularly touched to receive a congratulatory telegram from Limavady Urban District Council.

The presentation was made by King George VI at Buckingham Palace on July 2. Conolly invited Helen and Lucius to accompany him, but Lucius had to back out at the last minute because of work commitments, and Peggy's mother, Lillian

Edgcumbe, took his place. It is perhaps significant that Peggy herself was absent. Describing the scene to Eileen, Helen wrote: 'The heat was withering, and we sat one and a half hours in the quadrangle before the ceremony without a spot of shade… but it would have been worth sitting on the floor of Hell to see it. Dear Conolly took his (medal) so nicely, most dignified and charming looking. There is quite an art in getting the pace right and the salute and managing to halt in front of the king exactly, without making it too hasty or too shuffled. He said to me afterwards: "You know, there are so many others who deserve this far more than me."'

Helen, the proud sister, did not want the day to end, and she and Conolly decided to make the most of their visit to London. During a celebratory ice cream tea at Gunter's tea shop in Berkeley Square they were amused to find themselves sitting next to the exiled King Zog of Albania's sisters, who lived at the Ritz and were known by the press as the Zoglets.

To Conolly all this must have seemed an auspicious start to his conversion. Since May 3 he had survived Holland, beaten the odds at Boulogne, been honoured by the King, and retained the love and respect of those nearest and dearest to him. During that long hot summer of 1940 he could have been forgiven for thinking that from now on it would be plain sailing, and that any small problems associated with the tenancy of Drenagh could be quickly resolved. If that was his belief, he could not have been more mistaken.

It was not until the autumn that he notified the family solicitor, Alexander Ingram, who was an executor of Maurice's Will as well as a trustee of the Drenagh settlement, that he had been received into the Catholic Church. Ingram made his feelings clear in a brief but dramatic letter to Helen in October, telling her he was 'much surprised and distressed' to have heard her brother's news. Then came his dramatic verdict. As a result of the religious clause in the 1927 resettlement, he said, Conolly had 'irrevocably forfeited for himself and his family all interest in Drenagh and the rest of the settled property.' Drenagh was now Helen's, and she would receive all dividends and rents from the estate provided she legally acquired the name McCausland within a year as the resettlement required.

Ingram made it icily clear where he stood on the issue. 'It will be a matter for you to decide whether you ought to join with your brother in seeking to defeat your father's wishes by installing an RC at Drenagh than which, as I'm sure you know, nothing would have given him greater pain and which he has done everything possible to prevent by provisions in which Conolly concurred.'

Conolly would later hotly dispute that he had concurred in anything at all, but in the meantime the genie was well and truly out of the bottle. War hero he might be, but as word spread of his conversion, so the condemnation grew among the less tolerant sections of the Protestant community. Feelings ran so high that on Lundy's Day – the commemoration every December of the shutting of the gates of Derry against King James II in 1688 and one of the most important celebrations in the Protestant calendar – an effigy of Conolly was burned outside the Drenagh gates. (When protestors reappeared outside Drenagh the following year, Conolly brilliantly defused the situation by walking down to the gates and asking if he might have the honour of lighting the first match, a request to which the cowed and embarrassed crowd readily acceded before creeping silently away).

Helen and Lucius were as shocked and perplexed as Conolly by the turn of events. In the thousands of words they had exchanged in letters between each other since Conolly's conversion, there had been no mention about the possibility of them taking over Drenagh. The thought had apparently never occurred to them, for they had assumed all along that even in the most drastic scenario the estate would simply pass to Marcus. Besides, despite Drenagh's magnificence, neither had any wish to leave Great Amwell. Only the previous January, Helen had told Lucius in a letter that her life at Great Amwell with him was one of 'infinite and complete happiness.' Apart from anything else, moving to Ireland would be hard to reconcile with Lucius's powerful new job at the Bank of England. More importantly, both wanted to avoid a family rift. Equally, they recognised that if the law made it impossible for Conolly to live there, it would be their duty to up sticks and move to Drenagh, home to the McCauslands for more than two centuries. They clearly hoped it would never come to that.

One thing was plain to everyone: matters could not be left as they were. To ignore the forfeiture clause and let things carry on unchanged might have sounded simple in theory, but Ingram for one would clearly not let such a course go unchallenged. Besides, what might be acceptable to Conolly and Helen now might not be acceptable to their respective children in years to come. After all, if Ingram was right, Helen and Lucius's children were now in the line of succession, not Conolly's and Peggy's, and might reasonably lay claim to their inheritance when they were older. To pretend nothing had happened could be to store up trouble for the future.

Over the next eight months Helen and Conolly looked for a way out of the quandary. In correspondence with each other they discussed the possibility of Helen giving up her rights under the settlement, but lawyers advised them it would be extremely difficult to make such a course of action legally watertight. It would be one thing for Helen to surrender her own entitlement, but quite another for minors to be stripped of their rights in a way that was guaranteed not to unravel. Conolly meanwhile, having sought legal advice on whether his children as well as himself were bound by Clause Fifteen, wrote to Helen in February 1941: 'It is clear that all ideas of attacking the Deed on the basis of its unfairness to Marcus and Fania are quite useless.'

Seeing which way the wind was blowing, Lucius, who was once again away in Washington, wrote to Helen in June: 'About Drenagh and poor Conolly I will not comment, since you, most wisely, did not try to broach the subject in your letter. But I take it that we will almost certainly have to inherit. May we be worthy of the dear place; or rather may I, for you most assuredly will.'

With Helen having no room for manoeuvre, the onus was now on Conolly to suggest a way forward. Anxious to settle the matter, Lucius wrote to him in September 1941 stressing that his only two options were to accept the resettlement or go to court to try to get the forfeiture clause set aside. If he chose the latter route, he should do so soon, 'otherwise you might prejudice your case by apparent acquiescence.'

Unfortunately for Conolly, the second option already looked like a lost cause. In a letter to Helen, Conolly said he had been advised by counsel that 'there is not an earthly hope of us upsetting the deed of settlement.' That appeared to settle the matter, and after nearly eighteen months of to-ing and fro-ing, Conolly finally threw in the towel, accepting that he had lost Drenagh and that his father's wishes had prevailed. 'You are now in undisputed possession,' Ingram wrote to Helen. (Conolly did not know that the trustees of the settlement had received an opinion in 1940 from a barrister named Poole advising that the forfeiture clause was vulnerable because it went beyond Maurice's original intention).

If Conolly seemed to have surrendered without much of a fight, it may have been because there were other matters on his mind. Although he managed three brief visits to Drenagh between April and August 1941, the war was keeping him busier than ever. In June, following exercises on Salisbury Plain, the Irish Guards became part of an armoured division, and part of Conolly's job was to oversee training in the manning and operation of tanks.

That was not the only distraction. Many marriages came under strain during the war and Conolly's was one of them. His relationship with Peggy had hit a rocky patch and the birth in October of a son, Antony, conceived when Conolly was far from home, served to highlight the gulf that had opened up between them. It was perhaps significant that his diary entry for March 21 1941 failed to mention that it was Peggy's twenty-ninth birthday, an uncharacteristic omission by a normally doting husband.

If a defeatist streak now tainted Conolly's thinking, it would not have been surprising. Perhaps, for a time, he even stopped caring that much about Drenagh. He looked briefly at a scheme for jointly farming the estate with Helen, but lawyers ruled this out as impractical. One way or another, the fight had gone out of him, and he told Helen that as far as Drenagh was concerned he 'gladly and willingly' stepped out of the picture, adding that he would remain responsible for the day-to-day running of the estate until she was in a position to take over.

To all intents and purposes, Drenagh was now Helen's, and it followed that her eldest child, ten-year-old Mark, was next in line to succeed. Conolly began paying Helen an allowance for his continued 'occupation' of the property, and she in turn paid him £9,000 for Drenagh's farming implements, stock and crop with money borrowed from Eileen.

Peggy evidently found it harder than Conolly to accept what had happened. A letter from Eila to Helen at the end of 1941 hinted that she, Peggy, was upset at what had happened and had vented her anger on Helen. 'I am so terribly distressed to hear that Peggy is behaving this way,' wrote Eila. 'I'm afraid it must enrage and hurt, but it will pass I'm sure. I feel in a way quite cut off from all this, though I loathe to think of you being so unjustly attacked.'

Eileen meanwhile, once so preoccupied about Drenagh's future, quickly became reconciled to the changed situation and appeared relieved by the turn of events. She wrote to Lucius early in 1942: 'I would love to live (with you) at Drenagh if I could be of any use, and a hot water system could be installed which I would insist on paying for in lieu of rent. I could look after the dairy and garden, or at least keep an eye on them and the house. I would feel I am doing something whereas here (at Ardnargle) I am only spending everything on myself. If I was of any use I would feel I was doing a war-time job and helping to keep the beloved place together.'

Yet even now Conolly could not quite close the door on Drenagh, and wanted to keep his options open. In his mind there was still a comma at the end of the sentence rather than a final, irrevocable full stop. He wrote to Ingram saying that although he no longer felt in a position to mount a challenge, he wished to make it clear 'that by accepting the settlement I hope to make things easier for you and the other trustees, and I do not wish to prejudice any reopening of the case by me or my descendants at some future and more favourable time.' Ingram replied that he was glad Conolly had dropped the idea of a legal challenge, but he failed to confirm with him that he meant to give up any claim irrevocably, a lapse for which he was later criticised by the Court of Appeal.

In a separate letter Conolly told Lucius that while he was not disposed to bring an action, he would appeal the case 'should the law change or the administration of it in that part of our country ceases to be in the hands of those who now control such matters'. (He was presumably referring to the possibility of Ireland being under the control of Dublin, or perhaps even Berlin). In the same vein he told Helen that 'as for the future, it will be entirely in your hands and Mark's when he comes of age.' This implied he still had some hope that when Mark – the new 'remainderman' - reached the age of 21 in eleven years' time, he and his mother might resettle the property on Conolly.

All that remained now was for Helen and Lucius to change their name by Royal Licence to Thompson-McCausland as a legal condition of Helen taking possession of the estate. In addition the family chose a motto for the name of Thompson-McCausland, taken from Psalm 24 – *Domini est Terra* – the Earth is the Lord's. The College of Arms in London charged them £170 (about £5,000 in today's prices) for the change of name, which was duly announced in The London Gazette and the Belfast Gazette.

> *Whitehall,*
> 16th April, 1942.
> THE KING has been graciously pleased to give and grant unto Lucius Perronet Thompson, of Great Amwell, in the County of Hertford, Esquire, and Helen Laura his wife, daughter of the Right Honourable Maurice Marcus McCausland, late of Drenagh, Limavady, in the County of Londonderry, Lieutenant of the said County, deceased, His Royal Licence and Authority that they may take and use the surname of McCausland in addition to and after that of Thompson, that he, the said Lucius Perronet Thompson may bear the Arms of McCausland quarterly with those of Thompson and that such surname and Arms may in like manner be taken, borne and used by the issue of their marriage, the said Arms being first duly exemplified according to the Laws of Arms and recorded in His Majesty's College of Arms otherwise the said Royal Licence

and Permission to be void and of none effect.
And to Command that the said Royal Concession
and Declaration be recorded in His Majesty's said
College of Arms.

Helen, Lucius and their children were now required by law to use the name Thompson-McCausland, and when their sixth child, Virginia, was born the same month, the Garter King of Arms, Sir Gerald Wollaston, whose daughter was a family friend at Great Amwell, inquired of them why the notice of birth was not in their new name. Young Mark, returning to his school for the summer term, was teased by his fellow pupils when they discovered that he had acquired a double-barrelled surname and was heir to an estate in Ireland.

There matters looked set to rest. More than four years after Maurice's death, and nearly two years after Conolly's conversion, the future of Drenagh finally appeared to have been settled. The line of succession had changed from Conolly and his descendants to Helen and *her* descendants.

Although this was far from the end of the matter, and the real turmoil had yet to begin, for the time-being family harmony was the order of the day, and when Conolly visited Helen at Amwell Grove in August they spent a happy afternoon in each other's company. 'The dear creature was in good form,' Helen told Lucius. 'We talked much and he was greatly interested in your news and views.' Lucius's war-time work with the Bank of England had taken him to Canada earlier in the month and he was amused to discover that his hosts at a farm outside Ottawa had just sacked an Ulsterman for 'indolence and dishonesty.' He was from Co Derry, Lucius reported jocularly, and his name was McCausland.

Chapter Ten

Change of Heart

Mark, the first-born of the clan, was fed on wartime oats and bran,
Which made him what he is, so fine, a most worthy son of mine.
And then to Amwell, in the war, with half the ceiling on the floor,
Nor from enemy planes, Mein Gott, just the inevitable dry rot.

From a poem written for Helen Thompson-McCausland by her cousin Denis Gibbs in honour of her seventieth birthday in 1973.

Helen and Lucius were in no hurry to move into their new Irish home. Lucius's work for the Bank of England, seen as crucial to the war effort, frequently took him abroad, often to the U.S.A., and when not travelling he needed be in London on a regular basis. During this period he took part in the development of exchange control, and accompanied Maynard Keynes to the pre-Bretton Woods conference in New Hampshire, which led to the founding of the International Monetary Fund and the International Bank for Reconstruction and Development, both vital to rebuilding the international economic system. He also worked closely with the brilliant and raffish Montagu Norman, who was appointed Governor of the Bank of England during the war and led the Bank during the harshest period to date in British economic history.

In addition Lucius and Helen threw themselves into the war effort at home. They made over the extensive lower ground floor at Amwell Grove to evacuees, and Lucius was on regular fire-watching duty in the City of London. During one typical week he was up until past three a.m. on three consecutive nights checking that the wardens were at their posts. It was after one such busy night that he learned that his daughter

Virginia had been born. Moving to Drenagh was simply not on the cards until the war was over.

That said, he and Helen were keen to demonstrate their commitment to the estate, and they holidayed there in the summer of 1942, in large measure to reassure the staff and retainers by their presence that they had a secure future and that the family had no intention of abandoning them. All five of the newly-named Thompson-McCausland children went with them. Mark, Marianne, Benedict and two-year-old Teressa were old Limavady hands. The elder three had gone to live at Ardnargle in the summer of 1939, Mark and Marianne having attended Limavady Academy until they came home for Mark to attend prep school in 1940. Tessa had been born there in December 1939 and Benedict stayed on until the summer of 1941. Only for the baby Virginia was it a debut visit.

Mark and Marianne went riding every day and saw a lot of the numerous servicemen – both Royal Air Force and U.S. Army – who were using the estate as a war-time base. Drenagh had been requisitioned by the Ministry of Defence in 1940, and the presence of so many strangers on the estate heightened the feeling of upheaval the family already felt. Airmen had broken the urns in the Italian garden, and RAF officers had pinned maps to the walls of the drawing-room, ruining the exquisite wallpaper designed by Conolly Thomas's wife, Laura, more than half a century earlier. Much of the household furniture had been thrown haphazardly into the stables. 'Oh, the Hepplewhite chairs,' sighed Helen as she gazed at the broken jumble of family heirlooms. The Americans, perhaps surprisingly, were more considerate than their British counterparts. They took Mark and Marianne for rides on their jeeps and gave them jars of sweets which all tasted strongly of cloves but were sweets none-the-less in ration-restricted Britain.

If the children enjoyed the company of the American servicemen, they enjoyed Eila's company even more. Their adored aunt had a beautiful voice, and they loved hearing songs from her large repertoire wafting through the house. They eagerly awaited her days off from the Wrens in Derry, and often met her off the bus in Limavady when, if they were lucky, she too rewarded them with sweets, obtained in her case from the Free State where there was no rationing. The children loved congregating in her room before breakfast, climbing into her bed and playing games, an exciting contrast from the more formal activities of the rest of the household. (In due course Eila had two children of her own, James, born in 1946, and Helen-Mary, born in 1948).

The children's McCausland cousins also joined them for a time, and Mark and Marianne were mystified when ten-year-old Marcus solemnly told Mark: 'I don't mind if you have Drenagh.' The two Thompson-McCausland children knew nothing of the legal dramas of the two previous years, although they were aware that things had changed and that there was sometimes a downcast and difficult atmosphere in the house.

Marcus said something else intriguing at around this time. The adult conversation one day turned to the telling of fortunes, a subject in which they were all interested. (It was, after all, a fortune teller who had predicted great happiness for Helen and Lucius). Marcus turned to Marianne, who was standing with him away from the grown-ups on the front steps, and said: 'Look at my palm. It has an M on it.'

'M for Marcus,' replied Marianne.

'No,' said Marcus with a mischievous glint, 'M for Murder.'

Marianne thought little more of the remark until nearly three decades later when she was to recall it with shocking clarity.

In August 1943 Helen returned to Limavady, initially accompanied by Lucius, basing herself with Eileen at Ardnargle while she prepared the way for permanent occupation of Drenagh. Inez Macrory (Pat Macrory's aunt and a fellow leading light in the Limavady Brownies) lent her a trap and a chestnut pony, Dolly, to enable her to travel the two miles between Limavady and Ardnargle, and she proved a big hit with the children. Mark in particular enjoyed riding her along Drenagh's paths, although he was once nearly decapitated by a telephone wire stretched between two stone pillars.

In the meantime, Andy Lowden, Drenagh's faithful estate manager, met Helen at Ardnargle to discuss her plans for settling full-time into her childhood home. He was loved and respected by the family, who regarded him as efficient, knowledgable, amusing and kindly. To Helen's delight, he was able to report that Drenagh's boiler was working well and that the bedrooms were 'beautifully hot.' So far, all seemed to be going to plan.

The following month Conolly and Peggy arrived with their own children – Marcus, Fania and Antony - to help Helen sort out and allocate the furniture and household items, staying first at the Red Cottage at Magilligan, and later at Drenagh itself. With Peggy's help Conolly piled all his possessions from Cumber House into the Orange Room, placing in the saloon anything he thought Helen and Lucius might want to buy from him. Peggy went about the task of clearing the chimney pieces and cabinets of china ornaments – some of which had been earmarked for Eileen – and packing them away in cupboards. She also labelled all the furniture and pictures to ensure everyone got their correct allocation. There were only two items which Helen and Conolly both wanted – a serpentine table in the hall and a watercolour – but these clashes were resolved amicably. 'I hate it, but it must be got through,' Helen told Lucius in a letter.

136

The sorting and packing was an Augean task. Quite apart from the wrecked gems in the stables, much of the furniture had made its way over the years into cottages on the estate, and some had disappeared altogether. On one occasion Andy Lowden intercepted a van full of Drenagh furniture leaving the lower drive gate. The new gardener, a man named Buchanan, was said to have been behind the clandestine plan to deprive the family of many heirlooms.

Keen to show that everyone was getting on well together despite the awkward circumstances, Helen told Lucius: 'Peggy is admirable in the way she is tackling the choosing, sorting, packing etc and in trying to trace the missing furniture.' Nevertheless, both Helen and Conolly found it emotionally gruelling to see the house become emptier and more inhospitable by the day. Conolly, who was on just six days' leave, found the ordeal as debilitating as his sister. Like careworn peas rattling round in a gigantic pod, they became increasingly depressed by the coffined silence of once vibrant rooms. 'Conolly could not face much of it, poor dear man,' wrote Helen. 'It was heart-rending. He and I had a long walk in the glen and we wept together.'

At one point Helen began suffering from flu-like aches and pains. 'Feeling that Drenagh had done for me and that I should not be able to manage it I fell into a despair – though equally great was my relief and thanksgiving to find I was suddenly perfectly well after two days with no sickness or aches left. It was so good to think it wasn't the beloved Drenagh but only a mild form of gastric flu. I was rewarded when the rain ceased and the sun came out like a fanfare, flooding Drenagh and its lands with colour and radiance.'

By early November 1943 most of the work was complete and Helen and Lucius began mulling over the practicalities of living at Drenagh once the war was over. They decided that

Eileen should live with them, allowing Eila to lead a more independent life at Ardnargle, although they were determined that Eileen should live by their own rules and not hers. 'Mammy would be happy at Drenagh,' wrote Helen. 'But we must not let her run the house as her methods would be very different from ours. I thought of her perhaps planning the garden – this she would love.'

Visits to large country houses in Ireland had given Helen other ideas for improving the house and gardens and her initial reluctance about taking over Drenagh was increasingly giving way to enthusiasm. 'I picture us gardening together on spring evenings,' she told Lucius. 'How wonderful to think that we can always garden and that every year there will be a spring.' During his travels, Lucius had encountered a new-fangled contraption called a Servidor at the Statler Hotel in Washington. This enabled clothes for washing and ironing to be collected from bedrooms without the guests being disturbed. 'I think that we won't change over to Servidors at Drenagh,' he joked.

So far, given the potential for ill-feeling, the transfer of Drenagh from Conolly to Helen had gone as smoothly as possible, with little or no acrimony or obstruction on either side. Eila for one was so pleased with the way things were turning out that she was moved to write to Lucius: 'The decision you and Helen have taken over Drenagh makes me realise more and more what a very fine pair you are. It is a real sacrifice but I feel that all the generations of McCs who have lived in it and loved it will bless you for it, as I shall too.'

Eila's well-meant words tempted fate, for at this point all the carefully laid plans began to unravel. The catalyst for the sudden upheaval was Peggy, who had never been able to accept that the change in the line of succession was inevitable. Her concern all along had been not so much about herself and Conolly as for young Marcus, whom she felt had been wrongly deprived of his inheritance. That, at any rate, was how she expressed her unhappiness to Conolly, but it is equally possible that deep down she felt cheated herself and was using Marcus as a screen for her anger. Whatever the case, she felt it constantly, like an amputee with a phantom limb, a ghost irritant that was impossible to ignore. Never a day went by when she did not brood over what she saw as a hideous injustice, and helping Helen to clear the house served only to stoke her feelings of grievance. Her parents, the future Earl and Countess of Mount Edgcumbe, with whom she had been seeing out the war in Hertfordshire, encouraged her in the belief that Marcus had been wronged.

Although she and Helen had talked about the line of succession while sorting out the furniture, Helen was unaware of the full extent of her feelings. In the first week of November 1943 Helen wrote to Peggy thanking her for all her hard work and emphasising that she and Lucius had no wish to see Marcus lose out because of the forfeiture clause, but that their hands were tied by the law. It was a letter she bitterly regretted writing, for one way or another Peggy misinterpreted her words and understood them to mean that Helen and Lucius's top priority was to find a way for Marcus to have Drenagh.

Peggy's excited response arrived by return of post. 'I was so cheered by your letter. For the first time since all this unfortunate business started I feel that you really mean that you'd *like* Marcus to have the place. You see I have never been able to bring myself to accept it as inevitable. It has been my unshakable belief all through that something could be done about Marcus. I still believe it and always shall. I know there are difficulties, risks, disappointments entailed, but where there is a will there is a way. I've always thought the 'will' was missing not the 'way.' Now you have given me hope that the 'will' is there. Is that wishful thinking?' I won't say, or write, any more now except that my hope is high. You need never feel that talking about Drenagh is opening a wound. It is raw and wide open always. I sometimes wonder if I shall ever forget even for a day. Now you have made me believe that it can be buried and forgotten in a way I never dared hope would be possible.'

Helen was dismayed and flustered by the tone of Peggy's letter. While open to the idea of Drenagh being held in trust for the foreseeable future on the off chance of a change in the law, she knew that neither she, Lucius, Peggy or Conolly had the power as things stood to change unilaterally the line of succession, which was now headed by her own five children. Realising that she had unwittingly instilled false hope in Peggy, and sensing that a watershed moment had been reached, she wrote a 'confessional' letter to Lucius.

'I explained (to her) in simple language what you had told us about re-settlement when Mark was 21, ie that…we had no power to alter the line of succession (as I understood it). I felt that this can never have been explained to her, from things she has said, and that I would make one last desperate attempt to get it straight in her mind. Hoping to make her see that it wasn't <u>our</u> intention to do poor Marcus out of anything, I suggested that she should ask somebody who knew something of the law to explain it to her in legal language, trusting that she would see then. Unfortunately this has set up such a wild flutter of hope in the poor girl who has interpreted it that we are willing for Marcus to have Drenagh whereas we can do nothing about it. I wish we could set her mind at rest and that she could get peace.'

The exchange of letters between the two women had come at a particularly bad time for Helen. Lucius was in America, and she had recently been admitted to hospital in Belfast with a serious gynaecological problem. She was now recovering from a successful but gruelling operation, which had left her at a low ebb both physically and mentally, and she was not best placed to cope with this unexpected development. If she harboured the hope that nothing would come of Peggy's new-found optimism, she was soon to be proved wrong. Days later she received a letter from Conolly which, as she told Lucius, 'shook me out of my cocoon of peace.' Conolly told her he had read her letter to Peggy with 'joy and delight' and that he saw it as a clear expression of 'will' towards Marcus. He added to her consternation that Peggy had forwarded the letter to his lawyer, a Belfast barrister named Cyril Nicholson.

Helen was embarrassed that a 'rather intimate' letter intended for private consumption had been passed to a third party, although she was confident that it contained nothing compromising or inaccurate. A day or two later she was startled to receive a telephone call at the hospital from Nicholson himself, who said he would like to come and see her. Helen agreed to meet him and spent the morning before he arrived reviewing the Drenagh case in her mind, vowing to herself that she would 'ring the bell and have him shown out' of her room if he became hectoring or bullying. As it turned out, she was pleasantly surprised, finding him 'most considerate and quiet and untiring.'

She told Lucius after the meeting: 'Naturally he pressed Conolly's claims – this, as he said, entirely unsolicited by Conolly – but at the same time he sees the difficulty for us and seems to understand with great sympathy. It cleared my mind considerably talking to him. Apparently nothing can be done till Mark is 21 (as we knew) and I think Cyril's only weapon is to appeal to our sympathies. But I see more clearly now, at least I feel more strongly that Mark must come before Marcus. My beloved, you will not worry over, or be distressed at this. It is very good for me to go through it.'

In a subsequent letter she added: 'We must go through the (legal) documents again. I don't see that anything different can be done, neither does he (Cyril Nicholson), to alter the clause,

141

but it will show Peggy and Conolly that we are not blindly grabbing all within our reach, and if Peggy will <u>not</u> see, then to hell. What is a little sad is that Conolly has now come under her sway, and now writes about having high hopes.'

Nicholson's intervention – friendly and civilised though it appeared on the surface - did not go down well with Lucius. He thought it poor form for the lawyer to have visited Helen in hospital, and never fully forgave him for calling on her so soon after the operation when she was in a highly weakened and vulnerable state, and then staying for what he considered to be an excessive seventy-five minutes. He concluded Nicholson was not a man he could properly trust, an assessment which became increasingly significant given the prominence of Nicholson's future role in the Drenagh dispute.

Meanwhile the stakes were about to be upped yet again. A day or two earlier, Helen had written to Conolly gently chiding him for, as she saw it, failing to explain to Peggy how the forfeiture clause worked and why it excluded Marcus from the line of succession. Peggy's lack of understanding of the clause, she felt, lay at the heart of the problem. Unfortunately this letter backfired too. Conolly showed it to Peggy, who reacted with fury, accusing Helen in a letter of resorting to abuse and of doing everything she could to prevent Marcus from having Drenagh.

A mortified Helen told Lucius: 'How true it is that we should not let 'the sun go down upon our wrath.' To demonstrate, a letter arrived from Peggy letting loose a two-years-store of vitriol and gall! I was positively glad to get it (after I had finished ricocheting from the shock!) feeling that she will be a lot better now. Poor Peggy, she wrote in defence of Conolly to whom I had written accusing him of having left her in ignorance of the full meaning of the clause. She said that Conolly had never let her abuse me (not that I ever thought he had) and had never spoken of me with anything but gentleness and affection. However she seized the opportunity to 'draw her big lunge' and let me have all her opinions about us!

'Poor girl – it was just like banging the doors, and one can't feel any rancour at it, only relief that she must have slept really well for the first time for two years after letting all that off her mind. If only one could be sure that some other Devils won't enter in. Unfortunately her family are the worst possible people for her to be with and are utterly irresponsible over the things they say.

'I wrote back to say how genuinely glad I was that she had told me her thoughts and let her know that Drenagh was not bereft of burdens, responsibilities and partings for us, and went on to say that it is Drenagh that matters, not <u>who</u> lives there but <u>how</u> they live, and that Drenagh must be served so that in its turn it may serve…not for its own glory, but to God, the King and the State.'

Helen emphasised to Lucius in the letter that in an ideal world Drenagh would not be theirs to run and worry about, and that the intransigence of the law was to blame for their predicament. 'My love, if only we could convince them, and get ourselves out of the clutches of the trustees – wouldn't it be wonderful if we could step back and feel our work there was done – and live at Amwell and be together always.' Aware that her letter to Peggy had stirred up a hornets' nest, she added: 'I promise you darling I will tread very carefully over Drenagh and naturally do nothing without consulting you.'

But her worries continued. Realising that the previously amicable transfer of Drenagh was on the cusp of turning into a full-blown family dispute, she told Lucius: 'I have been terribly saddened by Conolly's last letter and by my own foolishness in writing what I did to Peggy – Conolly now reflects her every word and has stopped thinking for himself.' Going along with

Lucius's suggestion that a period of silence was called for, she went on: 'I agree with you about not writing while we are in this inflammable state, and have said so to poor Conolly. But I am very sad and I cannot tell you darling how I am feeling without you and how greatly I long for you.' (Lucius was again in America).

By mid-December 1943 Helen was in the grip of a black depression. This was due partly to the after-effects of the operation but also had its roots in her concerns about Drenagh. She wrote to Lucius on December 16: 'I have re-read Peggy's letter. I now see it is a far more reasonable document than I had supposed. I had only taken in the part that hurt and now realise I left the rest unabsorbed. I have not written to her again, but I have apologised to Conolly for my hasty letter to her and asked him to pass it on. The actions of bedridden women are most unaccountable. I think they harbour a bunch of explosive nerves that are unknown to men. I have come to the conclusion that it would be wiser for me neither to talk nor write for six months, until I am well and in my right mind. I have no real grip of the facts and at the moment can be swayed by any emotion that cuts uppermost.'

Conolly responded promptly and magnanimously to Helen's apology. She was able to report to Lucius just before Christmas: 'I had a charming letter from poor old Conolly. I'm afraid it is Peggy's unfortunate influence when he is with her that has him not thinking straight…Conolly accepted the situation during the time they were somewhat estranged (that much he has said) but now feels differently towards Peggy and I suppose has drifted towards her views.'

As 1943 drew to a close, an end to the conflict in the wider world was a small band of light on the distant horizon, and people were daring to hope that in a year or so the war would be over. The Drenagh conflict, by contrast, was hotting up.

Chapter Eleven

Preparing the Ground

Little prisoner fraught with fear
I will keep you, for your song
Of life and joy I hold most dear

From 'To a Blackbird Caught in the Greenhouse', by Helen McCausland, 1920s.

Conolly's capitulation to Clause Fifteen had lasted barely two years. Now, at the beginning of 1944, he had the bit between his teeth again and wanted Drenagh back. Peggy's championship of Marcus's cause was not the only reason for his stiffened resolve. The end of the war was still a long way off but an Allied victory now looked certain and his thoughts and dreams were returning increasingly to civilian life in his beloved Ulster. Coupled with this, he and Peggy had overcome their personal difficulties and the marriage was firmly back on track. To his great joy she had told him he was to be a father again in the summer. (A boy, Patrick, born very prematurely, had died after two hours the previous year). When peace came, what could be more rewarding than to go back to his roots and raise his young family at Drenagh?

Peggy, meanwhile, was determined to compensate for the marital turbulence of earlier years and wanted to do everything possible to make Conolly happy. Though less enamoured of Drenagh than he was, she now began a concerted effort to find ways of restoring the estate to her husband and, in due course, her son. For the previous two and a half years correspondence between the lawyers had focused on the division of Drenagh's income between Helen and Conolly. Now it reverted back to how Conolly could be re-installed there.

Although Peggy was prepared to accept that the courts would never set aside the forfeiture clause, she insisted it would be simple for Helen to enter an arrangement under which the estate would for all practical purposes be restored to Conolly and his heirs. Early in 1944, in a letter from her parents' rented home in Hertfordshire - Holwell Court - she made this wish clear to Lucius.

Lucius did not reject the proposal outright. Despite all the work and expense that had gone into transferring Drenagh to Helen, he remained open to suggestions, but very much doubted that a return to the status quo was feasible. Intent on avoiding a fudged agreement which would 'lay on Drenagh the curse of a disputable title', he wrote to Edward 'Wee' Brown (a partner of Alexander Ingram who had taken over the case following Ingram's death in 1943) asking if Peggy's proposal could be made to work. In doing so, he said, he and Helen were guided by three principles:

- Everything possible must be done to prevent bitterness and feuding between the two families.

- For this reason he and Helen would co-operate in any sound arrangement which Conolly or his advisers might suggest to restore his rights.

- He and Helen would on no account be parties to a patched-up arrangement which did not produce a clear-cut settlement and a 'sound and indisputable title' to those rights.

He added: 'To prevent bitterness, we feel that some account must be taken of the impression in Mrs McCausland's (Peggy's) mind that there is some simple arrangement by which, if my wife were sincere in her profession of goodwill, would restore her brother's rights in the McCausland estate…the main question on which I should like your advice is whether there is any means at all by which my wife could, by a clear-cut and indisputable arrangement, restore her brother and his heirs to a sound title.'

Brown's response was not encouraging. He pointed out that no arrangement to restore Drenagh to Conolly and his heirs would be simple or could be carried out without court approval. He went on to identify two problems. One was a provision in the Drenagh settlement known as a 'restraint on anticipation.' Such provisions were not uncommon and were usually designed to stop a woman bargaining away her future. Although it might be possible to persuade a court to remove the provision in question, said Brown, for the moment it prevented Helen from settling the property on anyone else while she had a living husband.

The other problem – much more intractable – was the one that had preoccupied Lucius all along. As things now stood Mark was next in line to succeed, but he was still a minor. It would be eight years before he was old enough in law to renounce his rights or otherwise, and in the meantime no one else could properly make the decision for him. Even a generous cash payment to buy out his interest in the estate might not win court approval.

To complicate matters further, his twenty-first birthday was not necessarily the cut-off point. If, when he came of age, Mark signed away his interest in a valuable property which would otherwise become his, the law would be 'very ready' to listen to a plea of undue parental influence if the resettlement was later challenged. The only safe way to proceed was to wait until Mark had reached an age where it could be reasonably assumed that he knew his own mind, such as when he was married or had settled down to a long-term career. That could be as much as fifteen years away.

Brown added: 'The fact that a particular settlement causes disagreement between members of a family is not grounds for pronouncing it to be invalid in law. Very many Wills, and a considerable number of other dispositions, give rise to family dissention. The fact that the exercise of his rights by a minor, or by some person on his behalf, would give rise to envy or hostility of his near relatives might be taken into consideration by the court in determining what was in his best interests, but I do not think it would weigh very much.' He added pointedly: 'As Mark's guardian, you are not concerned with co-operating with anyone or assisting in maintaining good relations between persons. You are bound to consider his interest and his interest alone.'

Lucius put these points in a letter to Conolly in February, emphasising that 'if I am correctly advised on these matters, there is nothing that can be done now or for a number of years to come.' He stressed that it was a 'difficult and delicate' situation, which had not be created by any action of Helen's let alone Mark's. He added: 'Helen, no less than you, is bound by the (1927) settlement and the law. I am sure that it is only wise for all of us to accept that hard fact and to look on it and all related facts with as level and as true an eye as we can. If we do not do so it will only complicate later decisions. May I therefore ask you to consider whether you are seeing the facts with quite a level eye when you speak of 'Marcus's inheritance'? Surely the crux of the whole difficulty is precisely that it is not now Marcus's inheritance.'

He continued: 'Ready as we were in 1940 and 1941 to do anything which might leave the title and succession with you, it has gradually been borne in on all of us (or at least on Helen and me) that there is nothing we can do now or for a considerable time to come.' Conscious that he sounded terse, Lucius concluded: 'I find that a letter of this kind unavoidably phrases itself in rather formal terms, and I ask that that should not be interpreted as an intended chilliness. We have to deal with facts and facts are cold things.'

To muddy the waters even further, Helen was now positively looking forward to moving into Drenagh. At the end of January she had visited the estate for the first time in three months (her weakened post-operative state had kept her away for most of the winter) and was enchanted by the snowdrops in the Glen, which she described to Lucius as 'a delicious sight, full of peace and promise.' In February she wrote to him: 'I still have my dark moments over Drenagh. Are we worthy?'

While the two sides struggled to find a way out of the morass, matters became yet more difficult. Enter, stage right, a blocking Cerberus in the shape of Sir Norman Stronge, one of the trustees of the Drenagh settlement and a staunch Protestant. Stronge had been a close friend of Maurice McCausland, and he chose this moment to throw an unconciliatory spanner into the works.

Captain Sir Charles Norman Lockhart Stronge, 8th Baronet, was a distinguished figure in Northern Ireland. In 1916 he had acquitted himself with honour at the Battle of the Somme as adjutant of the 10th Inniskillings. His name was the first to be mentioned by Field Marshal Sir Douglas Haig in his dispatches of the battle, and later in the war he won the Military Cross and the Belgian Croix de Guerre. Entering politics, he was elected an Ulster Unionist MP for mid-Armagh in 1938 and was subsequently made a member of the Privy Council of Northern Ireland, and Speaker of the Northern Ireland House of Commons. He had also been High Sheriff of County Londonderry, preceding Conolly in this post by three years. Tall and distinguished, he wore double-breasted, chalk-stripe suits and always sported a neatly clipped moustache. Nominating him as Speaker in 1945, Lord Glentoran said he came from a 'family which had been known for generations for its fairness, its courtesy, and its neighbourliness, and for that feeling of kindliness which is so essential to the Speaker of the House.'

Stronge's Protestant credentials were impeccable, which was one reason why Maurice had chosen him to be a Drenagh trustee. He was Sovereign Grand Master of the Royal Black Institution and a member of Derryshaw Boyne Defenders Orange Lodge of the Orange Order, both Protestant fraternal societies. Unsurprisingly he did not approve of Conolly's conversion to Catholicism. Heads of the McCausland family traditionally played a role in the wider community, and the public offices they had held over the centuries were not, in Stronge's opinion, suitable for a Roman Catholic. (Years later such views were to cost him his life).

Learning that the family was now trying to restore Drenagh to Conolly, Stronge wrote to Lucius saying he thought the whole issue had been settled and that it would be a great mistake to reopen it. He added: 'I feel from the Ulster point of view that you and Helen will be able to take a part in the country that Conolly could never take now. I do sympathise with you both in this business as it is very awkward, but you must look at it from the country's point of view and your son's, and what Maurice would have wished.'

Stronge's intervention was a significant blow to Conolly and Peggy's hopes. It was a clear signal that the trustees would block any attempt by the family to reinstall him at Drenagh. Conolly, however, was in no mood to back down and in the spring of 1944 he embarked on a bold new course. Despite the earlier warnings that the forfeiture clause was indestructible, he now decided to go to court in a bid to have it set aside, and instructed his lawyer, Cyril Nicholson, accordingly.

Nicholson was a powerful if controversial ally whose sympathies lay naturally with Conolly. Like his client he was both a Roman Catholic and unswervingly loyal to the Crown.

He understood the difficulties faced by a Catholic living in a predominantly Protestant country, and had devoted much of his early career trying to bridge the gulf between the two religions. This had included sending his children to Protestant schools, an action for which he had been severely criticised by his fellow Catholics.

Nicholson in turn engaged a solicitor named Eric Morrow, and the two lawyers began to prod and yank at the fabric of the Drenagh settlement, building a case round the fact that Maurice had not been bound by a similar forfeiture clause when he signed the previous settlement in 1897, and that the new clause had not been drawn to Conolly's attention, let alone explained to him, when he signed the 1927 settlement. Therefore, they argued, it was invalid.

In itself Conolly's case had considerable merit, but weighing against him was the fact that he had waited more than three years to bring an action. As Lucius had warned him in 1941, a long delay might be construed by a court as acquiescence, even allowing for the difficulties of mounting a challenge when the country was at war.

From the various army bases where he was stationed with the Irish Guards that spring and summer – Hawick in the Scottish Borders, Lingfield in Surrey and Fairmile Camp in Edinburgh – Conolly sent a flurry of letters to both his lawyers and to members of the family in preparation for a full court hearing in July 1944. His determination to go down this costly and uncertain route was underpinned by Peggy's unswerving support. Peggy had by this time become *Lady Margaret* following her father's ennoblement on the death in April of his cousin, the 5th Earl of Mount Edgcumbe. Conolly, meanwhile, had been promoted to Lieutenant-Colonel and had been made commander of the 2nd Battalion of the Irish Guards. Possibly these changes of status helped to boost his confidence.

Despite his promotion, Conolly evidently had plenty of time on his hands. He was an enthusiastic member of the regimental choir, and sang Mass with it every Sunday. He went frequently to the theatre and cinema, and in his long letters to Peggy he described in great detail the plot-lines of plays and films he had seen. Certainly he was unimpressed by the hero of El Alamein, General Montgomery, who visited the brigade at Hawick in February and addressed the men in his familiar clipped voice from the top of a jeep. 'No one can deny that he is a brilliant general and possesses a strong personality,' Conolly told Peggy, 'but it is not the personality of an English gentleman and that is rather obvious.'

Perhaps sensing that he was about to play a momentous role in Drenagh's history, he began to write his life story in a buff-coloured army exercise book. 'Don't forget to send my autobiography,' he wrote to Peggy after forgetting to take it back to his base with him on his return from leave. 'Some day I may be seized with the urge to continue.'

On Nicholson's advice he started to drum up support from close relations who, because they were further down in the line of succession, were 'interested parties' and beneficiaries and those whose opinions might help to sway a judge. He concentrated his efforts on five cousins – Denis, Joanna, Tom and Michael Gibbs, and Marcus 'Spike' McCausland – asking them to state in writing that they had no objection to the forfeiture clause being set aside so that he could be reinstalled at Drenagh. Contacting them was a time-consuming business because some, like Michael Gibbs, were overseas, but Peggy was a willing helper and he used her as a conduit to speed up the process. He advised her to save money by sending them 'night letter' telegrams – cheaper than normal telegrams – at a cost of five shillings (25p) for thirty words. In his spare time he painstakingly honed draft messages which got across the points he wanted to make in thirty words or less.

Almost every day he wrote to Peggy with fresh advice and suggestions. Of Joanna Gibbs, who lived in London, he wrote: 'You could get her on the telephone and explain what you wanted her to do (provided she was willing) and by her consent one could strengthen Morrow's arm. I have written to this effect to Michael and Spike and that leaves only Tom to be canvassed…Denis is a certainty.'

One by one the answers he wanted trickled in. 'I am enclosing the letter from Spike,' he told Peggy. 'I think it is quite one of the most pleasing I have ever had. No nonsense about 'wider implications' etc. but just an honest assurance of 100 per cent support…he certainly came in with a big hand, bless his heart.' Later he wrote: 'Joan has been most prompt – *an exemplary relative.*'

Thanking Peggy in a letter for her 'tact and persuasion' in helping to gather the statements, he apologised if he sometimes seemed tetchy and ungracious. Acknowledging that many of his friends had been killed or wounded in the war he told her: 'I cannot help feeling how much I have to be thankful for – and yet I grouse so much, and am jealous and discontented. God knows I have everything I want and stand in need of.'

That was not strictly true, of course, for he felt he could never be entirely at peace cut off from the umbilical cord of Drenagh. All the happy memories of the pre-war 'Golden Age' came flooding back when he had lunch there during a fleeting visit to Northern Ireland in May 1944 to meet Cyril Nicholson and other lawyers connected to the case. 'You will remember how lovely it looked the first year we were there and it was looking just the same today,' he told Peggy. 'The blossom is quite unbelievable and rhodo's, cherries, azaleas etc seem to be out together this year. Mrs Lowden (*the estate manager's wife*) had got the house beautifully swept and garnished, with flowers in the hall, which made it look very nice and welcoming.

Tomorrow is the fourth anniversary of my being received into the 'Una Ecclesia' and I am bicycling into Limavady for the early Mass.'

There was a moment of light relief during his visit when he regaled some of the Drenagh staff with a vivid description of how men of the 1st Battalion of the Irish Guards had taken part in the Anzio landings in Italy that January, and had fought their way northwards through Carroceto and Campoleone until they reached Rome. On hearing the word 'Rome', the eyes of Conolly's rapt Protestant audience lit up and their thoughts turned as one to the Pope. 'Did you get him?' they asked excitedly.

While Conolly was in Ireland, a new stumbling block to his hopes emerged. One of the 'interested parties' – his own younger sister Eila, whose backing in court he believed would be an invaluable bonus – resolutely resisted his attempts to win her over. Torn between loyalty to her brother and to her father's wishes, she did not know which way to turn, although she conceded she thought Marcus should be next in line to succeed. (Eila had begun a romance with Sir Norman Stronge's cousin, Mac Stronge – they would marry the following spring – and it is possible that this influenced her thinking about the case).

Conolly spoke to her several times at Ardnargle, where she was still living with the widowed Eileen, and became increasingly frustrated by her attitude. He wrote to Peggy: 'I have put the question to Eila but she wishes to remain neutral and will return no answer. I will have to ask Cyril (Nicholson) how he thinks the court will construe such an attitude. Poor old Eila...it is rather typical. However, she assures me she wishes Marcus to succeed to Drenagh, but considers it 'dishonest' to set aside the clause. I have urged her to think again and try to make up her mind.'

A day or two later he was even more scathing. 'Poor old Eila is very pulled down and depressed. I really feel terribly sorry for her and I am afraid she has worked herself into an awful state over the proposed legal proceedings. She has never had a clear-thinking brain and this combined with a 'Scots conscience' and all those sad complexes makes her rather difficult to talk to. I felt very strongly that it was best to leave her alone and perhaps if all the other parties came into line she may decide that the living are more important than the dead. I feel very sad about her and indeed about the whole thing which is distressing for Mammy as well – but even she told me she thought that a case should be brought for Marcus's sake and for yours.'

Subsequently Conolly thought he detected a shift in Eila's stance. He wrote: 'Eila's attitude in wanting Marcus to succeed and not caring where her own place in the list of 'successors' may lie, is tantamount to an entry on our side of the house, provided she will put it on paper. (But will she??!). However, I will try to persuade her, but you know what she is.'

With or without Eila's support, Conolly was already confident that he had enough 'interested parties' on board to launch his case with a reasonable chance of ultimate success. He even managed to convince himself that the settlement's surviving trustees – Norman Stronge and a Limavady solicitor named John Young – might yet decide not to stand in his way. Having visited Drenagh during that glorious week in May, he wanted it back more than ever. 'I had a wonderful week over there and only wish you and the children could have been there too,' he told Peggy. 'It would have just completed it.' But just as he thought he had done everything possible to prepare the ground for the coming battle he came up against yet another unexpected problem.

Chapter Twelve

The Wheels Turn

Oh Time, Can you forget
While yet
The young fresh green of May is here,
How soon Spring dies?
And by her bier
The drooping Summer quickly flies,
For brooding over all comes dark November.
Then, Time, remember,
Remember when the world is grey
How you proudly went your way
And would not wait
In May....

From a poem by Helen McCausland, May 1929

O h Conolly, Stop, Stop!' So went the opening sentence of a letter from Peggy to Conolly in the second week of May 1944. Like the Sorcerer's Apprentice who could not undo the spell in Goethe's famous ballad, Peggy could see everything spiralling out of control.

That she was losing her nerve was hardly surprising. Almost every communication from Conolly that spring had brought with it details of some new expense in connection with the court case, whether it was the sending of a batch of telegrams or the hiring of yet another lawyer. To Peggy it must have seemed that he had engaged the services of half the legal fraternity of Belfast, with a team of his own and another team acting on behalf of the 'interested parties'. Even the children, he told her, were to be separately represented in court. By his own admission the total costs would be in the region of £10,000, roughly the equivalent of £300,000 in 2013.

Peggy was horrified, particularly as there could hardly have been a worse time to start racking up bills. Marcus, now ten years old, was boarding at a £60-a-term preparatory school for Catholic children - Wellbury Park in Hitchin - and would soon be going to Eton, while seven-year-old Fania was due to go to a fee-paying convent that autumn. Antony, though not yet three, was also down for Eton, and that spring Conolly had written to his old housemaster, Francis Dobbs, asking for advice on which house would suit Antony best. On top of this there would soon be another mouth to feed, for Peggy was eight months pregnant. The mathematics were frightening. Conolly would still be paying school fees well into his fifties, assuming he had not bankrupted himself in the meantime.

Money was not Peggy's only concern. She was also worried that the legal action risked sparking conflict by creating opposing 'sides' among friends and acquaintances as well as the family. Conolly himself had fuelled this thought in numerous letters, as when he wrote to her from Limavady: 'I spoke to Flo-Lo (Florence Heygate) on the telephone. She is a weird old bird but anti-us, at heart, I am sure. Old Hal (Sir Henry Tyler) is definitely pro.'

Over the following days, Conolly did his utmost to assure Peggy that there was nothing to worry about, and in doing so he showed that he was not above using smoke and mirrors to bolster his case. 'My darling, what excitement you have got yourself into – but it must have been my fault for not explaining it all better. There is no need to be alarmed about poverty, penury etc.' Taking it as read that he would win the action, he added: 'You have acquired for £10,000 an Estate worth £120,000 which is not likely to lead to penury you will agree!?! So don't worry any more about it. I am so sorry I didn't explain it better.' In another letter four days later he wrote: 'I hope you are feeling much calmer about the case and the £10,000 – if it ever comes to that figure….all my love Darling and don't worry about this case – loathsome though it is.'

He also sought to calm her fears about splits and feuds. 'I explained (to you) it was not a question of sides but merely a matter of the place in the succession. How did you get the idea of sides out of my letter? I must have expressed myself very badly.'

In due course Peggy's worries faded and the letters between them turned increasingly to other issues, in particular the imminent new addition to the family, and what to call him or her. Young Marcus was excited too. 'My darling mummy and daddy,' he wrote from Wellbury Park. 'How are you? I am well-a-nuff thank you. Will you send me a telligramm when the baby arrives.' (Marcus had received naught out of a hundred in his history exam that term because his paper was 'completely spoilt by appalling writing and spelling.')

The new child, if a boy, was to be called Jonathan, but they were finding it hard to settle on a girl's name. Iona and Islay were considered and discarded. Peggy plumped for Dione (pronounced Deeonie) but Conolly rejected it on the grounds that it sounded like a brand of toothpaste, and for a time his favourite catchphrase became: 'Have you Dioneed your teeth today?' A week or two before the arrival, Conolly wrote to Peggy: 'Have you been thinking of names? I like Anne.' (St Anne, Our Lady's Mother, was one of his favourite saints).

After further long-distance discussion they plumped for Carolyn, and when Peggy duly gave birth to a daughter at Holwell Court in mid-June, an ecstatic Conolly wrote from Edinburgh: 'So it IS Carolyn. I could not be more pleased and happy. I found the telegram from Laire (*Peggy's elder sister, Hilaria*) in my pigeon hole at lunchtime and was simply thrilled. Oh I am so thrilled and so happy it is a daughter. I am sure Fania and Antony are beside themselves. The former will not know what to do with her excitement.' (Peggy's parents, the future Earl and Countess of Mount Edgcumbe, displayed markedly less excitement. On the evening the baby was born they went to bed with instructions that they were not to be woken unless the new arrival was a boy. The nanny went to their room anyway and informed them they had a new granddaughter. Peggy's mother did not stir, but her father said: 'Thank you, Nanny.')

Several days later both Conolly and Peggy began to harbour doubts about the name 'Carolyn.' 'I entirely agree with you about it as a name,' wrote Conolly. 'I am not really quite happy about it.' Setting off on a new tack he added: 'What do you think about Margaret Anne or vice versa?' Later that week he commented: 'I think we should stick to Anne because it is such a nice name.' Shortly afterwards the differently spelt 'Caroline' was back in favour. 'As a matter of fact, do you think Caroline Ann McCausland, or Ann Caroline?' asked Conolly, his to-ing and fro-ing parallelling on a smaller scale his changes of mind about the future of Drenagh.

At this point ten-year-old Marcus threw in his own mis-spelt thoughts, writing from school: 'I am very sorry but I do not like the name Caroline. It is too much like a sir-name I think. I hait it. Call her Anne Pamela or something desunt, but not Caroline.' In the end, despite Marcus's protestations, Caroline Anne were the agreed names, and Conolly sent Peggy a picture of St Joseph, the patron saint of children, to commemorate the event. 'All my love sweetheart,' he wrote, 'and every blessing. Your Ling, who loves you <u>very very</u> much.' (Peggy's sisters, Laire and Kitty, were with her at Holwell Court for much of the war. The three women produced so many babies between them that an acquaintance they met after the war, having seen the numerous birth announcements, assumed that Holwell was a nursing home).

The D-Day landings in Normandy on June 6 – the couple's 12th wedding anniversary – had been a further cause for celebration that month. 'The war news is wonderful, isn't it?' wrote Conolly. 'We seem to be making headway in France. Who would have thought that our anniversary would be chosen for the opening of a Second Front?'

But German retaliation was swift, and soon a new worry was exercising Conolly's mind. Just before the baby was born, the first flying bombs or 'doodlebugs' landed on London, and he became increasingly anxious about his family's safety in Hertfordshire. 'I worked myself into a fine state last night over the pilotless German rocket bombs,' he wrote on June 17, 'but this morning on reflection I realise that it is nothing more serious than the raids we have been accustomed to all along and it is the novelty of the things which had upset me. Well I just pray that none of them will come anywhere near Herts and that in any case an answer will soon be found to the whole affair.'

Later in the month he wrote: 'I see that the pilotless planes still appear to be coming over and pray that Herts is out of their orbit. Even so it must be very noisy at times, and unpleasant. I comfort myself with the thought that you have always slept through every raid that ever was!' In July a stray flying bomb destroyed a school in the Hertfordshire village of Essendon, where Peggy had spent much of her childhood. This prompted Conolly to write: 'I can't help feeling uneasy about you being down there with all this racket going on…I hope we shall soon get the whip hand of that infernal buzz or doodle bug machine.'

The Doodlebugs eventually forced Peggy and the children to decamp briefly to Scotland, where they stayed with friends until the scare was over, but it was young Marcus who put the matter into perspective. He wrote from school: 'Do you think those flying bombs or do-del-buggs are a wast? I do.'

It was not only the threat of flying bombs that disturbed Conolly's peace of mind. So too did comparatively minor domestic matters. When he heard that seven-year-old Fania had broken her watch, he wrote: 'She should be more careful with her things and not give a watch such rough usage. What a pious hope. I hope you have told her that she won't get any more nice presents unless she looks after them properly. Do you think it would be a good idea to say that she cannot wear the watch until she can tell the time, thus stimulating knowledge for which at the moment she doesn't seem to have any desire at all?' The issue of Fania's schooling and her lack of religious knowledge also preyed on his mind, and he was worried that he and Peggy had yet to decide which convent she should attend. 'The years are going by and of her religion she knows next to nothing. I cannot expect you to think this is unfortunate as I do, but it does worry me a bit for her own sake and in the future.'

Even Antony's adenoids were a niggling concern. 'One doesn't like the idea of shifting them but I am told it is quite a simple affair nowadays compared to some years ago.' When it came to Marcus, he was more phlegmatic. Although Marcus continued to commit literary genocide in his letters home ('inshendeary' for incendiary, 'evandulest' for evangelist, 'chockerlet' for chocolate), this amused rather than worried Conolly. He did, however, feel obliged to caution his son when he took him out for the day about 'telling Limericks of a dubious nature at school.'

Perhaps all these relatively trivial concerns were magnified in his mind by the far more portentous matter of the impending court action. In that same month of June he filed his case, serving writs on the trustees of the settlement and on Helen and Lucius, asking for the forfeiture clause to be set aside on several grounds, chiefly that it was against public policy and that he had signed the settlement by misrepresentation. 'The wheels are turning at last,' he told Peggy.

The wheels might have been turning, but not as smoothly as Conolly would have liked. The two trustees – Stronge and Young – now formally declared that they would oppose any attempt to transfer the estate back to Conolly on the grounds that 'it would be contrary to the intention of the deed and that it prejudices persons *(Helen and her heirs)* whose interests the trustees consider they are bound to protect.' This closed the door on an out-of-court settlement, and the stage was now set for a preliminary hearing in the Chancery Division of the Ulster High Court. On July 5 1944 Conolly travelled to Belfast where, two days later, he presented himself before Mr Justice Black in the High Court. 'Evidence before Black J,' he noted tersely in his diary.

The case was briefly opened and subsequently adjourned so that he could give evidence while on compassionate leave for that purpose, with the understanding that he was liable to be recalled to his battalion within forty-eight hours. Questioned in court by Cyril Nicholson, he recounted how his father had crossed to England for his twenty-first birthday in 1927 and told him he would have to sign a resettlement deed. Conolly testified that he signed the document at the office of his father's solicitor, Alexander Ingram, but it was not read to him and he received no advice about it. Nor was it ever suggested to him that he had any choice other than to sign.

He told the court he naturally thought he would succeed his father and that when he signed the deed he did not know it contained a forfeiture clause. The matter did not arise again until he married five years later. As part of his marriage settlement, his father increased his annual allowance from £400 to £600, but again 'it was not brought home to my mind' that the settlement would be affected by any change of religion.

Cross-examined by Mr Porter K.C., Conolly said he was brought up in the principles of his father's religion and was confirmed in the Church of Ireland. Two of his aunts had also changed their religion and had become Roman Catholics.

Mr Porter – Did you ever hear your father making any observations about changes of religion?

Conolly – I knew it was an unpopular move on our part, but I cannot recall any words he used.

Mr Porter – He expressed very strong disapproval?

Conolly – Yes, we never went into deep theological argument, but I knew he did not like candles on the altar. He said they were all nonsense, and I said I did not see anything wrong with them.

Mr Porter – Did you read the 'religious' clause in the settlement?

Conolly – I did not know that a 'religious' clause was contained in the settlement because, after reading the first twelve or fourteen lines, I could not understand the legal terms, and simply glanced over that.

The hearing was adjourned after Conolly had given his evidence, and there would be a long wait before the rest of the evidence was taken and a judgment given. Indeed, there would be no significant development in the case until after the war. Conolly's insistence on going to court, however, had not gone down well with Lucius, who viewed June 1944 as a watershed month which saw trust squandered. In an aide-memoire he pondered the future of the Drenagh estate and wondered whether he and Helen could run it any more successfully than Conolly. 'The trouble is,' he wrote, 'that (the month of) June has shown us his weakness and dissipated the hopes we had of him.' The reservoir of good will between the two sides of the family was beginning to evaporate.

Chapter Thirteen

A Dagger Pointed at my Heart

When I look back upon the years, I do so with such happy tears,
For all the tragedies and fun, which in the web of life are spun.
The Northern childhood's carefree days, when every moment
seemed ablaze
With Twos and Threes on Downhill's shore, or games of truth on
Drenagh's floor

From a poem written for Helen Thompson-McCausland by
her cousin Denis Gibbs in honour of her seventieth birthday in
1973.

Five years and five days after Conolly's conversion, the
war in Europe ended. Conolly marked the event (as he
noted in his diary) by downing two stiff whiskeys, but as
the nation celebrated victory against Germany on May 8 1945,
the future of Drenagh remained unresolved. The house was
in a state of limbo, more of a dusty mausoleum than a home,
mistreated by the servicemen who had used it for nearly half a
decade, and with no one in a position to lay full claim to it now
that peace had at last arrived.

A fortnight before the war ended, Helen and Lucius hosted
a wedding reception there for Eila following her marriage in
Limavady to Sir Norman Stronge's cousin, Maxwell, known
to all as Mac. Conolly was Best Man, returning the favour Mac
had done for him at his own wedding thirteen years earlier.

Eila, concerned about the potential for tension between the
two sides of the family, had considered holding the wedding in
Dublin to avoid any embarrassment. She wrote to Helen and
Lucius beforehand: 'My very dears, there are one or two snags
about the wedding being here (in Limavady). The main one,

of course, is Drenagh and the court case. The fact that Peggy and Conolly, and Marcus and Fania are coming may make it all rather awkward and uncomfortable, and I should just loathe any feeling of strain or friction for you and Mammy. It would spoil the whole day for me. It will be difficult enough to get through it as it is! Conolly and Peggy (whom it will not go easily with) will have to make up their minds that you and Mark and Marianne will be staying at Drenagh, and they will have to come here (Ardnargle).

'I am not at all sure that it wouldn't be better to have the wedding somewhere else – probably Dublin. It would make it a much quieter and more intimate affair – just family – that is provided the family will come down there. It would be putting a little more strain on their pocket, but perhaps they could stand it? I can think of no alternative. A wedding in Derry or Belfast would be almost nauseating! Limavady would be disappointed but I can't help that. Mac and I would far rather have a quiet wedding though it strikes me that the bride and bridegroom are the last people to be consulted! Mammy says to do what we like about it, and I'm sure she would prefer the wedding here, but I don't want her to have an uncomfortable feeling.'

In the event Limavady won over Dublin. Conolly attended the wedding in full military uniform, and while he and Helen gave every sign of being as close as ever during the celebrations, both must have found the situation strange and unsettling, with neither knowing which of them would eventually live out the rest of their days in their childhood home. Even so, it was a joyous occasion. War-time restrictions meant there was no petrol to be had, and Eileen, proud mother of the bride, hired numerous bicycles from a Limavady mechanic named McCaughey so that everyone at Drenagh could get about. Some six months later, just before Christmas, a slightly embarrassed McCaughey visited Ardnargle to have a 'wee word', saying, 'Mrs McCausland, you'll remember them bicycles you hired for the wedding? Well, the owners is wanting them back.'

If it took a long time for the bicycles to be returned, it took even longer for Conolly's legal case to be resuscitated. It was not until the summer of 1946 that the action he had begun two years earlier resumed in the Chancery Division of the High Court in Belfast. *The Northern Constitution* described it as 'perhaps the most important chancery action tried since the establishment of the Northern Ireland judiciary' nearly a quarter of a century earlier and predicted it would be a 'classic.' As a news story, it eclipsed Limavady's long-awaited Victory celebrations held the same week to mark the end of the war, which were largely wrecked by heavy rain.

The hearing lasted for eleven days. Conolly, still a serving army officer, continued where he had left off in 1944, giving further evidence under cross-examination about the infamous Clause Fifteen. Pitted against him were lawyers acting for the trustees of the settlement, who continued to oppose his bid to have the clause set aside. Lucius, intent on fighting Mark's corner, was also called to the witness box, while Helen, torn between loyalty to her brother on the one hand and loyalty to her husband and son on the other, adopted a neutral position and did not give evidence. To the surprise of many of those present, she and Conolly walked into the court room hand in hand, perhaps as much to bolster each other's confidence as to demonstrate family solidarity.

Much of the hearing was taken up by complicated legal argument. Two experts in canon law, Dr William Conway and Dr Arthur Ryan, were called to the court by Conolly's lawyers and expounded at length on the exact meaning of the phase 'become a Roman Catholic.' Part of Conolly's action rested on the contention that Clause Fifteen was not only too vague to have any meaning, but flew in the face of public policy.

The nub of his case, however, was that neither his late father nor the now dead Alexander Ingram had told him about Clause

Fifteen when he came of age. Maurice, he asserted, had told him the deed was simply a 'matter of form' and that he should not delay signing it, while Ingram later claimed he had been under the impression that Maurice had explained the clause's meaning to him. When, years later, Conolly had asked Ingram how he could get out of the clause, Ingram had said it would be impossible, adding: 'Anyway, you signed it.'

Conolly told the judge: 'If the religious clause had been explained to me I would never have signed the deed. Even if my father had pressed me, I would never have put my signature to anything so unjust…If I had known about the religious clause I would have regarded it as a dagger pointed at my heart.' He added that, come what may, he would still have converted to Catholicism even if he had known of the clause's existence.

Conolly then spoke at length about his father's trenchant views about High Church practices.
Conolly – My father was a strong supporter of the Church of Ireland, and he had no doubt in his mind as to what he believed.
Mr Justice Black – He was what would be called in England a **low churchman?**
Conolly – Yes.
Mr Justice Black – Very low?
Conolly – I should think so. My father, when things annoyed him, would express his views. I recollect my father's disapproval of some of the religious practices of my uncle, the late Reverend Reginald Gibbs. The Gibbs family occasionally stayed at my father's house and I remember Father commenting on their behaviour in church. My father did not dislike my uncle, but disliked his practices. My father might be described as an 'evangelical churchman' while I, in many ways, was gradually becoming higher and higher, and learned my prayers from a prayer book used by the Gibbs family. My father

did not like it, and said to me it was rubbish, or words to that effect.'

Warming to his theme, Conolly recalled Maurice's reaction to a newspaper report about a Church of England clergyman in Cornwall who had been sprinkled with holy water. 'He felt very strongly about such practices, and described the vicar as an ass. I tried, I am afraid rather feebly, to come to the vicar's defence, and that involved my father and me in a bit of an argument.'

Turning to the occasion after his marriage in 1932 when he finally looked at the deed of settlement containing Clause Fifteen, Conolly said he had had considerable difficulty interpreting a great deal of what was in the document.

Conolly: You know what legal documents are. (Laughter in court).
Mr Shiel KC (cross-examining): I don't. (Renewed laughter).

Conolly was on less sure ground when it came to his belated change of mind about challenging the religious clause, although Cyril Nicholson argued that the delay was 'both innocent and justified.'

Mr Shiel (cross-examining) – When your sister and brother-in-law changed their name, did that strike you as a final act purporting to show that the Thompson-McCauslands regarded themselves as lawful successors to the estate?
Conolly - I understood that might be the case.
Mr Shiel - You wrote a letter to your sister Helen in which you say that the Thompson McCauslands were entitled to think **they had been misled?**
Conolly - Not the word 'misled.'
Mr Sheil - That they were entitled to think they had been hardly used?

Conolly - Yes, at that time I felt very deeply for them, and still do.

Mr Shiel - Would you agree with me that your brother-in-law has acted most honourably throughout the course of this unhappy matter?

Conolly - Yes.

Lucius for his part told the court that his relationship with the McCauslands had always been of the most 'intimate, friendly and even affectionate nature.' He agreed that Conolly had never done anything to impair that affection and that 'he was a man of exceptional honour and integrity' who had never deceived him or Helen. He confirmed that in 1940 Helen 'was praying that the forfeiture clause might be set aside by some legal means' but that priorities changed when Conolly told her the following year that this could not be done. Lucius added that although he had no personal ambition to succeed to the estate, he did have such ambitions for his son once it became clear that Conolly had forfeited his and his family's interest in Drenagh.

Later Cyril Nicholson spent a day and a half arguing Conolly's case, making observations which led the judge to ask if he were accusing Alexander Ingram - and perhaps Maurice as well – of fraud. Nicholson denied this, but asserted that the two men had nonetheless kept Conolly in the dark about the clause because they feared he would not sign the settlement if he knew of its existence. Edward Brown, who sat in on the case, reported back to Lucius: 'Nothing was asserted directly by Nicholson against Conolly's father, but the implication that he also was a conspirator is inescapable from the argument.'

Mr Justice Black asked many questions during the protracted proceedings and undertook at the end of the hearing to deliberate carefully on the issues. His judgment, as it turned out, was a long time coming, leaving the family in limbo and in increasing emotional turmoil for another seventeen months.

Helen, in particular, had been upset by the hearing, and hated the sight of her brother being pitted against her husband and son in a public arena. It did not help that the evidence Conolly and Lucius gave did not fully tally, Conolly apparently having no recollection of Lucius's avowal that he had warned him in advance about Clause Fifteen, the obvious inference being that one or the other was not being completely candid. Seeking to calm the waters, Lucius's solicitor, Edward Brown, wrote to him on July 4 1946: 'I am sorry that your wife should worry about anything that happened in court. The conflict of evidence was inevitable, but it does not appear in the newspaper reports or at any rate does not appear in such a way as to suggest that anything highly controversial took place.'

In a subsequent letter Brown was more blunt, telling Lucius that Conolly had not come out of the ordeal of cross-examination 'with any credit at all.' He hinted that Conolly had been less than frank about exactly when he discovered the full meaning of Clause Fifteen, and that the presence of the words 'Roman Catholic' twice in the ninety-word clause should surely have aroused his suspicions when he first read it.

Since Brown was Alexander Ingram's successor, his comments about Conolly's evidence were not necessarily objective, but his views were echoed by Walter Topping, a Belfast lawyer who had represented Mark Thompson-McCausland at the hearing. He told Lucius: 'Your evidence had obviously been given with the greatest rectitude and frankness. I hope you will accept the view (which has been expressed by some of the onlookers) that it appeared that your attitude was not only the correct one in so far as you were your son's father, but also that it contrasted most favourably with the evidence given by the Plaintiff.'

Emotionally raw, and fearing that the family was being slowly torn apart, Helen was often close to tears in the days and weeks that followed the hearing. Her own solicitor, Hume Babington of Londonderry, sought to reassure her, writing on July 12: 'I fully appreciate your difficulty caused by your own benevolent attitude towards your brother on the one hand and your obligation to preserve the rights of your son, who is a minor, on the other. I feel sure that you will feel very relieved when it is all over as litigation of this nature is always most distasteful to those members of the family who have its interests at heart, and I sympathise with you in the position in which you are placed, which is not one of your making.'

Conolly too was concerned that the litigation was damaging the family. He was especially worried about the effect on Helen, and assured her in a letter that his love for her was 'undimmed.' He went on: 'I have nothing in the wide world against you, Darling. I have tried to make this as clear as I possibly could all through. So far from even thinking *one single thought* against you, I have so *many many* thoughts of all your sweetness, unselfishness, and of your tenderness, affection, and love for me that nothing would ever persuade me you would be capable of deceiving me or doing anything to hurt me in any way. *I know that you never would*. When you say you are close to tears it is more than I can bear. There is nothing wrong that cannot be put right.'

Peggy's father, Lord Mt Edgcumbe (known affectionately to his family and to Conolly as 'Farve') also weighed in, urging Lucius in a series of letters to settle the case as soon as possible because of the family bitterness it was creating. Lucius found his intervention unhelpful, believing his understanding of the case was naïve and simplistic. Apart from anything else, Mt Edgcumbe did not appear to realise that Helen was bound by the 'restraint on anticipation' provision which, as things stood, prevented her by law from settling the property on anyone else while she had a living husband.

Lucius wrote back: 'The present case must run its course. I wish I could convey to you some of my conviction that that decision is right. May I start from a sentence at the end of your letter in which you say that *this is eminently a family affair and not a matter for the law at all?* With all respect, I can only regard that as an over-simplification responsible for most of the bitterness which has already grown up. It can only mean that the legal obstacles are minor considerations which, given goodwill, can be disregarded.

'May I invite your most earnest attention to the facts? Neglect of them will only lead Conolly and Peggy to cling to the illusion that there is some simple way out which Helen and I can open or hold closed as we wish. That illusion can only lead to bitterness as the failure to find an easy way out will be attributed not to the facts in which it is inherent but to a supposed lack of goodwill on our part. To say that this is not a matter for the law at all is to disregard these plain facts. The origin of the whole affair lies in a legal document which binds the trustees and the beneficiaries in law. No good can come of an attempt to patch up an arrangement which does not take full account of that document and its provisions.'

While still prepared to reach a settlement that would not unravel legally and which did not compromise his children's interests, Lucius felt that Conolly was too ready to buy out Helen's interest in the estate on terms he could not afford and which would bankrupt him. 'I have constantly had to consider his interest as well as everyone else's – sometimes incurring Peggy's suspicions that I am merely casting around for reasons to refuse a settlement they are prepared to accept,' he told Mt Edgcumbe. (His concerns about Conolly's finances would have been confirmed had he seen a letter Conolly wrote to Peggy early in 1947: 'By the way you need not worry too much about money because I am still solvent at the Northern Bank with a credit of about £200.')

He told Mt Edgcumbe that since no settlement had been proposed that he and Helen could regard as sound, they should let the case run its course and await Mr Justice Black's judgment. He added: 'If he [Conolly] will but accept the decision of the court his acceptance will restore his peace of mind.' The correspondence ended on a bitter note, with Mt Edgcumbe retorting: 'That a (family) breach had been staved off up till a few weeks ago shows I think extraordinary magnanimity on the part of Conolly and Peggy.'

Anxious not to appear to be stalling, Lucius asked a tax expert for advice on an arrangement under which Helen would give up her rights to Drenagh, and in return for losing their places in the line of succession, the Thompson-McCausland children would receive a combined lump sum of £30,000. Of this, Lucius and Helen would contribute £5000 themselves, with the rest coming from the estate. Such an arrangement would have depended on a court lifting the 'restraint on anticipation', but long before matters reached that stage the idea became bogged down and led nowhere.

Irritated by the lack of progress, Conolly took out his growing frustration on Lucius, accusing him in October of having blocked all efforts to settle the case. 'So far as I am concerned,' he wrote, 'there is no question of a *feud* and I cannot readily believe that one has started (but) I wonder if you realise that every single attempt to reach a settlement of this case and keep it out of court and to reach some family arrangement - I repeat every single attempt in all these years - has been brought to nothing. This has been caused by the action of one person only and that person is you. You always found some reason for defeating everything - even your own suggestions. I have an idea that you are laying the blame for my present attitude on Cyril Nicholson who was supposed to have poisoned my mind against you. Your letter and several I have had from Mammy are pointers in this direction.

173

'I may be wrong in supposing this but if I'm right will you go back over the course of the trial and you'll see that how the whole history of your attitude stood out with clarity, culminating in an effort to get you to talk in language which I can understand. As far as I can see Farve's appeal (to you) met nothing but a similar crop of excuses. I do not know what he thinks but he is not a fool even if I am. As for hatred I have no such feeling for you. I have never found it easy to hate anybody, still less somebody who is married to Helen and is much beloved by her. There must be a lot to you, but I do wish you could be a little more human and not quite such a crank. I am not trying to be nasty in saying this but you will gather that I'm getting bored with your insinuations that I do no *thinking for myself,* so for heaven's sake stop looking for a whipping boy in the shape of Cyril Nicholson. Let us hope that there are days ahead in which all this will be over the horizon and forgotten.'

If Conolly seemed bitter and downcast, it may have been partly because he was once again far away from his family. He had been posted that autumn to Vienna to work for the Allied Commission for Austria, set up after the war to manage and control the defeated country. He found the job interesting enough and he had all the creature comforts he could want. His base was the exquisitely furnished Schonbrunn Palace, once the summer residence of the emperors, 'a miniature and much more delicate edition of Versailles' as he described it in a letter to Peggy. His office was a 'beautiful baroque boudoir' in which he sat on a Louis XV chair at a Benil table. Much of his work consisted of taking delegations of British MPs around Vienna and the British occupied zone, and introducing them to local politicians. He also went on trips to Prague and Budapest.

Despite the opulence of his surroundings, he felt more isolated than ever, and was acutely aware that his children were fast growing up in his absence. In a flash, so it seemed, Fania had gone from toddler to ten-year-old, while Marcus had

174

started his first term at Eton and was already on the sprint to adulthood. 'He should have a daily dose of malt cod-liver oil and malted milk tablets,' he wrote to Peggy in a rare and forlorn contribution to fatherhood on learning that Marcus had a chest infection and might not be eating enough. Caroline had learned to speak in his absence and was entranced by the big, square wireless at home in England which played Housewives' Choice at breakfast, and Children's Choice on Saturdays. She assumed the grill at the front was for talking to the man inside the set, although Antony scoffed at this idea. To prove her point, Caroline climbed on to a chair one Saturday morning and spoke into the grill: "Please will you play the Teddy Bears' Picnic?" It promptly did, and Caroline skipped round the kitchen in triumph in front of an open-mouthed Anthony.

Conolly, a family man through and through, was missing all this fun. He craved news from home, but difficulties with communications meant the news sometimes took weeks to arrive. The postal service was erratic at the best of times, and the cost of phone calls from Austria to the United Kingdom – £1 1s 9d (£1-09) for three minutes – was prohibitive. He discovered that calls the other way round – from the United Kingdom to Austria - cost only 15s (75p) for three minutes, a substantial saving on a six-minute call, but arrangements had to be made in advance by letter so that both parties were beside a telephone when the call came through. Sometimes the arrangements went wrong and the call was missed. 'My darling sweetheart, I rang you up last night just on chance but I was unlucky which was very sad,' he wrote to Peggy on one occasion. Even when everything went to plan, the conversations were stilted and rushed, and the operator would cut in after six minutes to tell them to end the call.

A note of near desperation was evident in a letter he wrote to Eileen on September 25: 'My darling Mammy. I have not had a letter or communication of any kind (barring one telephone call from Naples 3 weeks ago) since I left England. Something seems to have gone a bit awry somewhere but anyhow I hope and pray that you are all well. Do write to me when you have a moment. I am longing for news of everybody.'

In similar vein he wrote to Peggy: 'My mind is in a fair whirl as the posts are playing ducks and drakes with letters from England coupled with the fact that a letter of yours (plus one from Helen) arrived nearly a month after posting! The cocktail party sounded very great fun and I would love to see you with your hair on top of your head once more, like you used to do it.'

In November 1946 he poured out his heart in a long letter to Helen, making it clear that all he wanted was to be with his family at Drenagh, and regretting the differences that had arisen between himself and Lucius. He wrote: 'I have heard nothing yet concerning the Judge's decision but before I do so, I want to write to you to say that whichever way it may go I shall love you just the same as I have always done and that this is going to make no difference between us. I speak for myself of course, but I think I know that the love and affection you have for me is still as strong as ever – and, even though there is this difference between Lucius and me, it will not diminish – can you understand?

'My greatest longing in the world at this time is to go back to Drenagh, my home, and live there with Peggy and the children, no matter what difficulties may stand in the way. I am an exile here and in spite of all its advantages, its petty luxuries, everything that it can offer, I pray that when February comes I can leave it and go back to my house there to live, and die.

'But if that is not to be, I have got to try and take it as well as I can, and with the belief that having endeavoured to put the whole matter into the hands of God I have no choice but to accept what He ordains. I shall try to accept it as I know it should be accepted, and I hope I will succeed. I know that you are very miserable over the difference which is arisen between Lucius and me. In my last letter to him in reply to his I was very frank and I told him that it was no use his thinking my mind had been poisoned against him. There is no poison, but my mind is against him nevertheless. I do not think that it will last, and I know that it is a bad thing to have grievances against people especially kith and kin, but I just <u>cannot</u> help it.

'If I could understand why he thinks it necessary to do all this… but I just do not understand him and until I do so, the position might be made worse by argument. Hence it is better to leave the whole matter, but it makes me sad to think of there being anything between you and Lucius and me. If you are unhappy about this quarrel between Lucius and me, you may be sure that I am unhappy about it too. All the memories of visits to Amwell and the talks over the fireside, the porridge in the kitchen and the little things which I associate with both of you – I cannot bear to think of them ending just like that.

'There is nothing we can do about it at the moment - it is something which time only can heal. You do know however that I don't hate Lucius, and though I don't understand why he is always one jump ahead of me, when I am trying to keep in step with him, yet I believe the time will come when things will be as they were. In the meantime, please do not be unhappy and never forget that I love you very, very much.'

Helen, though normally sympathetic to Conolly's feelings, was not impressed on this occasion, and resented his comments about Lucius. She wrote to Lucius in Washington: 'A letter arrived from Conolly which I will not send. The leopard has not changed his spots. It's a silly letter and no use you fussing with it at the moment.'

As 1946 drew to a close, the two sides of the family – both acting with what they believed to be the best of intentions –

were growing further apart. On December 18 a lonely Conolly wrote to Peggy from Sacher's Hotel in Vienna: 'My darling sweetheart. No letter from you as yet although two posts have come in bearing Christmas cards and letters. However, every day I say to myself that I will surely hear something now.' He spent Christmas alone at a ski resort in the Tyrol, writing to Peggy on January 1 1947: 'A very Happy New Year to you darling and may it bring us every blessing and much happiness including our home together, a thing I long for more than anything else.'

Shortly after he sent this letter he added to his woes by breaking his leg while skiing. Simultaneously, a cylindrical-shaped package he had sent the family for Christmas arrived in England (it possibly contained German sausage). Three-year-old Caroline became convinced that the packaging containing the gift was Conolly's broken leg and she kept it carefully in the nursery cupboard for weeks. Every now and again she would gingerly take it out, half fascinated and half horrified. She was more than a little perplexed when Conolly finally came home – and lo and behold had two perfectly good legs.

Chapter Fourteen

Strained Relations

'If the law supposes that,' said Mr. Bumble, 'the law is a ass—a idiot.'

From Oliver Twist by Charles Dickens

On Wednesday February 18 1948, Mr Justice Black finally issued his ruling on the Drenagh case in the Ulster High Court. 'Black J gives judgment,' a nervous Conolly wrote in his diary beforehand. No one – lawyers and family alike - had dared to anticipate the result of his deliberations. All they knew was that the ruling had been a long time coming. Indeed, it might have been even longer had not Lucius complained to his lawyers about the delay, with the result that the Attorney General, Lancelot Curran, privately asked the judge to speed things up. The judgment, when it came, contained an extraordinary twist which took everyone by surprise and served only to prolong the agony.

The event had been keenly awaited throughout the province, and sparked almost as much interest as the resignation the same day of Eamon de Valera after sixteen years as Prime Minister of the Irish Republic. As the Northern Constitution reported: 'The importance of the judgment attracted to the court not only those directly concerned, but also many who anticipated that it would be a classic. They were not disappointed. Its delivery occupied two and a quarter hours, and the document, covering fifty-six closely-typed foolscap pages, ran into more than 16,000 words.'

Shortly before the judgment, Lucius had written a private note to himself which vividly summed up the anger and frustration he felt about the seemingly interminable saga, which was now about to enter its ninth year. It was a remarkable document, revealing as it did both his irritation with Conolly and his contempt for the lawyers and Catholic priests he believed had 'enslaved' his brother-in-law. Lucius remained of the firm view that he and Helen had been placed in an impossible position. Initially, as his note pointed out, they had not wanted Drenagh for themselves, and only took it on out of a sense of duty because, through no fault of their own, Conolly had forfeited his interest in the estate. They had put time, money and effort into Drenagh, and had planned their futures round it, only for Conolly to change his mind and want it back.

Part of Lucius's note read: 'In 1940/41 we did not want Drenagh. But neither did Conolly. He told us so. He was, as we now know, sick at heart and put up no effort when, if he wanted Drenagh, the effort should have been made. We accepted Conolly's decision and since then have allowed Drenagh to entwine itself more and more in our thoughts and lives. Hence our readiness to leave Drenagh has diminished. Meanwhile his readiness to give up has also diminished. We may reproach him with going back on a decision on which we relied to do many things important in our lives, but that helps nothing. The position has completely changed. Conolly has gone through the stages of:

1. 'I don't want it (1940/41).
2. 'I would like it if it can be arranged.' (1943/45).
3. 'Damn you, you are keeping me out of it.' (1946).'

Lucius then let rip at those he believed were ultimately responsible for the mess. 'We have seen Conolly pass into slavery to the lawyers and priests; we have seen him change his ground; and we have seen the inevitable result of that – his charges that we have deceived him and have never been honest with him. We know he has only a small chance of keeping Drenagh going and that his advent there will mean an advance of the Roman influence in Limavady and Ulster. And we now see, in him, what evil the Roman influence brings: slavery and self-betrayal.'

But, he asked himself, did any of this justify Helen and himself holding on to Drenagh? His note acknowledged that even if the Thompson-McCauslands won the case, the decision might be reversed in the Appeal Court or in the House of Lords. In that event, not only would he and Helen lose Drenagh, but there would be no hope of 'healing the breach' with Conolly and Peggy. Nor would there be any hope of Conolly making a first offer to Helen and Mark if he found he could not keep Drenagh going and had to sell up. 'Whatever we may decide to do or offer,' Lucius's note concluded, 'we must get Conolly to give us his full mind first. Our decision must be indisputably on the basis that Conolly has made his position plain this time.'

In another note to himself, Lucius wrote that the over-riding question was not what was best for the individuals involved, but what was best for Drenagh itself. 'The well-being of the estate is not mine and Helen's to give away. But we cannot be sure that Conolly will repeat his 1938-40 performance, or that we will be so very successful ourselves. If we really give weight to the estate and people we must either be ready to serve them to our full capacity or to do our best to satisfy ourselves of Conolly's capacity. The trouble is that he has…dissipated the hopes we had of him during the war.'

It was against this background of family turmoil that the two sides awaited the judgement of sixty-year-old Arthur Black, former Ulster Unionist MP, former Attorney-General, and a Judge of the Northern Ireland Supreme Court since 1943. The Belfast courtroom was packed as Black took his place at the Bench and began his ruling. He started by summarising the background to the case, remarking that the courts were generally unsympathetic to clauses such as the one that had been drawn up on Maurice's instructions, an observation that must have immediately raised Conolly's hopes.

He then embarked on a lengthy discourse about the meaning of the words *'shall become a Roman Catholic or profess that he or she is of the Roman Catholic religion.'* He found that the controversial forfeiture clause at the heart of the matter was valid, rejecting the contention of Conolly's lawyers that it was too vague and contrary to public policy. In short, the original wording, drawn up at Maurice's request more than two decades earlier, was sound.

Nor was he satisfied that Clause Fifteen had been inserted without Conolly's knowledge. He gave as an example Conolly's meeting at the Bank of England in 1939 when Lucius told him about the clause. Conolly's subsequent failure to remember the details of this conversation, said Black, indicated that his memory about when he was first informed of the clause's existence might also be faulty.

He next drew attention to the fact that, in his view, the clause took a more drastic form than was originally contemplated, so that a parent on his deathbed might deprive his own child by embracing the Roman Catholic faith. He pointed out the clause was not actually drafted until a few days before the settlement was drawn up for execution and that Conolly – who had been in England at all material times - had not had an opportunity of studying it in its final form. The clause was so unusual and stringent, said the judge, that Conolly should have had its meaning fully explained to him.

Crucially, he agreed with Conolly's assertion that he had signed Clause Fifteen 'under mistake or misapprehension', adding that the courts would not have upheld 'so unusual and so drastic a forfeiture clause' unless a competent adviser had carefully explained to the person against whom the clause would operate not only its precise meaning and possible effect but also his position and rights.' Conolly, he ruled, had not understood the clause when he signed the settlement. Had he challenged the clause in court as soon as he grasped its implications, he would have won his case and it would have been set aside. Put simply, Clause Fifteen was valid in itself, but it should not have come into force because Conolly had not had it explained to him. In essence – though Black did not put it as bluntly as this – Conolly had been duped. So far, so good for Conolly.

But there was more to come. The judge then turned to what he described as 'the vitally important' letter of November 18 1941 when Conolly told Alexander Ingram: 'I am writing to tell you that I no longer feel myself in a position to bring an action in the Courts against the re-settlement of 1927. I do wish, however, to make it perfectly clear that by 'accepting' the settlement I hope to make things easier for you and the other trustees, and I do not wish to prejudice any reopening of the case by me or my descendants at some future and more favourable time.'

The judge went on to quote Ingram's reply, sent the following week: 'I am glad that you will not proceed with the suggested application to the Courts for the alteration of the settlement, which I always felt sure could not be successful and would necessarily have led to the expenditure of very large sums in legal costs.'

This, said the judge, was the turning point, the defining moment. From then on everyone else involved assumed that Conolly had abandoned the idea of challenging the clause, and all their subsequent actions were based on the belief that he had acquiesced to it. Helen and Lucius, he said, took possession of Drenagh on the clear understanding that the Re-Settlement would not be challenged and that Conolly could not keep alive his right to challenge it merely by asserting it from time to time.

As a result, arrangements were made for Drenagh to be handed over to Helen 'on the most friendly terms.' Helen, for instance, paid Conolly more than £9,000 for Drenagh's furniture, stock, crop and implements. At not inconsiderable expense, she and Lucius had changed their name to 'Thompson-McCausland' as a condition of Helen taking possession of the estate.

The judge rejected Conolly's argument that he had only temporarily abandoned his claim and that he had the right to challenge the clause at some later date of his choosing. 'Once he had discovered the true facts and had been advised as to his legal position I do not think that Colonel McCausland was entitled to keep the matter unsettled in this way apparently for an indefinite period,' said Black. 'The mere assertion of a claim…will not serve to keep alive a right which would otherwise be barred.'

He added: 'I do not think that Mr and Mrs Thompson-McCausland would have gone into possession and taken the steps which they did if they had thought the arrangement was a mere temporary one.' Emphasising his view that the Thompson-McCauslands had acted entirely properly, he described Lucius as 'a witness of outstanding quality, obviously a gentleman of first class business competence, and in my judgment a gentleman of the very highest standard of honour and integrity.'

That appeared to be that. The essence of the finding was that Conolly could have successfully kicked Clause Fifteen into touch if he had acted promptly but that he had left it too late to do so. Accordingly, the forfeiture clause could not be set aside, and Conolly had lost his case. Drenagh was Helen's.

It was a pinnacle moment, and at this point in the ruling Conolly must have cursed himself for not having challenged the clause years earlier. No doubt he also cursed the lawyers who had advised him back in 1941 that there was not an 'earthly hope' of upsetting those ninety fateful words. As he listened to the judge, Conolly presumably thought that all was lost.

But Mr Justice Black had not finished. In the closing minutes of his judgment he added an unforeseen finding which threw everything into confusion again. He ruled that young Marcus was not affected by his decision. In other words, although Conolly had waited too long to bring his case to court, the delay did not affect Marcus's rights.

No one had seriously argued this point in court and Cyril Nicholson had only referred to the notion in passing in his closing argument. The judge himself admitted he could find very few cases of a similar nature, but reached the conclusion that this was the most just solution on the grounds that a child should not be bound by the legal neglect of a parent. Accordingly, under his ruling, Helen would have the estate until Conolly's death, at which point it would pass to Marcus.

While coming as a relief to Conolly and Peggy, the ruling left Helen and Lucius dumbfounded, placing them as it did in an invidious if not an impossible position. It meant Helen owned the property not for her lifetime, but for Conolly's lifetime, and that when Conolly died - whenever that might be - the property would revert to Marcus. If Helen died before Conolly, the property would pass to her son Mark before reverting to Marcus on Conolly's death. To Helen and Lucius it was a hopeless predicament. The idea that they should settle at Drenagh with their children, only to have to give it up again at some indeterminate date, was completely impractical.

Edward Brown denounced the ruling as 'bad logic and bad law,' and told Helen and Lucius they had strong grounds for an appeal. He wrote to Helen: 'You will have already appreciated how unsatisfactory is the nature of the interest in the property that remains to you and Mark. If you take possession you will not know the day or the hour when you may have to go. You might have to leave at a time when it was most uncomfortable or inconvenient to do so, and if Conolly were to die in your lifetime your son would never succeed at all.' Brown added that in the circumstances the court would be likely to approve any reasonable proposal Helen made to dispose of her interest in Drenagh.

Sir Norman Stronge, now the sole trustee of the estate following the death of John Young, took a similar view, writing to Lucius: 'It's the most extraordinary judgment, and I personally feel that you should appeal. You are responsible to Mark, and as things are at present, it does not appear to me to be a judgment that could stand in a court of appeal.'

Mark himself, who had just turned seventeen, summed up the difficulties in a letter he wrote to Helen from Eton, making the point that it would have been better if the estate had been returned to Conolly outright rather than for a gap in the line of succession to have been created. 'It is certainly an extraordinary judgment. It is a great pity that it should have been given to one side for a generation, only to be given to the other after that – it will mean another *break in the line* which, though perhaps not as bad as the one from 1940, will nevertheless pretty well undo any work which we manage to do during the time when it is in the family. It will be terribly easy to think "what's the use of doing such and such a thing" when it will probably be undone, or certainly not understood, by the successor?'

Conscious that the two sides of the family would have significantly different views on how to run the estate, he went on: 'It would be much better if they had given it back to Uncle Conolly, instead of allowing a state of semi-gap until Marcus succeeds. Do you think we would be able to have Marcus living with us for some periods so that he could pick up the spirit of our family, and so that he would understand and carry on what we did, instead of probably not seeing its point and possibly undoing it again? If we could bring him into the running of it he would probably feel much more responsible and would succeed, able to carry on anything done by us, instead of having to start up afresh, which would mean another jar to the whole machinery of the place.'

Mark's idea of sharing the running of Drenagh with Marcus – now aged fourteen and a fellow Etonian – might have sounded fine in theory, but Helen and Lucius knew it would never work. Lucius expanded on the problem in an aide-memoire: 'The situation created by the judgment is impossible. Helen's tenure is so insecure that the Thompson-McCauslands could not pull up their roots in England and devote themselves to running the estate.' He also noted that as things stood death duties would apparently be payable on both Conolly's and Helen's deaths, further depleting the estate's assets.

In another note to himself he wrote: 'There are now several people whose consciences are not quite clear. The wish for a clear conscience is leading them to transfer the reproach to us. Above all, therefore, we must not add ourselves to the number of those whose conscience is uneasy.

'This is a crisis in our own spirit. We have said that we will try to decide as Christians. That means that we must accept as our guide in all decisions the principles of Love and Truth, not of material advantage (including the advantage of the land and Drenagh people) or even *of what will be best for Conolly and Peggy in the end. Seventy times seven.* If we are deflected from those principles now we shall have made a choice of masters which will affect the rest of our life. Ye cannot serve God and mammon.

'At the same time we must not be deflected from the Truth. If we close our eyes to facts now we shall be in trouble later. Facts include our own feelings and if we take a decision now on the ground that certain feelings must not weigh, then we must be prepared never to let them weigh in future. I must let Helen express her full mind and not try to persuade her until she has.'

It did not take long for Helen to reach a decision. Three weeks after the judgment Lucius wrote to Sir Norman Stronge confirming that he and Helen would not appeal the case, and that the only sensible option left to them was to settle Drenagh on Conolly or Marcus. He wrote: 'We feel certain that if we appeal and win, the other side will take the case to the House of Lords. Then, even if we still win, the expenses will have mounted to such a sum as to leave the estate virtually crippled. It would be hard enough to run it successfully as it is without pouring more money away. Besides all this, we have all along told Conolly that we hoped he would not appeal, and that we ourselves would in any case accept whatever judgment was given in the first court. Conolly did not in fact undertake not to appeal. But we did, and for us that is final.'

He added: 'Having abandoned a career and connections here (in England) we would not know at what moment we might have to leave Drenagh and fend for ourselves again. And all the time we were at Drenagh we would have the feeling that whatever we did for the place might be thrown to the winds by our successor. I am sure you will understand that in these circumstances we feel there is no alternative to settling the estate back on to Conolly or Marcus, as it is their line and succession which is now in practice established there.'

In a bizarre postscript he referred to gossip in Northern Ireland about his own religious intentions. 'We have heard indirectly that there is a rumour in the North of Ireland that we are thinking of becoming Roman Catholics. No such intention exists or has ever existed in our minds'.

Chapter Fifteen

Endgame

The moon sails onward on the wings of night
Shedding her quiet glory o'er the world of sleep
Hill answers hill, flows on from sea to sea
The gentle radiance of her light,
And shadows deep.

Poem by Helen McCausland, October 1924

Over the following days and weeks Lucius considered several options for unscrambling the mess once and for all. After all, Drenagh was still his and Helen's problem to sort out, not anyone else's. One possibility he looked at was to find an outside tenant to run the estate, but as he pointed out in an aide-memoire: 'Such tenants are rare, and it would break the family connection.' Another was to install Conolly as a paying tenant – 'in many ways the obvious course' – but he doubted if Conolly could afford such an arrangement. Yet another was to turn Drenagh into a 'family community', with Helen, Conolly and Eila sharing the costs of the estate and splitting the income. This too presented problems. Such a community, he wrote, 'will need a leader, a president, or whatever is the right name for one with whom authority lies. This would make a community of Conolly and ourselves almost impossible.'

The distance that had grown between them vanished when Conolly visited Helen and Lucius at Great Amwell in the spring of 1948. The animated talks they had over the kitchen table did much to clear the air. Helen and Lucius – who had spent part of the previous summer at Drenagh with their children - had by now overcome their disappointment and accepted that the property was not to be theirs'. All three agreed the best way

189

forward would be for Conolly to buy out Helen and Mark's interest in the estate. Conolly wrote to them afterwards: 'I loved my visit to you and it made me so happy to feel the joy of reuniting with you again.'

Conolly's spirits had been buoyed by the completion of his Vienna posting and his retirement from the army. On his arrival back in Britain he had moved with Peggy and the children to Yelverton on the edge of Dartmoor. Their rented home, Pound Cottage, was barely ten miles from Mount Edgcumbe, the ancestral home of Peggy's family overlooking Plymouth South. (Mount Edgcumbe house had been destroyed in 1940 by a German incendiary bomb, along with priceless furniture and paintings, including several family portraits by Reynolds, and letters from Nelson to Emma Hamilton, and so the Mt Edgcumbes were living in the stables, which had been converted into a dwelling by the 5th earl.)

Conolly loved the drowsy pastoral beauty, the salmon-rich River Tamar, and the proximity of the broiling Devon and Cornish seas. He could easily imagine himself settling down in this part of the world if Drenagh continued to elude him, and for a time he looked at the possibility of buying a house near Mount Edgcumbe. Peggy, who was close to her parents and still looked to them for emotional support, would probably have preferred this option to moving back to Ireland.

But Drenagh remained Conolly's goal. Like his sister and brother-in-law, he had no wish to appeal the High Court judgment and he wrote to Lucius in April confirming this. 'I hope very much that you will not find it necessary to do so either, for the thought of throwing everything back into the melting pot would be an awful thing to contemplate. I am preaching to the converted in saying so, as you told me yourself.'

On the question of buying out Helen and Mark, he suggested than an actuarial assessment of their interest in the estate should form the basis of a deal. 'I know that you and Helen both agree that what we want is a family settlement. We value the peace and unity of our family very dearly and I know that your wish and ours is to make an end of this litigation at the earliest possible moment.'

As before, it was easier said than done. Helen and Mark's interest in Drenagh was independently valued at about £65,000, which was well beyond Conolly's means to pay. As Edward Brown told Lucius in a letter on June 30, 1948: 'To be quite candid, I think that Conolly may, in his anxiety to re-establish himself at Drenagh, incur indebtedness which would afterwards prove to be so burdensome that he would feel a resentment at having been forced to pay so dearly for what he may still think he ought never to have been deprived of. I mention this not because I think that you ought to facilitate him more than you are doing, but because I doubt whether the present plan, in the long run, is going to lead to happy relations throughout the family, which I know is what you and your wife principally wish for.'

Lucius now proposed various watered down settlements, and Conolly agreed to the last of these, a more realistic £38,000, which included £2000 for each of Mark's siblings. So far so good, but Conolly quickly foresaw another problem. No agreement could be reached without the approval of the trustee, Sir Norman Stronge, and Conolly forecast that Stronge would yet again be a barrier to progress. 'I should be interested to know what Norman has to say about the selling of the life interest and wonder if I am correct in anticipating considerable hostility to such an idea from that quarter?' he told Lucius.

Conolly was right to be worried. Stronge's position was the same as it had been in 1944. He said he had been advised by counsel that he could not enter into negotiations with the beneficiaries, and that he must carry out Maurice's wishes as expressed in the 1927 settlement. That meant never allowing Drenagh to fall into Roman Catholic hands and, as a result, he could not agree to any settlement which would result in Conolly taking over the estate. In keeping with Maurice's wishes, he added, he would appeal the High Court decision.

Lucius was as disheartened as Conolly by his uncompromising stance, not only because it meant yet more uncertainty, but because it would rack up more legal bills. In an effort to dissuade Stronge from appealing, Lucius came up with an ingenious suggestion, namely that Helen would be prepared to take some of her compensation from Conolly in the form of Drenagh land. Mark could then farm this land, and in that way at least part of the Drenagh demesne would remain in Protestant hands. That, Lucius argued, was the safest route for Stronge to take. If he went back to court, there was a chance the appeal would backfire on him and that Conolly would win an undisputed right to Drenagh.

But Stronge was adamant, repeating that he had no alternative but to appeal the High Court judgment. Venting his anger over Stronge's unbending stance, Conolly wrote to Lucius that summer: 'I have had about as much as I can stand of all this. I can hardly remember what life was like before all this began.' Acknowledging that Lucius had done his best to resolve matters, he added: 'I am very grateful to you and Helen that you've done so much to try and make it possible for me to start again where I left off in August 1939.'

Conolly for one suspected that Stronge had allowed his religious beliefs to cloud his judgment, and that his obstinacy was as much the result of prejudice as it was of honouring Maurice's wishes. He told Lucius: 'The kindest thing we can think (about Stronge's attitude) is that it is a sense of duty, while the unkindest is better left unsaid.' Conolly even went so far as to suggest that some of the lawyers in the case were driven by the same religious bigotry, blinkered knights of the Crusades, unable to resist the trumpet and the armoured steed. This suspicion reached the ears of Mark Thompson-McCausland's counsel, Walter Topping, who told a solicitor in the case: 'If the suggestion were not absurd it would be offensive.'

Conolly was not the only member of the family to feel frustrated. In July, out of the blue, his cousin and boyhood friend, Denis Gibbs, who was married to Peggy's elder sister Laire, wrote to Lucius: 'I am distressed at the thought that the Drenagh business still prolongs itself. No doubt everyone is distressed. Is (an appeal) really necessary? I mean is it really going to do anybody any good? Still less the estate itself? Is it too late still to save any further litigation and arrange the purchase of Conolly's life interest on a reasonable basis? Is all this of Norman Stronge's own making? Couldn't he be persuaded to accede to such an agreement? I am sure Uncle Maurice, could he tell us now, would not have wished it to go on like this.'

Though overtly friendly, and apparently aimed solely at Stronge, the letter seemed to imply that Lucius himself was impeding progress, and even hinted that he was encouraging Stronge's rigid stance. A suspicious mind might have concluded that Conolly or Peggy, or perhaps Peggy's parents (Conolly and Denis's joint in-laws) had put Denis up to writing the letter. Lucius's response was polite but firm. He stressed that the legal complexities of the case could not simply be swept aside, that no good would come of over-simplifying the issues, and that everything possible was being done to achieve a watertight settlement. Denis threw in the towel immediately and wrote back: 'I feel rather ashamed. I have always tried to be neutral in this matter, but I think you are right. I had come to be 'coloured' a bit by constantly hearing only one side of the issue. I will try to remain in the middle of the road in future. I am delighted at the arrangement you are all trying to implement.'

As it was, Lucius wrote to Stronge anyway and asked him to reconsider his position, but to no avail. Stronge wrote back: 'I know how awkward it all is, but as Trustee for Maurice, and as your son is still a minor, I feel bound to appeal. I am convinced there is no alternative.'

Of greater irritation to Lucius was Conolly's barrister, Cyril Nicholson. Lucius believed the lawyer had 'poisoned Conolly's mind' against him and had become a significant block to progress. He was particularly angry over what he felt was Nicholson's rudeness towards Drenagh's estate manager, Andy Lowden, during a legal conference in Belfast to discuss the estate's future. Things had become so bad that Lucius could no longer bear to be in the same room as Nicholson. Refusing to attend further meetings with the barrister, he told Conolly: 'My opinion of him has been confirmed by his treatment of Andy Lowden. It is not hate that I feel for him. That would imply an obsession or at least a fairly frequent occupation of my mind with him, whereas in fact I have very little thought about him.'

Conolly, for his part, faced a new problem, made all the more pressing because Peggy was pregnant again. The lease on the cottage in Yelverton was due to run out at the end of 1948, and since it seemed unlikely that the case would be settled by then, he needed to find somewhere else to live. His thoughts now turned to settling back in Northern Ireland, and he wrote to his cousin and fellow old Etonian Sir John Heygate, the eccentric owner of the Bellarena estate near Magilligan, asking if he could rent his large Georgian house for a year. Bellarena, which was only ten miles from Drenagh, had once belonged to McCausland forebears, and to Conolly it would almost be like coming home. Heygate at first appeared to be amenable to the suggestion, but then lost interest and failed to respond to

Conolly's letters. Conolly privately described him to Lucius as 'weak as water, though not caring much for it as a beverage.'

The Bellarena idea having fallen through, Conolly came up with a new proposal. Why not simply move into Drenagh itself? He wrote to Lucius: 'The absurdity of a situation where a furnished house is allowed to remain empty while one of the beneficiaries is left homeless is too ridiculous for any reasonable being to consider. I have to spend a lot of money taking furnished houses while Drenagh, with my own furniture and household goods, sits entirely empty. It isn't good for Drenagh either! Could anything be more fatuous?'

Although the appeal had yet to be heard, Helen and Lucius raised no objection, and agreed he should have the run of the house and gardens provided it was clear that this would in no way compromise Helen's interests. Conolly was quick to accept this olive branch and returned to Drenagh with their blessing on December 16 1948. He happily agreed to the conditions that he would be responsible for any tax liabilities and that he would look after Eileen's requirements, as Helen and Lucius had done. His seven-year exile was finally over.

He wrote to Lucius: 'I do not think you need fear any friction between us. I am not given to quarrelling with people and I think we both possess some tact, and know how to express ourselves without pomposity and giving offence. I shall never forget Helen's generosity in making it possible for me to return to Drenagh and I would not think of trespassing on her interests, or permitting anyone else to do so.'

Peggy and the children followed him to Ireland a day or two later, leaving behind a considerable degree of chaos at Pound Cottage. A note requesting compensation for missing, damaged and broken household items listed, among others: 2 pudding basins (cracked) 1 wine glass (broken) 4 liqueur glasses (broken)

4 white saucers (broken) 1 egg cup (broken) 3 primrose fruit dishes (broken) 1 meat plate (broken) 5 cheese plates (broken) 7 Crown Staffordshire tea cups (broken) 1 wash basin (cracked) 1 mallet (missing).

Not that Drenagh itself was in any better shape. The house where Conolly and his family spent that Christmas was very much in the third league of stately homes, sadly lifeless like a glass eye in a beautiful face. The saloon, drawing room and morning room were locked and shuttered. Many of the floorboards had dry rot, the curtains were full of holes, the carpets were threadbare or non-existent, and paper was peeling off the walls. Grimy windows looked out on to lawns that were spongy to the feet and punctured with mole hills and worm casts. Evidence of the wartime military occupation was all too starkly obvious, from penciled scrawls on the passage walls to old Nissen huts still standing in the park. The remains of smashed alabaster jugs on the drawing room floor seemed to suggest that R.A.F. servicemen had played skittles with them during the War.

The most distressing manifestation of neglect was an infestation of fleas. All the beds had to be sprayed with DDT, and camomile lotion was rubbed over the children's bodies to ease their itching. After a day or two of enduring this purgatory, four-year-old Caroline announced that she wanted to move to another house. When asked why, she replied simply: 'There are too many dusty old chairs.'

Yet all was not lost. The peacocks still strode around the lawn, and the garden continued to provide figs, peaches and nectarines. Clear, delicious drinking water still arrived in a churn from the spring in the Glen. Under the watchful eye of the old rocking horse, standing proudly on its huge rockers upstairs, the Passage Game was revived and was once again enjoyed by grown ups and children alike.

Unfortunately, Drenagh's legal problems were still far from over. Early in 1949 the Appeal Court announced its decision in the 'McCausland case.' The appeal was heard by only two judges - the Lord Chief Justice, Sir James Andrews, and Lord Justice Babington - because all other members of the Appeal Court had been involved in the case when they were counsel. Even Babington had ties to the family, having attended Maurice's funeral eleven years earlier.

Both judges agreed with the High Court finding that Clause Fifteen would have been set aside had Conolly challenged it sooner, but they disagreed on the key issue of whether he had left it too late to start litigation. Andrews, who took two hours to read his judgment, concurred with the High Court finding that by acquiescing to Clause Fifteen in 1941 Conolly had ruled himself out of a future attempt to have it set aside. He sympathised with Conolly to the extent that he had been 'a young man with no legal training or experience left entirely to his own resources to endeavour to fathom what must have been to him the gloomy and confused depths of legal phraseology.' He said a qualified legal adviser should have explained it to him, but that to rescind the 1927 resettlement deed now, after twenty years, 'would produce a state little short of chaos, and an injustice far greater than that which exists with the deed as it stands.' He also backed the original ruling that Marcus's rights were not affected, and said Clause Fifteen should not apply to him or to anyone else in the line of succession.

Like Mr Justice Black before him he went out of his way to praise Lucius. 'Never was I more impressed with correspondence in any case that has come before me than I have been with the tone and Christian spirit of Lucius Thompson's letters. They are, indeed, the letters of a high-minded, honourable English gentleman, who evidently preferred the happiness of his family home (in England) to all the McCausland property, with the material advantages, but also with the serious responsibilities which its possession would entail.'

Babington took a different view of the case. He said Conolly's abandonment of his claim in 1941 was largely dictated by his military commitments and was temporary only, giving him the right to challenge Clause Fifteen at a later date. He stressed: 'He did not at any time either confirm the deed or abandon his claim to challenge it, or acknowledge it to be binding on him.' Since the judges were split on this key issue, the status quo remained, and the High Court decision was left intact. Drenagh, therefore, was still Helen's and would pass to Marcus on Conolly's death. Nothing had changed.

The abortive appeal cost £4,500 in legal fees (around £100,000 in today's money), blowing another large hole in Drenagh's diminishing assets. Even Norman Stronge, clearly embarrassed by the outcome, now concluded that a quick settlement to the case was essential and that no more money should be frittered away by appealing to the House of Lords. 'I think that everyone has had enough,' Edward Brown wrote to Lucius.

A distressing by-product of the appeal was that it created further ill-feeling between the two sides. Conolly and Peggy felt it had strengthened their position, partly because one of the judges had said that Conolly's delay in bringing his action should not have affected his right to challenge Clause Fifteen. In addition they felt Marcus's position as heir to Drenagh was now unassailable unless Norman Stronge appealed to the House of Lords, a manoeuvre which no longer looked likely. Cyril Nicholson went even further, claiming Helen's interest in Drenagh had been greatly depreciated by the appeal.

The upshot was that Conolly felt the £38,000 he had agreed to pay the Thompson-McCauslands - £20,000 for Helen, £10,000 for Mark, and £2,000 for each of the other four children – was too high. He made it clear to Lucius he wanted to re-consider this figure, while Peggy – encouraged by her parents who thought no payment should be made at all - was increasingly of the view that the entire estate should be handed over to Conolly lock, stock and barrel with little or no compensation.

Andy Lowden, Drenagh's estate manager, told Lucius in a letter that it was unfortunate that Conolly and Peggy had been allowed to occupy the house before everything was settled. 'The psychological effect alone is a factor, and particularly so where Peggy is concerned,' he wrote.

In the first week of March 1949, Lucius wrote to Conolly reminding him of the terms they had already agreed on to settle the case, but Conolly dug his heels in and wrote back: 'When I read your letter, I could almost hear the heavy tread of a bailiff in the hall, but I am sure I would be wrong in thinking that your letter was intended as a pistol at my head?! You are quite right in thinking that I do not want any further litigation – but neither am I afraid of it if it has to be. I want a settlement according to the new circumstances which have arisen as a result of the judgments given in the Court of Appeal.'

Six days later Peggy let rip in a no-holds-barred letter to Helen: 'I will try to put before you, clearly, the McCausland as opposed to the Thompson view of Drenagh. I am certain in my mind that if I had in the past more often spoken out, much misunderstanding could have been avoided. After all, in settling anything fairly, it is essential to understand *the other side*. As you know we have always held that Drenagh *belongs* to Conolly. We still do hold that, and it has been successfully proved in court to be a just and true tenet. Three judges have now given verdicts on this point, and none of the three have held that anything *except* delay gives you any claim whatsoever to Drenagh, and one of the judges discounts your claim altogether.

'If you pause for a moment and look at this thing from a moral or legal point of view, you will see that your rights rest upon the one fact that Conolly delayed in bringing his action. Had he brought it in 1940 Drenagh would now be his entirely. You, therefore, hold that which is Conolly's because he was extremely ill-advised as to the true position, also indeed maliciously misled by Alex Ingram in 1940. If you think back to that year you will know that often weighty calls upon his time, his mind and his life came between him and the possibility of bringing family litigation into court. Upon such false and slender base does your case rest. Now we have arrived at a point, with the appeal behind us, when it is necessary to look again at the problem in a new light, and you MUST realise that for us, with the shadow of the appeal gone, there is new light.

'Any agreement Conolly might have signed (with you) before the appeal would have been to ensure against the risk of Marcus losing all. The risk was forced by Norman Stronge who refused to be party to any settlement, and had his appeal succeeded, what then? Marcus's claim has been upheld. He is now in an unassailable position. The responsibility of having Marcus's future to consider is therefore gone. He is unquestionably the rightful heir. That leaves your rights against Conolly's rights to be considered.

'One phrase in connection with this crops up constantly and it is a false phrase. You talk of 'my life interest' meaning your own. Have you a life interest? You have Conolly's life interest. It terminates with Conolly's life not yours. And for this thing that is Conolly's you propose to take £38,000 out of the settled income of the estate! It is not a sum that one would lightly toss aside in a moment, and you profess surprise, horror and even disbelief when Conolly proposes to give this matter further consideration. Remember it is now <u>his</u> problem, no longer his and Marcus's.

'We do not want further litigation, but we are not afraid of it. The only thing now to be feared is misunderstanding and ill-feeling. You must in all fairness let Conolly take time to consider this thing, and try to see it as we do, even if only for a moment.'

Lucius was incensed, not only because he thought Conolly and Peggy were reneging on their earlier agreement, but also because Conolly had seemed to hint in a separate letter that Helen and Lucius were split over Drenagh's future. He wrote to Conolly the next day: 'If you start out bargaining, we would get into a position of antagonism which will I believe end by forcing you to go to the Lords. Finally, if you think there is some difference between Helen's attitude and mine in all this, please put it away from you like poison. During the first case I know that Nicholson sowed that suspicion in your mind. You know Helen and me. If the insinuations succeed they will result in husband and wife being set apart from each other. If they fail, which they will, they may well set brother and sister apart, finally and without mending.'

He went on to remind Conolly of 'Helen's generosity' over the settlement terms, and warned that if he reneged on the deal she would let out Drenagh and sell her interest in the estate on the open market. He also warned Conolly that to keep the dispute going would benefit only the lawyers. 'Prolonged litigation over a considerable estate,' he wrote, 'is always recognised as a lawyers' paradise – a *killing* as it is called. The method, which is easier to recognise when one sees it applied to others than when it is applied to oneself, is to encourage the belief that victory is assured in the next court and that duty to one's dependants enjoins just one more effort.'

Despite his no-nonsense tone, Lucius was still prepared to compromise, and at the end of April he made a new offer - £12,000 for Mark, £10,000 for Helen and £2,000 for each of the other children. He pointed out that the actual cost to Conolly, taking tax savings and other factors into account, would be much less than the £30,000 total. He added that he preferred settlement to litigation, but if it came to litigation he and Helen would engage the best counsel they could to defend their children's interests.

The last sentence apart, Lucius's letter was in the main conciliatory. Indeed, throughout the litigation there had never been anything approaching a complete breakdown in relations between the two sides. Even when the atmosphere became tense and fractious – and this only happened occasionally – none of the key players forgot that family came first. Letters that carried tough and uncompromising messages were almost invariably topped and tailed with news about the children and other family gossip.

Conolly replied that he liked the 'friendly and reasonable' tone of Lucius's latest letter which 'I feel to be more like your real self.' He regretted very much 'my ill-expressed and stupid letter which caused much of the post-appeal trouble.' He added: 'I am sure we all, you and Helen, Mammy, Eila…all of us, want to see the thing settled now and for ever, and though it is never possible to please everybody we must at least aim at that as near as possible.'

Although Conolly was inclined to accept Lucius's new offer, his lawyers were less amenable. Cyril Nicholson thought that £30,000 was too much and considered £10,000 to be an adequate figure. He told Conolly to sit tight and do nothing for the moment. Not for the first time, Lucius felt Nicholson was being unnecessarily obstructive. He wrote to Edward Brown: 'I confess to some astonishment at what I take to be Nicholson's effrontery in discovering difficulties…which were not thought any obstacle at all last year.' Brown agreed with him. 'Nicholson is anxious to maintain the fallacy that you have unjustifiably extorted from Conolly a huge sum. He is incapable of seeing anything but the monstrous grievance which he affects to believe Conolly has.'

In May 1949 Peggy gave birth to her fifth child, Piers, and negotiations stalled for a while, perhaps as a direct result of her being removed from the fray. Then, in August, Conolly wrote to Lucius suggesting a £20,000 payment to be split fifty / fifty between Helen and her children. Lucius rejected this and repeated that Helen would sell her life interest on the open market if there were signs of delaying tactics. He wrote to Brown: 'Between ourselves, my own reading of the situation is that Conolly wants a settlement, but has had so many objections raised (perhaps rather irresponsibly) within his own family and in-laws that he does not quite know what to do next.'

The sum they finally agreed on was the £30,000 Lucius had suggested several months earlier, although it took almost three years for the settlement to be signed. The figures for the children were based on what a court would be likely to agree was acceptable compensation for losing their place in the line of succession. Equally, the court needed to be satisfied that Helen's compensation was high enough to warrant lifting the 'restraint on anticipation' provision which prevented her from settling the property on anyone else while she had a living husband.

Once again the lawyers involved acted less than diligently by wrongly assuming that the court had the power to approve the settlement while the Thompson-McCausland children were still minors. In fact they had to wait until Mark was twenty-one in 1952 before the agreement could be approved by the court, and the settlement was not actually signed until the middle of 1953.

Not that the cost to the Drenagh estate came to anything like £30,000. Helen treated £6,000 she had received from her mother as part payment, and either waived her other £4,000 or returned it later. In due course Mark also returned his own £12,000. The remaining £8,000 balance was reduced further by tax savings, added to which Lucius gave Conolly five years to pay the bulk of it.

The final sum, of course, was dwarfed by legal fees, which totalled many tens of thousands of pounds. Even as the negotiations neared completion, the lawyers kept throwing up obstacles, causing Lucius to write to Conolly in October 1949: 'It seems to me that, in a no doubt well intentioned effort to make things difficult for us, they are risking making them impossible for you! Above all, and from both our points of view, we must get this settled as quickly as possible. I find it hard to believe in the difficulties they are now discovering.'

That Drenagh survived and remained in McCausland hands was no thanks to the lawyers in the case. From start to finish, and in more ways than one, they cost the family dear and came within a whisker of bankrupting the estate.

Chapter Sixteen

Peaceful Days

Ah, my love,
What strength this quiet garden hath to break
The city's yoke of cares, and setting free
The soul, to lap it in tranquility

From a poem by Lucius Thompson, August 1933

With the case finally over, life for Helen and Lucius steered a peaceful and happy course. Having five children to raise, they needed a larger house, and Drenagh's definitive removal from the equation made them look more earnestly for a suitable English property. In 1952 they moved into Epcombs, Hertinfordbury, a large Georgian house set in forty acres in a village near Hertford and under twenty miles from Amwell Grove. With a garden said to be designed by Humphrey Repton, and a large lawn that swept from the terrace to the River Mimram, this was a paradise for all the family, who could bathe, punt and fish in the river, and in time go for romantic walks through the adjoining wood and along the river path.

Helen and Lucius restored the garden, cleared the river walk and, long before the days of garden centres, transformed the stables garden across the road into a market garden. The children helped the gardener prick out bedding plants in the holidays and were later allowed to graft roses with a high success rate. Ever practical, Lucius installed his own central heating in the house, buying radiators from a scrapyard, together with a boiler and some copper piping. Every weekend with the same handyman/gardener he hammered, sawed and drilled, making holes in ceilings and floors, but success followed his endeavours and the house became notably more comfortable thereafter.

Epcombs provided the perfect setting for large family gatherings, and the Limavady McCauslands (known as the McCs) were regular guests of the Thompson-McCauslands (the T-McCs). All differences created by the court case were long forgotten. Indeed among the children such differences had never existed, for both sets of parents had gone to great lengths to prevent the younger generation from picking up any negative feelings about the past.

Each year family from Ireland would arrive for Chelsea Flower Show, Fourth of June, Henley, and the Eton and Harrow match at Lords. Fania's 'coming-out' dance was hosted at Epcombs by Helen and Lucius in 1955. Marcus based himself there for much of 1959. A grateful Conolly wrote: 'My darling Helen, I want to thank you very much being so kind to Marcus who seems to have spent most of his time driving across England, kidnapping aeroplanes *(Marcus was a keen aviator),* and being in bed with suspected flu. You and Lucius have both been very good to him and helped him greatly in every case and at every turn.'

Another excitement that year was Benedict T-McCs selection to row for Cambridge in the Boat Race. As a keen oarsman himself, Lucius followed his training closely, travelling to Cambridge before work and cycling along the towpath following the trials. When the crew moved to Ely, he again followed when he could. Alas, when the great day came, Oxford ended a four-year losing streak and beat Cambridge by six lengths.

MarkT-McC, the one-time future heir to Drenagh, having spent several years in industry after his graduation from Cambridge, felt drawn to train for the Anglican priesthood. He entered the Community of the Resurrection at Mirfield in Yorkshire in

1957, and in a letter to Conolly, his Godfather and confidant, said he was sad to be training for Orders that Conolly, as a Roman Catholic, could not regard as valid. Conolly responded: 'To weigh the validity of Holy Orders is not in my hands, but should you ever find yourself in Orders which have attracted no shadow of doubt, then lay part of the blame on your old uncle who prays for you every day.' In his role as priest, Mark was to play a significant part in all future family occasions of joy and sorrow, whether Protestant or Roman Catholic, marrying, baptising, burying and preaching, and giving valued support in every case.

Just as the McCs were regular visitors to Epcombs, so the T-McCs were frequent visitors to Drenagh, and their journeys across the Irish Sea on the Liverpool ferry remained a highlight of their year. None of the pre-war magic had been lost. To the younger children Lucius always seemed to be in a good mood from the moment they set off, although they still had to stop to picnic or be sick. They passed the long journey singing folk songs like *Cherry Ripe, Early One Morning* and *Green Grow the Rushes O* and playing a game called 'legs', as the car wound along the single carriageway roads through every village. Each side of the car won points for the number of 'legs' portrayed by pubs on their side of the road. 'Coach and Horses' or 'Red Lion' brought shouts of triumph. 'Queen's Head' and 'Devonshire Arms' sparked groans.

In those early post-war years Helen and the children based themselves with Eileen at Ardnargle for a month or more every summer, while Lucius joined them when he could. The younger children stayed at the Red Cottage with a nurse for part of every visit and were largely unaware of Catholic and Protestant issues in the family: but they knew that singing or humming *Lillibullero* - an old Irish song satirising the sentiments of Irish Catholic Jacobites - was strictly forbidden.

And everyone that won't go to Mass
Lillibullero bullen a la
He will be turned out to look like an ass
Lillibullero bullen a la

Most days they walked into Limavady along the cinder track
which ran beside the railway line to the station, a particularly
exciting experience on market days when cattle were being
loaded and unloaded on to the trains. They hired bicycles from
the same Mr McCaughey who had supplied bikes for Eila's
wedding and, when of driving age, cars from RJ Pattison Nutt
in Main Street. Almost always they stopped at 'Daddy' Maxwell
in Main Street for an ice cream, which came as a 'slider' or a
'cone', a treat unknown in ration-restricted England They were
always greeted with: 'Are yous on your holidays just now?'
from a welcoming Daddy Maxwell.

There were regular visits to Drenagh, where now a picture
of the Madonna hung over the central hall fireplace. Conolly,
ever congenial, told them to treat the house as if it were
theirs. Peggy, though outwardly no less welcoming, pointedly
introduced Tessa and Benedict as 'the Thompsons' for years
afterwards, apparently unable to accept or even to comprehend
that their name change had been a legal requirement and was
not through any wish of their own. That aside, all children
were given free rein to enjoy themselves. They rode Fania's
numerous ponies, took out the Yellow Bounder, and played all
manner of indoor and outdoor games. When required, they
helped to bring in the harvest, gathering the sheaves into stooks
to dry. Bathing and picnics at Magilligan continued to be a
highlight of each holiday, now with exciting wartime detritus to
be found there: aeroplane parts, lifejackets, huge coils of barbed
wire, and posts sunk into the sand to repel invaders.

Eileen left the Red Cottage to Helen and Eila in her Will so that they could keep a 'foothold' in Ulster and after her death in 1955 it increasingly became the focal point of T-McC visits, all the more so because of the freedom of actually staying there, often in the company of their Drenagh cousins and other friends. After a night or two at Drenagh, The T-McCs would move in laden with fruit, vegetables, turf, logs and the blanket trunk. Life at the Red Cottage, as it had been for previous generations, was simple in the extreme and in complete contrast to that at Drenagh - no water, no drains and no electricity. Drinking water, cold and clear, was collected from a spring at the Umbra, under Benevenagh, and pennies were flattened on the railway line en route. Rainwater for washing and washing up was collected from the roof into a tank. A turf and wood fire valiantly tried to keep the party warm, and an Elsan provided adequate lavatory facilities. Cooking was on a paraffin stove and later two calor gas rings. They collected milk in a billy can from Mrs Deighan at Benone Farm before walking to the shop to collect their daily provisions. They spent blissful days bathing, walking, surfing, sliding down sand hills, and hunting for cowries, which were used as currency for candlelit games in the evening. On many days a party arrived from Drenagh bearing tea, with scones, strawberry jam and cream. 'French and English' – a rowdy flag game - would take place on the 'Galloping Green' in among the flax stooks, helping them to warm up after a bathe. Reading, making music, singing, cards, and pencil and paper games filled the evenings, and the Red Cottage became an extension of Drenagh itself.

Another highlight of the summer holidays was the huge joint picnic outings to Donegal and Inishowen with the Drenagh household and other friends and relations, often involving a boat trip up Lough Swilly. Visits to the Roe and Regal cinemas in Limavady were another favourite, taking the bus to Limavady. With the arrival of the automatic gramophone and 33rpm long playing records featuring Jimmy Shand, Conolly and Peggy initiated the legendary Reel parties at Drenagh every Saturday night in the holidays. Families and their guests from all around would join in and Naval families stationed in Derry swelled the numbers. Many lasting friendships were made, picnic numbers swelled and romances blossomed.

Life for the T-McCs in rural Hertfordshire was no less rich and fruitful. Helen and Lucius quickly established themselves in Hertingfordbury as stalwarts of the village, the church, and the community at large. In 1965 Lucius became High Sheriff of Hertfordshire. He kept up his reading of the classics whenever possible. Following an operation for a hernia in January 1958, he wrote to his brother Gerald: 'I read Sophocles' Electra, finding that Greek came back to me much more quickly than I would have expected. The first 300 lines made me think what a hypocrite I must have been to say the kind of things about Greek tragedy that one used to say in essays; and the next 1200 swept me off my feet – magnificent!'

Lucius also coached students at the Balls Park Teacher Training College in Hertford in the appreciation of poetry, and on summer evenings groups of girls (known as 'the swans') sat on the terrace at Epcombs reading poetry aloud. In addition he taught Latin at the Working Men's College in Camden Town, one of Britain's oldest adult education institutions, where he had taught English as a young man. In due course he became Chairman of the college, and later its principal, giving it (in the words of one his obituaries) 'courteous, genial and effective leadership.' He was Chairman of the Governors of his old school, Repton, skilfully managing the school's resources so that money was available when needed, and introducing innovative ways of mixing Arts and Science disciplines within the school.

Both he and Helen gave strong support to the ecumenical movement within the Church. With his financial expertise,

Lucius was able to offer valuable advice to the Church of England, especially in the diocese of St Albans, latterly under Bishop Runcie – later to become Archbishop of Canterbury - with whom he became close friends.

Following his important work at Bretton Woods, he remained an influential figure in the financial world at large, being an Adviser to successive Governors of the Bank of England, from 1949 to 1965 including his Cambridge contemporary, Cameron 'Kim' Cobbold. As 'banker' to the Government in post-war Britain, the Bank of England played a crucial role in determining the country's economic direction, attempting to deal with inflation and sterling weakness by credit and exchange controls, and trying to keep a fixed exchange rate. As Chairman of the Bank's powerful Finance Panel, Lucius played a prominent part in shaping and pursuing these aims, and in the 1950s he was offered a CMG (Companion of the Most Distinguished Order of St Michael and St George) for his work in this field. He was told by Cobbold that those working in the Bank did it for honour not reward (though shortly after these fine words the climate must have changed when Cobbold himself accepted a barony) and Lucius had to wait until 1966 when he retired from the Treasury to receive his CMG.

Throughout the 1950s and beyond Lucius continued to be deeply involved in international banking and funding, travelling regularly to Washington and being closely involved with, among others, the International Monetary Fund, The International Bank of Reconstruction and Development, and the General Agreement on Tariffs and Trade (GATT). In 1962 he contributed to the so-called 'Maudling Initiative', which was aimed at establishing a Mutual Currency Account on which member countries could draw. Reginald Maudling (then Chancellor of the Exchequer) was known to say that it should have been called the 'Thompson-McCausland Initiative'. On his retirement from the Bank of England, Lucius was invited by the

Labour Chancellor, James Callaghan, to work in the Treasury as a consultant on international monetary problems, which he did for three years. After his retirement he kept his hand in as a director of an American credit information company, Dun and Bradstreet, and as Chairman of both Moody's Investors Service and a small oil company, Tricentrol.

During all this time Lucius's devotion to Helen remained undimmed. On their thirty-third wedding anniversary in 1963, he sent her a telegram from Italy: 'Was ever better bargain made than this?' In 1965, as they entered their thirty-sixth year of marriage, he cabled her (again from Italy): 'Wilt thou take Helen thirty-six times? Yes.'

Lucius had grown to love Italy, holidaying there frequently with Helen at the invitation of their good friend, Oliver Roskill. With his background in classics, he felt a strong urge to find somewhere of their own where he could practise the language that had evolved from Latin. For two years they rented a house near Volterra in Tuscany before finding the place of Lucius's dreams – a derelict hilltop farmhouse where the fields fell away on all sides and the views were magnificent and far-reaching. Lucius set about redesigning it as a comfortable family house, and in due course he and Helen were able to entertain large numbers of friends and relations there every summer, and as often in the spring and autumn as they could manage. Lucius continued to read Latin and Greek, and the sight of him looking over the harbour at Syracuse with tears running down his face as he quoted from Thucydides during what was probably his last trip abroad, left a deep and lasting impression on his son-in-law, Angus Armstrong.

Lucius's health began to deteriorate after a routine operation to remove some polyps resulted in peritonitis. He never fully recovered from this complication, and eventually moved into a nursing home in Saffron Walden where he died in February

1984. The Governor of the Bank of England and former Chief Cashier, Leslie O'Brien, wrote to Helen: 'He brought a very special personality (to the Bank) and many great qualities from which we all benefitted and much enjoyed. I remember especially the great intellectual stimulus he gave to us all and his great courtesy.'

Among others who wrote was Robert Runcie, who was by then the Archbishop of Canterbury: 'He was a dear and unforgettable friend of our whole family,' he told Helen. 'My conversations with him gave me penetrable insight into his goodness, his faith and his immense integrity.' Of Lucius's great love for Helen, he wrote: 'He was always aware of what you were doing and feeling. The arrangements for his next telephone call with you (from Italy) always had the highest priority.' In similar vein, Lucius's brother Gerald wrote: 'You were the adored centre of his life from the first time he met you. He was trying at times, as all we Thompsons are, but how faithfully you guarded the treasure entrusted to you.'

For Helen at eighty it was the end of a sixty-year love affair. "At least I won't be on my own for long," she told the family. There she was wrong. She carried on for another sixteen years, acting as a focal point for the family and village, gardening, writing letters, entertaining and inevitably shopping for the large number of her weekend visitors. When osteoporosis made mobility an issue, she acquired an electrically-driven wheelchair and a stair lift which spun her round the three corners of the stairs into the hall below with great dignity and allowed her to retain a remarkable degree of independence. She was cajoled into wearing an 'Aid call' button round her neck, but more than once when she ventured far into the garden to visit the hens or look at the border and tipped out of the chair, she would not push the alarm button until she judged it was a convenient time for someone to come and help her, commenting "I was quite happy smelling the grass and listening to the birds." Her combination of mechanical aids allowed her to use most of the downstairs rooms every day, and she would explain to her numerous visitors that she "just wanted to see how they were."

From her wheelchair she hosted the weddings of three granddaughters and continued to open the garden, and often the house, for a variety of local good causes. Among these was the Hertford Civic Society, whose evening of madrigals in the garden, romantically sung from the steps on the far side of the river, was very nearly her undoing when she contracted salmonella poisoning from a quiche at the supper which followed. Happily, she made a full recovery, and she remained the centre of family and village life until her death nearly a decade later, her mind still sharp and her sense of humour as keen as ever. She took on the task of organizing new kneelers for the church, each with a dedication label on the back. When Virginia made one with the words: 'Dedicated to Helen Thompson-McCausland of Epcombs,' Helen added her own comment '…who is not dead yet.'

In the week before she died, when she was suffering from an infection for which she refused to take antibiotics, she would open her eyes and report "Still here" to whichever daughter came in to open the shutters. When her faithful Italian carer, took her favourite cardigan to the wash, she said: "Do be quick. I rather want to die in that'

She finally died in 2000, six weeks before her ninety-seventh birthday. Despite some niggling health problems throughout her long life, she had outlived Conolly by thirty-two years and Eila, who had died of cancer in 1976, by twenty-four years. It is interesting to reflect that had she clung on to Drenagh after the war she would have had to relinquish it again under the terms of the High Court ruling while she still had a third of her life to live.

Chapter Seventeen

Time moves on

We had joy, we had fun, we had seasons in the sun.
But the wine and the song, like the seasons, all have gone.
(popular song)

After the end of the legal case, Conolly and Peggy settled into life at Drenagh with enthusiasm, confident at last that their future there was secure. Peggy set about decorating the house, overseeing the transformation of the dining room, drawing room and main bedrooms, the creation of new bathrooms, and the conversion of the extensive back premises into flats to be let to servicemen from Ballykelly. She moved the kitchen from its former distant position into a room behind the dining room, and had the central hall painted in Wedgewood blue. In the evenings she often played the piano for the children, the music echoing around the hall and up the stairs.

The post-war value of Conolly's stocks and shares was just over £16,000, yielding £800 in dividends. Given that the portfolio he inherited in 1938 was worth around £70,000, and that the T-McCs had returned most of their compensation, this gives some indication of the amount harvested from the estate by lawyers. By 21st century standards this was probably the equivalent of a seven-figure sum. It was a heavy price to pay for his conversion to Catholicism, but Conolly never appeared to dwell on the cost.

The sale of some of the estate's outlying properties, including Dunbeg to the west, Greystone to the south and, most significantly, Bell's Hill for development to the east, enabled him to thaw out the iron frost of insolvency, even if it brought Limavady lapping against the estate wall. In addition, the Robert Ogilby family trust (known as 'Ogilby Aid'), funded by rental income and later the sale in 1964 of property in Woolwich formerly owned by Eileen's father, Robert, provided Conolly and many other members of the family with a regular and sustained income. Lucius was the Trust's chairman, and December's AGM in London was timed to take in both Smithfield Show and a dinner at Epcombs for the 'Founders Feast' on December 6, honouring Henry VI, founder of Eton and Kings, Cambridge.

At home Conolly spent a part of each day writing letters at his desk in the library, a combination of place and pastime from which he derived much contentment. He often reflected in these letters on the halcyon days of his youth. Not long after Eileen died of heart failure in 1955, he wrote to an acquaintance: 'I like to think that they are happy together – my mother, my father, Grimes – and all the grand old people of my early days, in Heaven.' (For her part, Eileen had remained devoted to Maurice's memory for the seventeen years that she outlived him. Long after his death she wrote to Eila of a stroll round Drenagh: 'How Daddy would have loved it. He walked beside me all the way, as he always does in the Glen.')

For most of the rest of the day Conolly was out and about on the estate, seeing to its affairs in the way he had hoped for and expected since he was a boy. The welfare of Drenagh's workforce was important to him, just as it had been to his father. Every Christmas Day he set off after lunch to visit the cottages and lodges on the Drenagh demesne, a gesture which earned him love and respect in equal measure.

A sociable man, he often found an excuse to go to Limavady. He always attended meetings of the Urban District Council, of which he was an enthusiastic member, marking every session for the year ahead on his calendar and arranging visits to England around them so that he rarely missed one. His voice on the council was always one of moderation and good sense.

Afterwards he enjoyed regaling friends with tales from the council chamber, mimicking the voices of his fellow councillors to great effect. (In later years he kept a picture of the hard-line Unionist politician Dr Ian Paisley pasted to the underside of a Drenagh downstairs lavatory seat). He found another outlet for his love of mimicry by appearing regularly in productions of the Limavady Amateur Dramatic Society.

His many other forays into public life included chairing the Roe Anglers' Association, the Limavady War Memorial Trust, the Fruithill branch of the North Derry Unionist Association and the Limavady Old and Handicapped People's Committee. He was also president of the Drummond Cricket Club and a member of the Royal Society for the Protection of Birds. As an active member of the British Legion, he was largely responsible for the provision of the United Services Hall in Limavady.

His dedication to the local community played a large part in bridging the religious divide, and demonstrated to Protestants that the 'other side' could be human too. He wanted as many people as possible to enjoy Drenagh and allowed regular public access to the gardens on Open Days. Even so, his Catholicism remained a hindrance in his life. In 1951 he stood to be selected as the Parliamentary candidate for the Ulster Unionists in Derry, but the Ulster Unionist leader Hugh O'Neill correctly warned that 'the local parochial outlook might be fatal to your chances.' By the same token, few invitations to formal occasions adorned Drenagh's mantelpiece in those post-war, post-conversion years. Religious prejudice in Northern Ireland lived on.

Not that this affected the atmosphere at Drenagh. Once again, it was a happy family home, with a constant stream of visitors, swelled during the holidays by the children's friends and cousins. Fania's wedding in 1958 to Denis Mahony – the first wedding at Drenagh since Eila's in 1945 - was a typically splendid occasion, and the house and garden shone at their best.

Visitors were always made to feel welcome, although it was not unknown for Conolly, in Peggy's many absences, to forget who they had asked to stay. One long-term guest was Gill Hordern (later Gill Sargent), whose father was vicar of the parish of Maker near Mount Edgcumbe. Gill was 'volunteered' by Peggy to do holiday cover as a radiographer at the Roe Valley Hospital, and ended up living at Drenagh for more than two years, becoming almost a member of the family. One day she and Conolly were chatting by the window when a car drove up, causing Conolly to leap to his feet with a strong suspicion that it contained arriving guests. He and Gill rushed upstairs to find beds, and while Gill sorted out bed linen, Conolly galloped down stairs before walking calmly to the front door and greeting the visitors with a warm "How lovely to see you", and never a hint that he had not known they were coming.

In the house itself the two constants were Nanny Grieve, who had been with the family since 1941, and Miss Irwin a later import. In the early days Nanny Grieve held sway in the nursery domain along the upstairs back passage keeping Caroline and Piers under some sort of control. "Nanny hasn't taught me to like it," was Caroline's response to food she did not want. Another time Piers, wanting to take pot shots at a baked bean tin with his air gun, asked: "Nanny, would you mind holding this tin while I shoot at it?" A trained nursery nurse, Nanny Grieve was firm, fair, humorous and perceptive. The children adored her, although her relationship with Peggy could be strained, and she would sometimes justifiably complain that the latter was always off 'gallivanting' somewhere. As a girl Nanny Grieve had badly injured her eye when she walked into the shaft of a cart while returning home from school. Her mother, a First World War widow earning £12 a year, could not afford an operation to repair the damage, so

218

that Nanny Grieve had a squint and wore glasses. Despite this, it was said that she had many male admirers.

Miss Irwin's kingdom was the kitchen from which she produced resplendent meals for whatever numbers appeared. Tea was especially memorable and was laid out on a large trolley, still in use, to be taken in the library or morning room unless numbers dictated the dining room. She was also the source of endless picnic teas for outings. Early on it became an obvious and accepted fact that she was 'not quite herself' at the full moon. One morning Gill Hordern lifted the silver lid for the usual cooked breakfast only to find beneath it a solitary scone. In the absence of any other breakfast, she and Conolly solemnly shared the scone. Miss Irwin respected Conolly, but took against Peggy. One of life's blunter trowels, she once informed the latter as she put her head round the kitchen door to ask if she needed any provisions from Limavady: 'When I sees your face through that door I just want to die.' On another occasion, when Conolly and Peggy were both ill, she took two bowls of soup to them in bed. Conolly's was full to the brim. Peggy's was almost empty.

In 1961 Miss Irwin had a bit part in one of the more dramatic events in Drenagh's history when two brothers from County Down caused a massive explosion which all but destroyed the kitchen. Sven and Gordon Mackie had been befriended by Marcus, probably during a drinking session at the Alexander Arms, and whenever they went on one of their regular wildfowling expeditions in the Foyle Estuary he insisted they stay at Drenagh rather than pay for rooms at a local hostelry. On the night in question, Marcus was in bed with flu, and Conolly and Peggy were fortuitously away. Arriving late, the brothers set about drying out the powder for their punt gun shells, placing a ten-pound tin of powder in one of the ovens of the electric cooker which stood in an island unit in the centre of the kitchen. This, they wrongly claimed later, should have been a safe procedure, since the powder would not burn unless it came into contact with a naked flame or red hot metal.

Ignoring Colonel Peter Hawker's advice in *Instructions to Young Sportsmen in all that relates to Guns and Shooting*, published in 1824, that 'it is not a good idea to dry gunpowder on a plate before the open fire or to dry powder in the flask on the hob of a chimney while having supper,' they joined Marcus upstairs. Some time later Miss Irwin came into the kitchen with a rice pudding, unwittingly placed it in the same oven, and turned up the heat to full blast. In due course the oven's heat melted the solder holding together the canister, and the powder ignited.

A huge explosion blew the oven and rice pudding to smithereens, sent the kitchen windows flying on to the lawn, brought down the ceiling and filled the downstairs rooms with smoke. Fearing the worst, Marcus came running downstairs in his pyjamas, gazing in stupefaction at family portraits hanging drunkenly on the walls of the adjacent dining room. Luckily no one had been hurt, and the two brothers worked round the clock for a week to repair the damage before Peggy and Conolly returned. Perhaps inevitably, word went round that the explosion was the work of Protestant extremists who wanted to burn out the Papist McCauslands. Miss Irwin must briefly have wondered whether it was something she had put in her rice pudding.

Peggy, for her part, had little to do with Miss Irwin's rice puddings and other culinary offerings. Her diet consisted mainly of products recommended by a controversial American nutritionist named Gayelord Hauser. His books *Look Younger, Live Longer*, published in 1950, and *Be Happier, Be Healthier*, published in 1952, were her bibles. Undeterred by Hauser's brushes with the law over allegedly fraudulent claims, including his contention that blackstrap molasses (in which he had a business interest) could re-grow hair on bald spots, Peggy followed his advice to 'add years to your life' by consuming regular concoctions of brewer's yeast, wheat germ, yogurt, skim milk and black treacle. This was but the first of many 'healthy' and often rather cranky diets she pursued for the rest of her life.

Attractive, energetic and a magnet to the young, Peggy loved master-minding expeditions and picnics for Drenagh's many house guests, as well as organising the famous reel parties, which happened every Saturday night without fail in the holidays. To Caroline in particular she was a goddess, a blend of strength and earthiness which made Caroline feel safe and lucky. To the staff at Drenagh, Peggy was *M'Lady,* which her grandchildren later morphed into *Lardy.* (Conolly was known as 'Granolly'). She and Conolly designed the Moon Garden and both spent happy hours clearing brambles and undergrowth.

Peggy's attitude to Drenagh and Ireland remained essentially the same as it had been when she married Conolly in 1932. Ulster could not provide the excitement and glamour she sought, and her frequent trips to England to stay with her parents at Mount Edgcumbe, where she had housed a number of her 'healing' friends nearby, (known by Conolly as 'Spooks'), were one manifestation of her restless spirit. By the mid-1960s, with four of her children married, and with a growing number of grandchildren she was spending less and less time at Drenagh.

So, as the years went by, her interest in Drenagh became ever more limited, and the house often had a neglected air. Damage went unrepaired and broken appliances were seldom replaced. Guests noted that the bathrooms were often without soap and the lavatories without paper. Visitors awaiting pudding at meal-times were liable to be given empty bowls and told to go and forage for themselves among the fruit trees. During the Summer of Love in 1967, half-clad flower people – friends of Piers – added to the Bohemian if exotic atmosphere, turning night into day and vice versa. Anthony Henman, today one of the world's leading experts on drugs use, had his first experience of exotic substances in the Drenagh Billiard room. On one famous occasion the Drenagh cattle devoured some marijuana leaves the hippie brigade had left out to dry, with colourful results. The escapades of the flower people elicited a request from Conolly to England for them to stay at the Red Cottage rather than Drenagh. This was willingly granted by his anxious sisters.

Conolly, now mostly alone, led a far from pampered life. Evening meals usually began with powdered soup acquired in large quantities from a Cash and Carry in Derry. This might be followed by liver, chops, or fish fingers, together with any vegetables that happened to be left over from lunch. Sometimes his supper was a single sausage accompanied by a few spoonfuls of limp vegetation. During Peggy's long and frequent absences, he often seemed distracted and low in spirits, and his sisters in particular became very concerned about his well-being. . 'He was sweet and gentle, but not quite of this world,' recalled one of his daughters-in-law. He habitually shaded his eyes and rubbed his head as if in pain. He was clearly sickening. Conolly, while enjoying the peace, would wander around the house, rather distracted, looking for company, and would often go into Limavady to find it.

He and Peggy spent Christmas 1967 in Portugal, and on their return Conolly finally admitted and began to complain of persistent headaches. By the beginning of February the pain was so severe and so frequent that he took to his bed with the curtains and shutters closed because he was unable to tolerate the light. Peggy called in faith healers but to no apparent effect, and the last Conolly saw of his beloved Drenagh was when he was carried downstairs on a stretcher to be taken away for specialist treatment in London. Surgeons there found an inoperable brain tumour and, with nothing more to be done, he was moved to a Christian home at Burrswood in Kent where he was lovingly cared for until his death in April. Peggy was allowed to stay at the home to be close to him, and his wider family were able to visit him there. Courteous to the last, he would emerge from semi-consciousness on their visits to offer them lunch or tea.

Part of his obituary in the Belfast News Letter read: 'He was one of those complex yet simple, stern yet gentle, spiritual yet human personalities rarely thrown up in Irish history. Deeply religious and, as is often the case with such men, a fine soldier, he was dedicated to his career and the Irish Guardsmen he commanded. Often at odds with his conscience, he took the massive step (in Ireland) to change his religion. His motives for changing may be questioned but those who knew his principles can never question his integrity.'

Conolly was returned to Drenagh where the family made their personal farewells as his coffin lay in the saloon surrounded by flowers, his statue of St. Anne and candles. The coffin was carried from the house draped in the Union flag by his three sons and two sons-in-law and placed on a farm cart followed by a piper and drummer from the Irish Guards and drawn by past and present employees of the estate. Heads bowed, members of the family walked behind it to the beat of the muffled drum for the mile and a half journey to St Mary's Roman Catholic Church, and were joined as they entered Limavady by members of the British Legion.

After the service, many townsfolk joined in the procession as the cortege proceeded from St Mary's RC Church to Drumachose Church of Ireland Parish Church, while scores of others stood silently beside the road. Had there been no other evidence of the love and respect in which Conolly was held, and the powerful influence for ecumenism his life had demonstrated, then this was testimony indeed. A great-niece later met one of those who had stood by the road as a boy and who vividly remembered the impression the dignity and silence of the procession had made upon him.

Conolly was laid to rest beside Maurice in the family plot in the Protestant churchyard, a poignant reunion of a father and son whose differences on religion in life now melted away in death. Later a memorial service was held at the Guards Chapel in London with music played by the Band of the Irish Guards. On both occasions the family hymn of St Patrick's Breastplate was sung, as it had been at Conolly's wedding thirty-six years earlier.

On Lucius' advice Conolly had bought a large acreage of prime land in East Anglia to hedge the inevitable death duties, and its sale after he died enabled duty to be paid without crippling the estate further. There the good fortune ended, and his death at the early age of sixty-one was the first in a series of family tragedies. He was succeeded by thirty-four-year-old Marcus who, though a Roman Catholic, was not bound by Clause Fifteen since both the High Court and the Court of Appeal had ruled that he should not be penalised because of a parental mistake. He was the ninth McCausland (including Helen) to succeed to the estate and his tenure turned out to be the shortest.

Marcus was an engaging and entertaining if somewhat unruly character who, like Conolly, had joined the Irish Guards after leaving Eton. His career with the Guards was rich in drama. On one occasion he was charged with demonstrating a night attack to visiting top brass from Europe, including Germans. Nothing happened for more than an hour. Then, just after 11 p.m., the headlights of three sets of vehicles being used in the exercise were switched on and off, followed almost immediately by a high-pitched shriek. It transpired that Marcus had gone to relieve himself (hence the headlights to show him the way) but had done so on an electric fence. It was antics like this that helped inspire the character of Bumbo Bailey in Andrew Sinclair's 1961 novel *The Breaking of Bumbo* about a young subaltern's exploits in the Guards.

Certainly Marcus's life perpetually steered an unconventional path, and after his military service he acquired a biplane, a four-seater Thruxton Jackaroo, which he used for visiting friends in England and taking holidaymakers at Portrush for joy rides. At one stage he even toyed with the idea of starting up his own Ulster Airlines. Crop spraying also interested him and he had the plane adapted for this purpose. He gathered potential clients for a demonstration, including councillors, Ministry of Agriculture officials and farmers, and herded them into an enclosure to watch. Unfortunately he failed to take note of either the air speed or the wind direction and when he pulled the lever to start the spray – which was appropriately orange - the whole lot blew straight into the crowd.

Subsequently he was encouraged into an interest in forestry and took charge of the Drenagh sawmills, having completed a forestry course at Forde Abbey in Somerset, the home of Conolly's friend Geoffrey Roper. 'I think I knocked some sense into him but I doubt it will last,' the genial Roper reported to the family.

In 1961 Marcus met June Macadam during a skiing holiday in Austria. Though Anglo-Argentinean, June had Irish roots, her father's family having come from Donegal and her mother's from County Wexford. She did not fall instantly in love with Marcus, but she watched with amusement and a degree of awe as his tall, slender frame snaked down the ski runs dressed from head to toe in black, usually after the consumption of several glasses of schnapps.

They met again in London, and Marcus invited her out to dinner. Admitting he was 'skint,' he took her first to a party hosted by friends in Eaton Square, where he placed a hat on the piano and sat down to play. Like Peggy, he was an excellent player, having more than fulfilled one of his prep school reports – 'Piano: half asleep but could be quite a good pupil' - and before long his friends had tossed enough money into the hat for him to take June out for a slap-up meal.

Later that year June and her sister Binny accepted Marcus's invitation to stay at Drenagh. Marcus took June to a ball in Dublin, and was soon head over heels in love. When June stayed at Drenagh again in November 1961 he drove her to the sea at Benone during a tearing gale and asked her if she would marry him. After a moment's thought June replied: 'I think I will' and they were married in Buenos Aires the following April. (Conolly was delighted at the wedding to spot what he thought was an old Etonian tie and spoke animatedly to its wearer about Eton until he realised he was an Argentinean who spoke not a word of English).

Marcus and June spent the first four years of their marriage as tenants of Pat Macrory at Ardmore Lodge before moving into Shell Hill, a wooden cottage on the Drenagh estate. This was their home until Conolly's death two years later, when they moved into Drenagh itself. That same year saw the first of the Civil Rights disturbances, which in turn led to 'The Troubles' that were to blight Northern Ireland for three decades and give rise to the most shocking event in Drenagh's long history.

In 1970, with violence in the province spiralling out of control, the British Government created the Ulster Defence Regiment, a reserve force which, like the disbanded 'B' Specials, was designed to assist the regular armed forces in defending life and property in Northern Ireland against attack and sabotage. Marcus, who was now the father of three small children – Conolly Patrick, Shane and Marianne – considered it his duty to become an officer in the UDR. Like every McCausland before him he was committed to the union with Britain, as demonstrated by his chairmanship of the Limavady branch of the Ulster Unionists. He was particularly keen to set an example to fellow Roman Catholics, many of whom were deterred from joining the UDR because of IRA threats. Initially, Catholic recruits accounted for just eighteen per cent of UDR membership, and this would dwindle to three per cent in later years. His decision to join the regiment was instrumental in costing him his life.

In January 1972, the notorious Bloody Sunday tragedy in Derry took place, in which British troops shot dead thirteen unarmed civilians. By this time Marcus had been in the UDR for two years, but had now decided to resign because he could not reconcile his membership of the regiment with the British Government's policy of internment without trial. He maintained that Republicans were good people at heart and were only rebelling against the establishment because unionism had failed them. He had told his family of his intention to quit the UDR, and had written but not actually posted his letter of resignation.

In February of that year June took their second son, Shane, to visit her parents in Argentina leaving Marcus at home with Conolly and Marianne.

On the afternoon of Friday, March 3, Marcus took a punt gun onto Lough Foyle to shoot duck with Sven Mackie (who had been responsible with his brother for blowing up the Drenagh kitchen) and Major Robin Bullock-Webster of the Irish Guards. In the early evening he returned to Drenagh where he saw his farm manager, Jim Smith, and arranged a breakfast meeting the next day, before heading out again to dine with friends in County Donegal.

At around 9.30 pm he met his friends in a restaurant in Fahan, returning in the early hours to their house overlooking Lough Swilly, where the conversation and the drink flowed on. It was not until 4.30 a.m. that he climbed into his English registered car and headed back towards Limavady, recklessly taking the

route through the fiercely Republican Creggan estate, which
at that time was a no-go area for troops and police. Maybe the
lateness of the hour and the conviviality which had preceded it
contributed to his taking a wrong turn, but he was stopped by a
foot patrol of the Official IRA. On advice from their superiors,
Marcus was escorted at gunpoint to an IRA centre nearby. Here
twenty-year-old Ronald O'Neill was told to take away Marcus's
car and set fire to it. At around the same time eighteen-year-old
William Kelly saw Marcus taken into a back room by senior
members of the Official IRA. Here Marcus was questioned for
several hours.

At around 9 a.m. on 4th March a bricklayer working at St
Joseph's Orphanage in Derry saw two Ford Cortinas containing
several men drive past from the direction of the Creggan
estate. Shortly afterwards he heard two shots in the Braehead
Road, and saw the cars being driven back towards the estate.
He went to the back gate and found Marcus's hooded body
lying at the roadside. He had been shot twice in the back of the
head. Protected by troops, police officers began house-to-house
inquiries but within minutes they came under heavy gunfire
from the Creggan estate and were forced to retreat. As a result,
Marcus's murder was never fully investigated.

The Official IRA, soon to be disbanded because of local disgust
at their activities, claimed responsibility for Marcus's death
stating that he was shot and killed because he was a member of
the UDR and, furthermore, that he was involved in intelligence
work for the British Army. The British Army refuted this
statement, which, as everyone who knew Marcus could have
testified, was nonsense. (He was the third Catholic member
of the UDR to be murdered by Republicans, and the first to be
killed in Londonderry) and it was a bitter irony that he had
been on the point of handing in his resignation when he met his
death.

No one was ever charged with his murder, although some years later Ronald O'Neill was convicted of stealing and setting fire to Marcus's car, and William Kelly confessed to withholding information about what had happened. Another man, suspected of being one of the two killers, was arrested in 1973 but was released without charge. Five years later he was shot dead at his home in Greysteel by an unknown assailant. The second gunman is widely believed to have been a high-ranking member of the Official IRA, who went on to become Adjutant General of the even more murderous Irish National Liberation Army. He died of cancer in 2007.

Marcus' body was returned to Drenagh and, like his father's before it, lay in the saloon surrounded by flowers and candles. Here the shocked family supported each other and made their farewells in private during what had otherwise become a very public occasion. Armed police surrounded the house, guarded the gates, and stopped and searched every visitor, in an uncanny throwback to Edward Carson's visit to Drenagh six decades earlier when the house and grounds were guarded by members of the Ulster Volunteer Force. Once again, only four years after Conolly's death, a coffin draped in the Union flag was borne from the house, and once again was pulled through the streets of Limavady by estate employees to St Mary Roman Catholic Church. Hundreds attended the funeral, and for all of them it was a gruelling, chilling and frightening occasion. For the family it was the most dreadful event of their lives, not just because of the senseless slaying of a greatly-loved husband, brother and cousin, but because of the tense and grim atmosphere then pervading the whole of Northern Ireland. (A total of 497 people, including 130 British soldiers, died in 'The Troubles' in 1972, more than in any other year).

June, who had been told the news of Marcus's murder shortly before she boarded her plane home from South America, was in deep shock, while Peggy, who had been badly hurt in a car crash in London days before, missed the funeral altogether. Mark Thompson-McCausland, was asked by the family to preach on this most difficult occasion and rang the Catholic priest in Limavady"I'm Marcus McCausland's cousin, I'm a protestant clergyman and I'm to give the address. When would you like me to do it?" "It's the McCauslands want you to give the address, I don't want you," he was told. Mark enquired further "Will you allow me to give the address?", the priest gave a gruff affirmative, but hung up without reply when Mark asked when in the service he should speak.

In the event Mark began his address by saying: "I'm Marcus's cousin and I bet you I'm the only protestant clergyman to have done three Lough Derg pilgrimages". (The Lough Derg pilgrimage in County Donegal, an important event in the Roman Catholic calendar, is reputed to be the most challenging pilgrimage in the Christian world, and includes three days of almost continuous fasting with just one meal of black bread and tea every twenty-four hours, walking barefoot over gravel and rocks to various stations, and a 24-hour vigil of prayers and liturgies during which sleep is forbidden.) Mark preached on 'Perfect Love casteth out Fear' and the priest sat in the vestry with his feet up and the door open for all to see he was no part of it. The most charitable view of his behaviour was that he was terrified of reprisals, for the fear and dread, even among the province's priests and clergy, were palpable.

After the service Marcus's coffin continued its procession from St Mary's Church to the family grave at Drumachose Parish Church in complete silence. Some of his hotter-headed friends talked darkly about forming an armed raiding party and going into Derry to find and 'finish off' his killers, but good sense prevailed over their understandable anger. If there was one consoling aspect to the whole terrible story, it was that although Marcus had written his letter of resignation to the UDR, he had not posted it. This meant he died 'on active service', which in turn exempted the estate from death duties. Had it been otherwise, a second demand for death duties within four years would have probably forced the family to sell Drenagh[2].

In July 1973 Peggy, by now living in County Donegal, announced that she wanted to visit the Bogside to meet her son's killers. Speaking at the World Assembly for Moral Re-armament at Caux in Switzerland, she said: "I really don't feel bitterness but what I've often felt during this last year was an urgent feeling that I must go into the Bogside to meet the people, the men, who quite deliberately did what they did and bring to them the feeling I have of unity with them as human beings."

She did not achieve her ambition, and in due course she left Ireland to settle in Warwickshire. She died there in 1988, but not before more tragedy blighted her life. In 1980, her second son Antony, by then on his second marriage and running a pub in Finchingfield, Essex, died of cirrhosis of the liver. Like Marcus, he did not live to see his fortieth birthday. Three years later Peggy's son-in-law Simon Weatherby – Caroline's husband – died of kidney failure, leaving Caroline a widow at under forty. Simon quoted Julian of Norwich in his final diary entry: 'All shall be well, and all shall be well, and all manner of things

---

[2]   By a macabre coincidence, Marcus was one of three people involved in the Drenagh court case who subsequently died at the hands of Republican terrorists. Nine years later, in January 1981, Sir Norman Stronge, the trustee of the Drenagh settlement, and a barrier to many attempts to find a solution to the problem, was also murdered by the IRA at the age of eighty-six. He and his son James were watching television in the library of their home, Tynan Abbey in County Armagh, when members of the Provisional IRA broke into the house armed with machine guns and grenades. Father and son were shot in the head and the house was burned to the ground. (In a curious twist, Eila's son James succeeded to the title). It was a deep irony that Stronge had been one of the relatively few officers in the Ulster Division to have survived the carnage at the Somme in 1916, only to be killed by his fellow countrymen sixty-five years later. The Roman Catholic politician Austin Currie declared that 'even at 86 years of age, Sir Norman was still incomparably more of a man than the cowardly dregs of humanity who ended his life in this barbaric way.' Sir Norman was buried in Tynan Parish church in a joint service with his son. The Queen sent a telegram saying that she and Prince Philip were 'deeply shocked' by the murders.

A third victim was Helen's counsel during the case, Maurice Gibson, once described by Lord MacDermott, the Chief Justice of Northern Ireland, as the best lawyer at the Bar. In April 1987, some four decades after the Drenagh case ended, 73-year-old Sir Maurice – by now a Lord Justice of Appeal - and his wife Cecily were killed by a remote-controlled car bomb as they drove into Northern Ireland after a holiday in the Irish Republic. As Gibson's car reached the border, he stopped to shake hands with the Garda security escort who had completed their part of the assignment. Seconds later, as the couple drove towards a waiting RUC escort, an explosion threw their vehicle across the road, killing them instantly.

shall be well.' Mark Thompson-McCausland took both funeral services.

During those dark years a terrible cloud seemed to hang over the McCausland family, but one bright and steadying light was the marriage in 1974 of Marcus's widow, June, to forty-three-year-old Brigadier General Peter Welsh. As commander of the 2nd Battalion the Royal Green Jackets during an eighteen-month tour of Northern Ireland, Peter had seen much of the conflict in the province at first hand. Five weeks before Marcus's murder, he observed the unfolding Bloody Sunday tragedy in Derry from a helicopter. Always a voice of moderation, he had voiced his concerns beforehand about the presence of units of 1st Battalion the Parachute Regiment at the civil rights march which sparked the disaster. The Paras were renowned for their toughness, and Peter's misgivings proved well-founded when they opened fire on unarmed civilians. In his report into the tragedy, published nearly forty years later, Lord Saville commended the 2nd Royal Green Jackets for the restraint and proportionality with which they had responded to the rioting that day. Peter was awarded the OBE at the end of his tour of Ireland, to add to the Military Cross he had won in Borneo for his 'inspirational' courage and calmness under fire.

In the wake of Marcus's death, Peter played a crucial role in providing stability to the family, and to Drenagh in general. An accomplished footballer, cricketer, boxer, racquets player, squash player and a first-rate shot, he was a warm and generous man with a love of food and cooking. Although based in England until his retirement in 1986, he and June spent as much time as possible at Drenagh. Both worked hard to restore it to its former glory, helped by the farm manager, Jim Smith. This took considerable courage, for Peter himself was under threat from the I.R.A. and had been warned to stay away from Ireland. Like Marcus and Conolly Robert before him, he served as High Sheriff of Londonderry, and helped to organise fundraising events for many charitable organisations, including the British Heart Foundation.

June's own devotion to Drenagh, and her determination to see it passed down to a ninth generation, meant that when in 1995 she handed over the house to her elder son Conolly Patrick – the fifth Conolly McCausland to be installed there – the property was in excellent repair and back on a secure financial footing. In her own resolute way, she did as much as anyone in Drenagh's long history to ensure it stayed in McCausland hands. On vacating the house, she and Peter moved to another part of the estate, at Streeve Hill, where June remains to this day, doted on by her children and grandchildren. After Peter's death in 2011, at the age of eighty, Conolly Patrick spoke movingly at his funeral, praising his 'old-fashioned values of manners and decency' and adding: 'We owe him an immense debt of gratitude and lasting respect for making our family complete for nearly four decades'.

Sixteen decades after it was built, the house June passed on to Conolly Patrick in 1995 could still be justifiably described as one of the most beautiful in Northern Ireland. In keeping with its new role as a venue for weddings, parties, conferences etc., there are en suite bedrooms, a home cinema, and an indoor pool. Helicopters have even landed on the lawn bringing American guests from Derry Airport.

In almost every corner of the house the McCausland family's long history remains in evidence. Conolly Thomas's old library is still there, along with his scores of books, as, upstairs, is the rocking horse on which Helen, Conolly and Eila played as children, and the gong which called the family to meals. Portraits of long-dead ancestors – the first two Conollys, Marcus the great philanthropist, Conolly Thomas in his cricket whites, Maurice in the uniform of His Majesty's Lieutenant – look down from the walls of the house, as do many of their wives and children. Taking pride of place above the dining room mantelpiece is Robert, the entrepreneurial McCausland who started it all three hundred years ago. Had he known what lay ahead for his descendants – particularly those who lived in the twentieth century - he would have felt a mixture of delight, amazement, bewilderment, sorrow and pride.

****

In March 2014 financial pressures on Drenagh Estate finally brought this chapter of its story to an end. The house and land went into administration and were put up for sale. The news came as a shock to all those associated with Drenagh, and many were left with a feeling of bereavement. Even in their darker moments, it was not the ending they had expected.

One may hope that Drenagh itself will stand for centuries to come, a reminder of the momentous and extraordinary events that have taken place within its desmesne: the great beech tree in which 'Perseus' lived is still on the lawn – the same lawn where the second Conolly trained the Balteagh Infantry to see off Napoleon, and where 'Missy' watched her 'beautiful little peachick' in the 1830s, and where Maurice addressed his 'B' Special recruits in the 1920s.

The McCauslands may go from Drenagh, but their story is an indelible part of Ulster history. The house remains and the numerous branches of the family are still closely in touch, their closeness a testimony to the love between Helen, Conolly and Eila, who refused to be torn apart by the seemingly insurmountable machinations of the law.

Music when soft voices die,
Vibrates in the memory;

"To…" by Percy Bysshe Shelley

The Battle of Be'long

By Captain J.F.Marnon

Come all ye loyal Irishmen, the border is erased
By North and South a fighting man will equally be praised,
Set light to your tobacco boys, while I give you a song
Of Captain C McCausland at the Battle of Be'long.

In April 1940 there was trouble in Berlin,
Says Ribbentrop to Hitler 'God, you're getting' awful thin.'
Says Hitler to Von Ribbentrop 'I need a change of air'
'Be'long,' says he 'is the place for me, Be'long,' says he, 'sur-Mer.'

Says Ribbentrop 'Send Keitel in, we have to make a plan,
We'll leave Field Marshal Goering, he's a dozy idle man.'
Says Keitel 'If ye want Be'long we'll have to strike a blow,'
'We will, bedad,' says Hitler 'and begob we'll strike it low.'

'But listen,' says Herr Hitler, 'there's a point I'll stipulate,
I want the place in order, now ye mustn't break a plate.
Ye'll keep the town intact, and let me tell ye apropos
That if ye don't obey I'll take back your Iron Cross.'

Says Keitel 'It's a bargain! We'll be there without delay,
Address yourself Be'long-sur-Mer the 23rd of May,
We'll draw the French asunder, then ye'll have an easy trip
And peaceful sands will see ye take your paddle or a dip.'

The General was as good as his word until the twenty-first,
Herr Hitler swelled his chest with pride, Field Marshal Goering burst
And when they saw the Channel on the 22nd May
'Ach, Gott, Be'long ist etwas Geld fur marmalade,' says they.

235

Says Keitel to his Aide-de-Camp 'Immediately go down,
Arrange Triumphal Arches for me entrance to the town,
Instruct the French militia to get out and tell the maire
I'll choose me bed and breakfast at the Hotel d'Angleterre.'

The Aide-de-Camp came running back; says he 'I can't get in,
There's Belgians there in thousands, had I best ring up Berlin?'
Says Keitel 'Fire a mortar bomb, as soon as they hear the noise
The Belgians will skidaddle, it's the Belgians are the boys.'

'Go easy,' says the Aide-de-Camp, 'there's worse than that below
There's seven hundred English in the village of Outreau,
Intelligence says they've ne'er a gun or a hand-grenade, it's true,
But them's the Coldstream Guards for I saw Captain Pole-Carew.'

Says Keitel 'Holy Moses, that's the wildest man in Tip,
He's famous for his aiming from the shoulder or the hip,
Me bosom's in disturbance and already it feels the loss
Potential or contingent of me elegant Iron Cross.'

'But order up me squadrons and me batteries and me tanks,
Tonight we'll take the English in the rear and the flanks,
They'll not withstand bombardment like they did at Waterloo
So long as ye keep away from Captain Patrick Pole-Carew.'

The night was dark when forward went the Germans to attack,
Atrocious were the fusillades and shortly they fell back,
Said Hans to Fritz 'Who told us we were fighting them Coldstream!
The last time I saw lads like them was on the Shannon Scheme.'

'Be Jabbers,' said the aide-de-camp, 'meself was in the van,
The captain of the flank must be a famous fightin' man,
Intelligence calls him Ulster's own reply to Captain Paddy,
It's Captain C McCausland from the town of Limavady.'

Their talk was interrupted by a stentorious bawl,
And 'Gallagher' came a lusty voice, and 'Gallagher' came the call,
'God save us,' said the General, 'be cripes we're in a fix!
It's not the famous Coldstream Guards, be Jesus it's the Micks.'

Dismay and consternation filled the German High Command,
They sent for armoured tractors to come up and lend a hand,
They sent for all their aeroplanes and infantry of the line,
And the General sent for half a pint of Port and Brandy Wine.

Tremendous reinforcements reached the General in the night,
'We're twenty-five to one,' says he, 'there'll scarcely be a fight.
The Fuhrer's train arrives at noon, we'll have the town by ten,
And ne'er a trace himself will see of the bastard Irishmen.'

The sun came up, the trumpet blew and every cannon pealed,
The German tanks in hundreds surged across that battlefield,
The Irish Guards were forced to quit the outskirts of Outreau
But never a German soldier raised his head to see them go.

'Come on now,' said the General, 'We've got them on the run,
No longer need we reckon with that Company No.1.
Take note that Captain Murphy is already out of sight,
And I'll go bail that Madden has no stomach for a fight.'

So forward went the Germans and approached the village square,
When suddenly twenty muskets and a Bren gun rent the air,
Says Hans to Fritz 'It's still the Micks, who called this a withdrawal?
There's Captain C McCausland up behind the garden wall.'

'Herr General,' says the Aide-de-Camp, 'it's quarter after nine,
And Colonel Haydon's formed his men upon a second line,
Intelligence says there'll be a third, picked out by Major Ross
I bet ye're getting' flustered, now, about your Iron Cross.'

Says Keitel 'May the Divil take Intelligence down to Hell,
There's Maddon in the churchyard and there's Finlar in Portal,
The school for girls is Murphy's – God forgive me my mistake,
It's Captain C McCausland and the garden we must take.'

Says Captain C McCausland 'Boys, the range is thirty yards,
We'll teach them limbs of Satan to obstruct the Irish Guards,
For every shot they loose, me lads, we give them back the same,
And an extra one for Ireland's sake, or Conolly's not me name.'

The Germans concentrated every gun and every tank
From village square to garden wall the firing was point blank,
But every shot was answered by the rifles and the Bren
Of Captain C McCausland and his one and twenty men.

And every man that saw that sight pronounced the self same thing,
The stand remains unrivalled since the Siege of Mafeking,
Like Hougemont and Rorkes Drift the story will be told
Of Captain C McCausland with his gun too hot to hold.

From nine o'clock till afternoon they held the village square,
And later when the order came 'Withdraw in good repair',
The town they left in shambles and before the day was done
An Iron Cross was forfeit and a Military Cross was won.

And that's the way the Germans lost the battle of Be'long,
Fill up your glasses, boys, before the finish of my song,
Good luck to every Irishman from Cork to Lewtownards,
That sails away from Dublin Bay to join the Irish Guards.

Select Bibliography

War Diary, 2nd Battalion Irish Guards, May-June 1940, National Archives

Battleground Europe: Boulogne Jon Cooksey, 2002, Leo Cooper

In Search of Buchanan: From Anselan to President James Buchanan, Irene Martin, Rossnashanagh Publishing, 2011

The Landowners of Ireland, U.H.Hussey de Burgh, Hodges, Foster and Figgis, 1878

Irish Names of Places, P.W.Joyce, Pheonix Publishing, 1869

A Topographical History of Ireland, Samuel Lewis, 1837, S.Lewis & Co

Ordnance Survey Memoirs of Ireland (Roe Valley Central) 1833-5

The Irish Tourist, A.Atkinson, 1815, Thomas Courtney

The Strings Are False, Louis MacNeice, Faber, 2007

Carson, H Montgomery Hyde, Heinemann, 1954

Carson – The Man Who Divided Ireland, Geoffrey Lewis, Hambledon and London, 2005

Days That Are Gone, Patrick Macrory, 1983, North-West Books

Buildings of New Ireland (North-West Ulster) Alistair Rowan, 1979

Picturesque England, Laura Valentine, 1890, Frederick Warne & Co

The Diaries of Frances Lady Shelley, edited by Richard Edgcumbe, John Murray, 1913

My Dream of You, Nuala O'Faolain, 2001, Penguin

An Illustrated History of Limavady and the Roe Valley, Douglas Bartlett, 2010

The Breaking of Bumbo, Andrew Sinclair, Faber and Faber, 1959

Milestones in Murder, Hugh Jordan, Random House, 2002

Lost Lives, David McKittrick & others, Mainstream Publishing, 1999

A Shorter Illustrated History of Ulster, Jonathan Bardon, Blackstaff Press, 1996

Historical Enquiries Team, PSNI